DATE DUE

DISORDERED MOTHER
OR
DISORDERED DIAGNOSIS?

DISORDERED MOTHER
OR
DISORDERED DIAGNOSIS?

MUNCHAUSEN BY PROXY

SYNDROME

◆

DAVID B. ALLISON
MARK S. ROBERTS

≉ THE ANALYTIC PRESS

1998 Hillsdale, NJ   London

Set in Minion 11/13 by CompuDesign, Rego Park, NY

Published by The Analytic Press, Inc.
101 West Street, Hillsdale, NJ 07642

http://www.analyticpress.com

Library of Congress Cataloging-in-Publication Data

Allison, David B.
   Disordered mother or disordered diagnosis? : Munchausen
   By Proxy Syndrome. / David B. Allison, Mark S. Roberts.
   p.   cm.
   Includes bibliographic references and index.
   ISBN 0-88163-290-2
   1. Munchausen syndrome by proxy. I. Roberts, Mark S.
   II. Title
   RC569.5.M83A38   1998
   616.85'8223—dc21   98-34172
                                                            CIP

Printed in the United States of America
10 9 8 7 6 5 4 3 2 1

CONTENTS

PART THREE
THE CONSTRUCTION COMPLETED
The New MBPS Orthodoxy

FOREWORD

In Hans Christian Andersen's classic tale of *The Emperor's New Clothes*, two charlatans come to the Emperor's city, posing as weavers of such fine fabrics that only the truly intelligent can see them. The charlatans are hired by the Emperor, and in exchange they will receive gold and silk to weave the fabric. The ruse is simple enough: appeal to the intellectual vanity of the Emperor and his court. Each member of the Emperor's court in turn is sent to the charlatans' room to check on the progress of the fabric. Each returns to the Emperor "bedazzled" by the beauty of the fabric. No one in the Emperor's court wants to appear dim-witted and admit that there is no fabric to be seen. The ruse is complete on the day the Emperor is to show off his new clothes. There in the dressing room stands the naked Emperor, with his court and the charlatans, each gushing over the beautiful colors and textures of the nonexistent fabric. Although the Emperor can see that he is entirely naked, he too refuses to admit that there is no fabric to be seen. It takes the clear-minded honesty of a child to point out the nakedness of the Emperor.

I have often used this tale in closing arguments, because of the many wonderful parallels that exist between it and Munchausen by Proxy Syndrome. Since 1991, I have spent nearly 4,000 hours counseling, litigating, and defending these cases nationwide. I have consulted with the most preeminent medical scholars in the fields of genetics, microbiology, immunology, neurology, infectious disease, gastroenterology, psychiatry and more, only to find that the allegations against the mothers were as threadbare as the Emperor's new clothes. As a result of my work I have successfully reunited five families and have helped dozens of other attorneys nationwide do the same. In each of these cases, a child was taken from his or her mother because someone claimed that the mother "suffered" from Munchausen by Proxy Syndrome.

The essence of this "disorder," as described by the "hired gun" experts, seems to be that the mother medically maltreats her child to gain the attention or approval of doctors. The reasons given by these experts as to why a mother would do this smacks of misogyny or, as I like to call it in court, pure, unadulterated "mommy bashing." The reasons testified to range from "women are much more manipulative than men" to "women have become enamored with doctors as saviors, through the medium of daytime and nighttime medical soap dramas." Keep in mind that these "hired gun" experts are also professors of medicine in our nation's medical schools.

The problem is that the "hired gun" experts cannot agree on what to call this "disorder," much less agree on how to define it. These experts have alternately referred to this "disorder" as "Munchausen Syndrome by Proxy," "Munchausen by Proxy Syndrome," "Munchausen by Proxy," and "Factitious Disorder by Proxy." Each of these labels carries with it a vastly different definition, each more vague and equivocal than the next. Is this a mental health disorder residing within the mother? Or is it a description of an act of medical abuse of the child? Who gets the label, the mother or the child? There are many other important questions left begging for answers. Unfortunately, the relevant medical community cannot even agree on what the answers to these questions are.

The profile used to identify "perpetrators" of this disorder is equally pusillanimous. For example, one characteristic that consistently makes the lists of the "hired gun" experts is that the mother is convincing in her denial of the allegations. How is this predictive of anything? One can easily imagine a truly innocent mother testifying sincerely and convincingly about her innocence, only to have the judge check off one more element of the profile as having been met. Of course, if she is nervous about testifying in court and appears less than convincing, that will be counted against her as well. It is like the old childhood ruse of "Heads I win. Tails you lose."

The literature on Munchausen by Proxy Syndrome is replete with warnings that only those doctors and scientists who are well versed in the supposed permutations of this "disorder" can see it. In support of this dire warning, no less an expert than Herbert Schreier, M.D. cautions, in his book, *Hurting for Love*, how, during an interview of a mother accused of MBPS, he was once almost duped into believing that she was innocent. It was not until Dr. Schreier left the interview and had his faith reaffirmed by other knowledgeable doctors that he realized what was going on. With this type of dire warning coming from experts, it is no wonder that social workers, police, and eventually judges themselves get pulled into the ruse. Just as in *The Emperor's New Clothes*, nobody wants to admit that he or she just does not see "it." By the time a MBPS case gets to the judge, it is replete with dubious experts, social workers, detectives, and nervous treating physicians who by now have all jumped on the "Munchausen Bandwagon." Unless the mother is fabulously wealthy, she will be no match for the unlimited resources of the state, and her family will be destroyed.

With all this "evidence" amassed against a mother, few judges would be willing to admit that they just do not see this esoteric "disorder." In one case I am aware of, the trial judge acknowledged in her findings that she did not see Munchausen by Proxy Syndrome; however, she went on to enter the finding anyway. The judge's reasoning was that the state had provided her with more experts on the subject than the mother did. Indeed, some courts have held that all that is needed for a finding of Munchausen by Proxy Syndrome is a chronically ill child with baffling symptoms and a mother who fits the "profile" (see *In re Jessica Z*, 135 Misc.2d 250, 515 N.Y.S.2d 370 [N.Y. 1987]). In *Jessica Z*, the court unbelievably applied the tort doctrine of *res ipsa loquitur* (literally "the thing speaks for itself"). This doctrine is used in personal injury cases where there are no eyewitnesses to an injury-producing event. This doctrine further requires the defendant to have exclusive control over the thing or instrument that causes injury. Lastly, this doctrine holds that no other possible explanation can exist, except that the defendant must have been negligent in the control of the object. To have any viability, the application of *res ipsa loquitur* in the Munchausen by Proxy Syndrome setting would require the mother to have exclusive control over the child at all times. The application of *res ipsa loquitur* fails to take into consideration the doctors, nurses, therapists, technicians, fathers, grandparents, aunts, uncles, stepbrothers, and others who come into frequent, regular contact with the sick child.

Making sense of all this nonsense has been difficult until now. David Allison and Mark Roberts have done a masterful job of analyzing the historical context of Munchausen by Proxy Syndrome. They expertly guide the reader through the development of witchcraft and hysteria as precursors to the modern-day Munchausen by Proxy Syndrome. The authors deftly show how fear, prejudice, and distrust of women have been defined, classified, and codified into societal acceptance by the very institutions that have the most to gain from the exclusion of women. This is especially true in the field of medicine. According to a recent study (Doty. 1997), the majority of all health care decisions in the United States are made by women. Given the rapid advancement of managed health care in the last 10 years, health care professionals and their payors (read that as insurance companies) are "incentivized" to remove any woman who is perceived as overutilizing the system.

Allison and Roberts are at their best in this book when they bring the bright hot light of their critical thinking to bear on Schreier and Libow's work, *Hurting for Love*. Allison and Roberts point out, with tremendous insight, the internal inconsistencies, the lack of scientific support, and the sheer reification of supposed facts in Schreier and Libow's work. If society is going to take effective steps to eradicate child abuse, it needs something much more substantial than *Hurting for Love* before it steps in and destroys a family. Allison and Roberts's work set forth in this book is Exhibit "A" of that fact.

What Allison and Roberts have done here is not just fire a warning shot across the bow of the "Good Ship Munchausen." Indeed, they have fired an Exocet missile right into its midsection.

Thomas M. Ryan, Esq.
Chandler, Arizona

ACKNOWLEDGMENTS

The authors would like to acknowledge their sincere appreciation to the many individuals who helped us at various stages in the preparation of our manuscript, especially to John Kerr, who gave many substantive and extremely helpful suggestions concerning the theoretical development of our work. Our other editors at The Analytic Press, Paul Stepansky and Eleanor Starke Kobrin, also lent great support and their highly professional expertise to this difficult and controversial project. We would similarly like to express our thanks for the encouragement expressed by the faculty, students, and staff of our Department of Philosophy at Stony Brook University, with particular thanks to Edward Casey and Mary Rawlinson. We are most appreciative of those friends and colleagues who read the manuscript in its many phases of development, especially Anna Alexander, Babette Babich, Clive Baldwin, Paula J. Caplan, Andrew Haase, Donald Pruden, François Raffoul, Will Sinda, and Allen Weiss. We are especially grateful to Zvi Lothane, M.D., for his invaluable advice in the areas of pediatric psychiatry and psychoanalysis. Thanks also to Herbert A Schreier, M.D. and Phil B. for their helpful contributions. We are deeply indebted to the law firm of G. Tony Serra, Lichter, Daar, Bustammante, Michael, and Wilson, and particularly to Zenia Gilg and Kristen Wahadlo, for their assistance in dealing with the legal complexities of some of the court cases we examined. Finally, and with deep respect for the legal assistance he has provided to so many deserving individuals, we would like to thank Thomas M. Ryan for his expert advice and counsel on the present work.

INTRODUCTION

THE RECENT EMERGENCE OF THE MUNCHAUSEN BY PROXY SYNDROME "PHENOMENON"

First principle: any explanation is better than none.

—*Friedrich Nietzsche*

It may have escaped the notice of some, but more than 300 articles in a broad range of professional journals have witnessed the arrival of a peculiar new plague, a mystifying psychological disorder termed Munchausen by Proxy Syndrome (MBPS).[1] Briefly, the syndrome, like all syndromes, is characterized by a number of unusual signs and behavior patterns in the subject, but, with MBPS, it is particularly alleged that the common factor consists of a person's (usually a mother) inducing or feigning

---

1. Although the syndrome is often designated somewhat differently in the professional literature (e.g., Munchausen's syndrome by Proxy, Munchausen by Proxy, and Factitious Disorder by Proxy), we have here used the name preferred by Herbert A. Schreier and Judith A. Libow (1993a). Maintaining that the by proxy syndrome is not a variation of Munchausen's, they explain that this term is used to distinguish the by proxy syndrome from Munchausen's syndrome in general.

either physical or psychological symptoms—and sometimes, both—in another person (usually her child). Typically, in the course of the MBPS dynamics, the mother is said to produce a range of distressing symptoms in the child, but always with an eye toward obtaining subsequent medical attention for her child. The MBPS mother then enjoins the physician to perform unneeded and extensive examinations, as well as invasive procedures, on the child, thereby involving the doctor and hospital staff as unwitting participants in her deceptions. According to the standard descriptions of this syndrome, the mother typically denies any accusations of deception or of abuse of her child. Nonetheless, psychologists, psychiatrists, medical practitioners, and various other health care professionals are of a single voice in alerting the general public to the menace this syndrome represents: that it appears to constitute a major new form of child abuse. The warnings are indeed harsh, and medical authorities have attempted to mobilize public opinion so as to contain the damage wrought by this syndrome and to prevent its spread. Two researchers, who have been perhaps the most outspoken advocates for the diagnosis and aggressive control of MBPS, Schreier and Libow (1993a), write:

> The illnesses that have been presented in MBPS cover a remarkable range of organ systems and physical complaints . . . [including] some 100 different factitious or induced symptoms for which children have been brought to the attention of physicians, including abdominal pain, apnea, bleeding, diabetes, diarrhea, eczema, fevers, infections, lethargy, rashes, renal failure, seizures, shock, tachycardia, vomiting, and weight loss. And the list is expanding all the time, as new cases are seen and described in medical journals. Unfortunately, since these "illnesses" are nonexistent or induced by other substances or manipulations, they generally fail to respond to the physician's usual treatments, or show an unusual and unexpected course of recurrence or intensification. The medical picture tends to get progressively more complicated by the addition of new medications and invasive interventions as the physicians search for ever-more powerful treatments for these persistent "illnesses" [p. 15].

But the dire warnings do not stop here. To insure that these professional medical judgments be heeded by the greatest range of those who are responsible for protecting children, the FBI took the task upon itself to simplify and to disseminate this specialized information to law enforcement personnel throughout the U. S. In the official publication of the FBI we are told that today, the consensus is that MBPS is not rare, is notoriously resistant to parental psychotherapy, and carries a very grim prognosis. Approximately 10 percent of MBPS victims die. Unfortunately, more police agencies and medical professionals will be confronted with this form of abuse in the future. Hopefully, the information discussed here will alert law enforcement officers, especially those who deal with cases of abuse, to the warning signs of MBPS and will assist them in identifying the perpetrators and helping the victims [Boros and Brubaker, 1992, p. 20].

This information was communicated to social service agencies, family courts, counseling centers, and educational and health offices throughout the United States and elsewhere. There is a burgeoning popular literature on the syndrome, and several television talk shows have devoted time to its diagnosis, prognosis, and sufferers. Documentary exposure on TV has also extended to the dramatic videotaping of presumed MBPS mothers suffocating their children in hospital settings. The print media, in particular, have featured a number of stories on the syndrome itself and its effects on contemporary family life and have covered some of the more spectacular court cases involving MBPS. In short, MBPS has arrived, both as a pathology and as a popular phenomenon.

One of the most dramatic and widely covered of these cases was that of Ellen Storck. *The New York Times, Newsday*, and many other national and regional newspapers detailed her repeated court hearings from October of 1992, through May of 1994. A single mother of four, Ellen Storck was accused in July of 1992 by a physician at the Schneider Children's Hospital at the Long Island Jewish Medical Center of having induced apnea episodes in her youngest child, Aaron. The accusation was provoked by her response to the severity and aggressiveness of the type of treatment suggested by the physician. Following the outplacement of her son by Child Protective Services of Suffolk County and a lengthy trial in Suffolk County Family Court, Storck was adjudged of having neglected her child and of routinely subjecting him to unnecessary medical treatment. She subsequently appealed to regain custody of her son; but she was denied custody, and he was eventually transferred to live with family relatives in Ohio. Having consistently denied the charges of MBPS child abuse—Aaron himself likewise denied any abuse—and continually attempting to regain custody, Ms. Storck finally took possession of Aaron from her relatives in Ohio and subsequently fled with him to Florida. After several unsuccessful attempts to capture Aaron, a police SWAT team, entering through an air-conditioning shaft, finally cornered and recaptured the 14-year-old Aaron. He is currently residing in a group home, pending further litigation.

Popular interest in MBPS has been reflected in numerous articles that appeared in national magazines such as *Newsweek* and in discussions on TV "talk shows" and featured presentations. Other popular exposure of the syndrome has centered on two similar high-profile cases, those of Kathy Bush and Yvonne Eldridge. Bush's daughter, Jennifer, had visited the White House and had appeared in a poster for Hillary Rodham Clinton's campaign in support of national health care reform in the spring of 1992. It was later alleged that Kathy Bush was actually abusing her child by MBPS. The Bush case is still in litigation and will go to trial in 1999. Yvonne Eldridge, like the Bushes, was honored by the White House. In 1986, Nancy Reagan declared the Eldridges to be one of the six "great American families" for their foster work in caring for severely ill children—children born to substance-addicted mothers or who suffered from HIV/AIDS and multiple physical and mental disorders. In 1992 Mrs. Eldridge was also accused of child abuse and neglect, with MBPS as a determining factor in her indictment. She was tried and convicted on the charge, but now awaits a new trial tentatively scheduled for January, 1999. Both cases were of national interest, and accounts of them appeared on various television programs.

Remarkably, Munchausen by Proxy Syndrome did not exist as a disorder until 1977, when a British pediatrician, Roy Meadow, published an article in *The Lancet*, bringing two brief case histories of the syndrome to public attention. In doing so, he was incorporating a term and a tradition that was itself less than three decades old. Twenty-six years earlier, another British physician, Richard Asher, anecdotally—with the fabulist, Baron von Munchausen in mind—coined the term Munchausen's syndrome to describe the fanciful behavior of three other people, who would previously have been diagnosed as malingerers, hysterics, or hypochondriacs. The original Baron von Munchausen was an 18th-century German figure who was cast as the exaggerating storytelling hero of Rudolphe Raspe's (ca. 1789) novel, *The Travels and Surprising Adventures of Baron von Munchausen*. The three subjects Asher discussed repeatedly sought medical treatment for what he considered to be largely simulated and fabricated (i.e., nonexistent) illnesses. Thinking that such cases might prove to be costly and burdensome to administer—until one could establish that the subjects were in fact not ill and, hence, did not need medical treatment—Asher deemed it important enough to bring these cases to the attention of hospital officials, if only to warn them that there were such subjects and that they might be otherwise difficult to diagnose. In the end, Asher (1951) thought his effort to be a practical and helpful matter and that, almost as an afterthought, his notice might help facilitate the search for "a cure of the psychological kink which produces the disease [i.e., Munchausen's syndrome]" (p. 341).

From 1951 to 1977 the original Munchausen's syndrome aroused sporadic suspicion and attention among medical authorities, much of which centered on a series of published letters and brief papers responding to Asher's article. In the handful of technical articles that appeared during this period on the subject, Munchausen's syndrome was treated as a more or less unspecified factitious disorder among others and usually in relation to other types of common disorders, particularly malingering, hypochondria, and hysteria (see Cramer, Gershberg, and Stern, 1971, pp. 573–578; Curran, 1973, pp. 564–567). Once Meadow introduced the Munchausen's Syndrome by Proxy, however, locating the new disorder in a nexus of transferences between parent and child, and between patient and doctor, the by proxy syndrome seemed far more specific, and therefore far more accessible to analysis, understanding, and intervention. Given the immense increase in public awareness—and reporting—of child abuse cases (familial, au pair, and, especially, day care child abuse) in the 1980s and 90s, as well as the dramatic rise of reported cases or illnesses resistant to standard diagnosis, such as Sudden Infant Death Syndrome (SIDS), Shaken Baby Syndrome, Chronic Fatigue Syndrome, various stress-related disorders, and the like, MBPS became a focal point in the diagnosis of these confusing types of disorders. It offered itself as a model through which empirically difficult to ascertain cases could be explained. It provided a flexible dynamic that could detail aberrant behavior, abuse, sexual perversion, molestation, and so on within multiple dyadic relations, especially those cases in which the subjects' own motives could not be clearly recognized or understood. It remained for professional writers, medical clinicians, and psychiatric diagnosticians to codify the syndrome, to give it a defining set of signs and symptoms, and to assign sufficiently generalized etiologies to the disorder, such that it might emerge as a publicly recognizable phenomenon and so that appropriate intervention might lessen the frequency of this particularly insidious form of child abuse.

CHALLENGING THE MBPS CLAIM

The principal theme guiding this book is that adult Munchausen's syndrome and MBPS, by extension, are to be understood as diagnostic "constructions" or "fabrications" that reflect and embody institutionalized medical power; that is, the unquestioned professional authority to create and legitimize what are oftentimes simply scientifically indeterminate constructions (such as those factitious disorders whose existence is determined solely on a diagnostic level). At the outset, we should perhaps clarify the sense of this notion of "medical power." Physicians, to whom this book is addressed in part, are not accustomed to thinking in terms of power outside of certain limited contexts. To be sure, internal struggles over ascension in hospitals and medical schools involve questions of power. So, too, do external struggles waged with government regulatory agencies and, more recently and more significantly, with third-party payers. But the kind of power at stake here is of a quite different order. It pertains to the profession as a whole, its authority within society, and the scope it is granted to exercise that power without interference and, in some cases, to command resources and assistance from the other sectors of society. To combat typhoid, for example, requires the ceding of enormous power to the medical profession: to diagnose not only the ill but also, importantly, not-ill carriers of the diseases; to enlist public health authorities in quarantining the ill and carriers alike; and, finally, to enlist police and criminal courts when these strictures are violated. But for the physician the exercise of this kind of power is understood instrumentally, straightforwardly. What else would one plausibly do? And, yet, once a profession has been granted this kind of power, at least in certain domains, then it becomes liable to certain kinds of potential irrationalities that are always inherent in how power is created, maintained, and exercised in society. The exercise of power, as for example in combating an epidemic, need not be irrational; but, by the same token, once it has been granted, it acquires its own institutional momentum and its own internal logic by which its continued exercise is justified.

Social and cultural theorists, to whom this book is also addressed in part, have an advantage over physicians in that they are accustomed to thinking in terms of power formations within society and the kinds of practices and discourses by which those formations are created and then maintained. By the same token, theorists are accustomed to examining instances where the cumulative momentum of a particular social formation—say, restrictive commercial associations or the power of the clergy in Ireland—lead to dubious social practices that are nonetheless allowed to endure and that become blanketed with various institutionally self-serving rationales. Where social and cultural theorists have a relative disadvantage is in their lack of a practical understanding of the logic of medical reasoning, and most especially with the ambiguities that are actually encountered in clinical work. Nor are they likely to be completely familiar with the kinds of ambiguous, less than ideal situations in which physicians are often called on to act, such situations as working in a large urban hospital caring mainly for indigent patients. For these reasons, such readers—as well as the general public—are often likely to suspend judgment and accept medical testimony as more or less self-evident. The kinds of judgment that sociologists and historians are quite ready to make about, say, restrictive commercial trade associations or the power of the clergy in Ireland, they are not ordinarily prepared to exercise vis-à-vis the broad use of medical power in contemporary society, at least not in most cases.

A final paradox to be considered with regard to our invocation of "power" as an essential element in the construction of MBPS has to do with the social space in which this power is, in fact, often exercised. A factitious disorder, for example, is, by definition, a nondisorder, a simulation of a disorder. Most physicians would prefer not to become embroiled in such cases. Yet, who is better qualified to make the determination that a factitious disorder is or is not present than a physician, usually a psychiatrist, psychotherapist, or a psychologist? Thus it is that the physician is thrown into a situation that, unless he or she enjoys playing detective or prosecutor, is very much not where the physician wants to be. The physician is, in a sense, held hostage by his or her own professional responsibility. But it is in precisely such situations where the physician holds enormous power, for, by a single determination, he or she can both refuse care to someone demanding it and, if third-party remuneration or compensation is at stake, open the doors for prosecution for fraud. In fact, as we shall show, MBPS is generally found to be located within a socially marginalized population (although claims to the contrary are frequently made), involving typically poor women whose children are being attended to in less than ideal circumstances; and yet, by the same token, it is on this periphery that physicians enjoy enormous power and that, guided by a faulty preconception of what may be at stake in terms of the difficulties in diagnosing and treating the child's illnesses, physicians are in a position do real harm.

Our broader claim, then, is that MBPS and adult Munchausen's are not self-standing, verifiable, and specifiable disorders at all but rather, are brought into existence through a set of historically evolved discourses and operations that stem from particular medical institutions and individuals. As such, these discourses and operations tend to cohere over a period of time and coalesce into a medical model, itself driven by a set of taxonomic classifications and an underlying set of perceived social threats and cultural biases. Once these classifications are refined, reified, set into the recursive domain of professional literature, supported by statistical data and by physician consensus, and so on, the disorder becomes effectively "established." Or, as Jean Baudrillard (1983) said, "it is the map that precedes the territory" (p. 2). The adult Munchausen's and MBPS "maps," the broad set of taxonomic designations and signs, furthermore, serve as a means to provoke our recognition of its alleged subjects. In this sense, the Munchausen "map" signifies or denotes a readily identifiable group of so-called sufferers—who, we should add, are by and large powerless to resist their own classification and who typically have been traditional targets for the exercise of medical power and social control in any case: that is, women, the poor, "hateful patients," the homeless, drug abusers, the mentally ill, "derelicts." It is in these respects, then, that MBPS is able to establish its legitimacy and its social urgency. If there are historical precedents, appropriate taxonomies, statistical quantifications, sufferers and victims, then the disorder must be studied. And, since it poses a real threat, it must be contained. But, most important, and by the same imperative, it *must* exist.

BUILDING THE MODEL

One of the things we find to be particularly problematic about MBPS is the construction of the previously mentioned spurious and inappropriately conceived model, which enables it to be articulated as a disorder in the first place. To begin with, the model itself and the specifics it addresses are largely the result of an extremely complex set of relations between individuals and public and private institutions, as well as among a variety of disciplines, discourses, and other types of what Michel Foucault termed "power formations." Accordingly, in our view,

MBPS is not so much a precise and objective mental disorder, possessed of a unique set of determinant characteristics, as it is a generalized hypothesis advanced by a group of individuals and institutions with similar concerns and intentions, all of whom tend to collectively define and perpetuate its very existence as a disorder. The way in which MBPS is treated, the organization of the various institutional formations constructed around it, its power to generate discourses and mobilize various agencies, all serve to establish its uniqueness, its novelty, as a modern pathology. Thus, the constructed model, and even the informational claims initially made within the professional literature, are mediated by a broad variety of social, cultural, political, economic, and legal interests—interests that range from politically inspired "aggressive prosecution" of suspected child abuse cases to the zealous pursuit of medical insurance fraud—interests that, forcibly, dictate methodological procedures and motivate criteria for nosological analysis and for active intervention. Hence, even the specification of the disorder is rendered problematic at the very outset.

It must be understood that this confluence of influences is in large part predetermined, if not simply pregiven. In much the way Nietzsche (1974) claimed that the "founders" of religion are rather "finders" of already existent patterns of life, language, values, behavior, ideals, and aspirations—and thus lend systematic coherence and direction to these social and cultural patterns, rendering "new" sects and denominations out of them—so it becomes clear that not only MBPS, but many other "disorders," harbor deep historical and social predeterminations, underlying their appearance as "new" disorders.

> The distinctive invention of the founders of religions is, first: to posit a particular kind of life and everyday customs that have the effect of a *disciplina voluntatis* and at the same time abolish boredom—and then: to bestow on this life style an *interpretation* that makes it appear to be illuminated by the highest value so that this life style becomes something for which one fights and under certain circumstances sacrifices one's life. Actually, the second of these two inventions is more essential. The first, the way of life, was usually there before, but alongside other ways of life and without any sense of its special value. The significance and originality of the founder of a religion usually consists of his *seeing* it, *selecting* it, and *guessing* for the first time to what use it can be put, how it can be interpreted [p. 296].

In seeking to illustrate some of the characteristic motivations underlying the formation of MBPS, we have drawn on two historically antecedent "disorders," namely, witchcraft and hysteria. The two cases are particularly relevant to an understanding of MBPS because they anticipate a similar pattern of dynamic construction. On one hand, both disorders focus on their bearers, hosts, and purveyors: women. On the other hand, the disorders are held to threaten a fundamental (if only presumed) social stability brought on by a dramatic eruption of what will be held to be evil or madness. With both witchcraft and hysteria, the fundamental expression of a cultural and psychological fear of women is magnified into a complex, necessary, and pressing social and political need.

Some readers may well balk at the thought of comparing any contemporary medical diagnosis—no matter how odd—with the kinds of designations involved in accusations of witchcraft. For witchcraft simply doesn't exist, and to believe in it is simply irrational and superstitious. Nonetheless, we do believe in things that are often matters of unproved inferences. We readily believe, for example, that "chemical imbalances" are the root causes of certain "diseases" like depression. We believe this even though there are a residual number of cases of depression that don't respond symptomatically to the proffered pharmacological solution, cases that cannot always be distinguished from those that do. More to the point, we also tend to believe in a great number of inferences having to do with the existence, potency, and persistence of "unconscious" processes. And while no serious 20th-century thinker would doubt that, in fact, there can be powerfully determining motives affecting behavior that are nonetheless unconscious, this realm of inference is famously open to a great deal of faulty reasoning and faulty invocation, resulting in a fair amount of wrong, and often pernicious, belief. Moreover, the resulting false beliefs can have dramatic social consequences leading even to prosecution and incarceration of some people. The advantage, then, of thinking about practices like the persecution of witches, or the various kinds of treatment offered to women suffering from hysteria, is that it offers us comparison instances of how beliefs can become embedded in certain kinds of discourses and certain kinds of social practices, quite irrespective of their truth value or lack thereof. But before going further, here let us note expressly that the comparison with either witchcraft or hysteria by itself does not possess any specific evidentiary value in terms of the validity of MBPS as a syndrome. This is a separate matter, which we will take up at length later. The point, rather, is to familiarize ourselves with the kinds of social practices, atavistic social fears, various forms of perceived urgency, and so on whose dynamics can drive such constructions.

In the case of witchcraft, an immense apparatus was engaged to rid the dreaded evil: witch hunters, witch prosecutors, judges, witchcraft torture, widely circulated confessional manuals, ecclesiastical bulls, well-established trial procedures, witchcraft-spot "prickers," witch dousers, paid witnesses, exorcists, all were included in the drive to eliminate witches, not to mention the assistance lent by the provincial gentry, who stood to gain from the confiscation of witches' tainted properties. All this was initially subtended by the concerns of the church—to eliminate heresy, devil-worship, and evil, generally—and, in later cases, continued by the interests of the state, which stood to gain from the quelling of disorders and the elimination of potentially dangerous political enemies. In short, we hope to demonstrate that, even though witchcraft was a completely invented "disorder," it assumed the legitimacy of a dangerous public threat, which, in turn, generated an entire set of procedures to contain it, each thought to be of important and real significance within the culture and society of the times.

In the millennia-old case of hysteria, the lines were similarly drawn between women and the institutional structures meant to contain them. What had traditionally been seen as women's oftentimes disruptive, wanton, willful, and obliquitous behavior, was equated with a kind of generic—if not genetic—madness, one that threatened the stable life of the family unit and, by extension, the patriarchal social model as a whole. From ancient Egypt, through its Renaissance reconstruction, and well throughout the 19th century, hysteria was universally understood to be an "illness," and, by this very token, medicine was entrusted with its remediation. Such remediation would include a variety of medical procedures, among which numbered surgery, hospitalization, therapeutic techniques, medications, and so on, which were, if not less repressive, at least more humane than traditional folk or family treatment: physical abuse, enforced isolation, restraint, and the stigma of a generalized social opprobrium.

Charged to diagnose and to treat hysteria, medicine would proceed through a series of impasses, each of which would be "resolved" by continually expanding the medical model itself. While the authority of church and state remained relatively stable throughout the period of the "witch troubles," the medical model expanded dramatically. It moved from its initial diagnostic hypothesis of "womb displacements" to its explanation of the disorder according to the effects of the bodily humors, through the anatomically specific physiological and neurological models of "lesion-induced" behavior, to a relatively sophisticated medical understanding, which, at the close of the 19th century, realized that there was no organic cause at all of "hysteria." Hence, hysteria itself posed a dramatic challenge to the authority of the medical model. If an "illness" stubbornly persisted in women—with all its disruptive effects on the individual, family, and community, notwithstanding the care given to these hysterics by all the attendant institutions devised to treat them—and yet medicine could find no organic etiology whatsoever for this illness, then what, in fact, was an illness, and how could medicine be charged to cure it, especially if no one could determine precisely what it was? To all appearances, this difficult issue was resolved by Freud, who reduced virtually all etiological problems of hysteria to ideational or psychodynamic causes, which could be neither empirically recognized nor dealt with by the patient herself. The construction of hysteria, which had fallen into perilous straits, was to a certain extent rescued by Freud's invention of the unconscious and its unobservable, yet ineluctable, logic.

Having to confront the broadened concerns of psychodynamics, introduced by 19th- and 20th-century psychology and psychiatry (from Charcot, through Janet, Breuer, and Freud), modern medicine would have to extend its theoretical models of diagnosis, etiology, and treatment and offer the assurance of a cure, of remediation, to these new subjects. It was precisely this necessity that afforded medical psychiatry a greatly expanded field of operation, a position that enabled it to generate a whole new set of determinations, classifications, disorders, and etiologies. This would extend the authority of medicine beyond its traditional areas of application into the determination and control of a vast number of heretofore, nonmedical "behaviors." This extension was supplemented and effectively confirmed by the creation of a series of authoritative nosological manuals—most prominently, the various editions of the *Diagnostic and Statistical Manual of Mental Disorders (DSM)* and the *International Classification of Disease (ICD)*—which gave the appearance of widespread reliability and validity to psychiatric practice. With its newly found authority and comprehensiveness, medical psychiatry was in a position both to construct a whole range of "disorders" and to direct their treatment. Aberrant, deviant, and unusual forms of behavior would henceforth be designated as psychiatric "disorders," much as hysteria had come to be categorized under the older medical model.

A person who was formerly considered an academic "underachiever" would now be labeled as suffering from "Specific Academic or Work Inhibition," according to *DSM-III* (American Psychiatric Association, 1978) or *DSM-IV* (American Psychiatric Association, 1994); those who occasionally "blow their top" were now classified as having an "Isolated Explosive Disorder" (American Psychiatric Association, 1978, 1994), and so on *ad nauseam*. Obviously, and unfortunately, much of the nosological and taxonomic complexity introduced with this expanded authority over behavior—public and private—lacks serious scientific and medical foundations. Much of this classification is, in fact, a collection, a compilation, of individual and institutional affirmations and concerns, all subject to relations that, to a large extent, fall outside the field of medical science proper: in some of the more egregious cases, these concerns take the form of biases concerning sexual role behavior, gender determination, economic status, social class, race, education, social conformity, cultural convention, and, indeed, what is commonly understood to be behavioral "normalcy." Legend in this respect are such classified "disorders" as Homosexuality (*DSM-IIIR*, 302.90), Premenstrual Dysphoric (*DSM-IV* Appendix), Histrionic Personality (*DSM-IV*, 301.50), Dependent Personality (*DSM IIIR*, 301.60), Disorder of Written Expression (*DSM-IV*, 315.2), Noncompliance to Treatment (*DSM-IV*, V15.81), and so on. It is through this expanded authority, we submit, that one such prominent new disorder—MBPS itself—has come to be constituted as a "major illness," a "disease," that affects women, mothers, nurses, foster mothers, grandmothers—and even, in a few alleged cases, fathers.

HISTORICAL AND METHODOLOGICAL CONCERNS

To understand the construction of MBPS, we have endeavored, in Part Two, to articulate the alleged historical antecedents of factitious disorders generally.[2] In this respect, we have attempted to examine critically

---

2. In *DSM-IV* (American Psychiatric Association, 1994), Adult Munchausen's Syndrome and Munchausen by Proxy Syndrome are categorized under the terms

certain central aspects of the tradition. We argue that many of its vary-ing (and oftentimes, conflicting) interests and concerns testify less to medical science proper than to practical issues of administration, to the maintenance of social biases, to the exercise of punishment and social control, to the demand for theoretical hegemony, or simply, to the ordi-nary and uncomfortable persistence of personal conflict. The strategy of criticism focuses on elaborating as wide a variety as possible of these extenuating concerns, which are claimed to constitute the tradition that precedes MBPS, as well as to legitimate it as a specific syndrome.

Our critique of the MBPS construction begins with an examination of the work of George Cheyne and Hector Gavin, British physicians of the 18th and 19th centuries, respectively. These figures establish an ini-tial focus for our own reading of MBPS, since they are frequently invoked as being among the most prominent early theoreticians of hypochondriacal and factitious disorders—particularly Gavin, who appears in virtually every text with pretensions to trace the historical provenance of both the adult Munchausen's and the MBPS disorder. The trajectory leads us to examine the subsequent work of later 19th-century figures, such as Sir Benjamin Brodie and, again, Charcot and Freud.

The specifically modern construction of MBPS—beginning with the emergence of the adult Munchausen's syndrome—is subsequently examined through the texts of Karl Menninger (1934) (on "surgical addicts") and Asher's *locus classicus*, "Munchausen's syndrome," and is continued through the work inspired by this text. This literature is con-siderable, and it comprises a large number of letters and correspon-dence in the medical journals of the period, as well as articles and longer monographs. A careful review of these texts reveals a remarkable pat-tern of coherence concerning the problematic nature of the physi-cian–patient relation, brought about by the "deceitful" and "dangerous" ministrations of the "typical" Munchausen sufferer who seeks medical

---

Factitious Disorder with Physical Symptoms and Factitious Disorder by Proxy. Factitious Disorder by Proxy was placed in Appendix B, indicating the need for further clinical and diagnostic assessment. Factitious Disorder with Physical Symptoms, however, is contained within the main body of the *DSM-IV*. Generally speaking, factitious disorders are understood to be the presentation of false or self-induced psychological or physical symptoms without general concern for "gain." It is this lack of gain that presumably distinguishes factitious disorders from those associated with, for example, malingering and hypochondria, where gain is said to be evident.

assistance. Such patients appear to present themselves as suffering a multitude of feigned and self-induced disorders without any apparent motive for doing so, and this constitutes the principal axis of the adult Munchausen's syndrome. On closer examination, however, we found that virtually every "Munchausen" patient mentioned in the literature had a panoply of already existing physical, behavioral, and psychological disorders, not to mention that many were driven to seek hospitalization and shelter for reasons having to do with drug dependency, substance abuse, homelessness, poverty, or, quite simply, intense personal pain and suffering. That is to say, what at first glance appears to be a unitary syndrome defining a factitious disorder, plain and simple, at closer inspection turns out to be a veritable grab-bag designation of patients with a wide variety of very real and very severe troubles. Moreover, such patients would never be classified together outside of the putative logic of the superordinate description entailed in the adult Munchausen's syndrome.

Following the critique of the precedent literature concerning factitious disorders and the adult Munchausen's syndrome, we discuss a number of central problems that arise from the language and logic of the MBPS disorder: the problem of definition and recursivity (a procedure in which all present cases are defined in terms of previously accrued and constantly reiterated cases) in arriving at a classification; the formal understanding of what constitutes a syndrome or disorder; the logic of medical articulation; and questions of observation, validity, and verification. In relation to the language of MBPS, we attempt to focus on the laxity of definition in psychiatric nomenclature in general and, particularly, in that of adult Munchausen's and MBPS. Curiously, MBPS, which was stipulated as a syndrome by Meadow and others, assumes its medical and social "reality," its specific characteristics, largely on the basis of the initial stipulative definition. Indeed, it could be said that, in a certain respect, MBPS is defined "into" existence by virtue of the enormous amount of material written about it: each professional paper, report, case history, and review thus serves to "verify" the initial definition, to confirm the existence of subsequent "cases," and to act as a warning that the disorder is far more widespread and pernicious than had been originally suspected. The initial definition also is a means of ordination, since, by definition, the term syndrome provides for a broad clustering of otherwise unconnected "signs and symptoms," taken up under a single category or classification. What we attempt to demonstrate in this respect is that the defined category itself, and not the observed medical reality, constitutes the received legitimacy of the MBPS disorder.

What complicates any understanding of the disorder is the remarkably repetitive series of accounts about adult Munchausen's and MBPS and the striking recursivity of information (e.g., case histories and multiple diagnoses) used to describe it. The many cases so routinely refer to one another that a vague, all-encompassing model—characterized by an accreted stratum of "fact" and a rhetorical nomenclature used to articulate it—eventually overwhelms the specificity of each new presentation. Thus, the later cases are interpreted only in the corresponding terms of earlier precedent, such that what should be relevant empirical considerations to the case at hand are progressively marginalized, if not eliminated. Such a trajectory of standard and routine interpretation raises two subsequent problems. First, with the progressive elimination of collateral empirical data—that is, the failure to collect, to make use of, or even to take note of detailed medical histories, psychiatric records, specific socioeconomic conditions, informed personal histories, an understanding of marital relations, inquiry into possible spousal abuse—the case studies presented emerge as entirely abstract constructions, each of which, owing to the absence of distinctive empirical analysis, corresponds to the vague profile of all the earlier cases. Hence, the second problem follows in turn: the inability of practically everyone writing in the field to devise even a remotely plausible etiology for the MBPS disorder. To put this matter another way, given the great diversity of the patients involved—the variety of their personal lives, histories, personalities, socioeconomic situations—if the only thing they are alleged to have done alike is to injure their children to gain attention from physicians, then the question is, why do they do this? If we cannot find a consistently coherent answer, then the behavior, *if it does occur*, is merely an indication of some unacceptable moral or psychological deterioration, no different in kind from other indications and not worthy of being regarded as a syndrome at all.

THE NEW MBPS ORTHODOXY

With the appearance of Schreier and Libow's (1993a) definitive study of MBPS, however, the prospect of establishing a rigorous etiology for the disorder finally seemed forthcoming. They argue that MBPS is effectively a "perversion of mothering," one in which the MBPS mother would "fetishize" her own child in order to gain affection and admiration from her "caregiving" and "nurturing" physician. This claimed etiology permeates the entire work, which, in turn, becomes a somewhat labored exercise to establish its validity, to explain its agency, and thereby to determine the overall management strategy of MBPS. Indeed, one of the main purported goals of the text is to establish finally an objective basis for the diagnosis, prognosis, and treatment of the disorder.

Part Three of this book is devoted to analyzing these claims, to criticizing the underlying assumptions they rest on, and to examining the methodologies and data on which the authors' account is predicated. What necessitates this approach is that Schreier and Libow's (1993a) *Hurting for Love* has become the definitive "handbook" of MBPS medical diagnosis and treatment. Most significantly, it is the principal theoretical frame of reference for the juridicolegal prosecution of MBPS and constitutes, in part, the guidelines for child protective and social service agencies. Thus, it has had an enormous influence on both the professional and the public minds. Because of the largely uncritical acceptance of the MBPS theses, children have been outplaced, mothers have been convicted of "MBPS" abuse, families have been dislocated and broken up, and an entire general framework for the continuance of the "Munchausen" claim has been established. Our critique is thus pointedly directed to revealing a number of weaknesses in that text, among which are the central role of Schreier and Libow's proposed etiology for MBPS, the unwarranted—and ahistorical—transformation of the traditional doctor–patient relation into the mother–doctor dyad, the inexplicable and often theoretically self-serving use of such core psychoanalytic terms as perversion, transferential, sadomasochism, mothering (i.e., the psychodynamics of maternal behavior), fetishism, and the like in elaborating the etiology and dynamics of the disorder.

This unreflective construction of a theoretical etiology (out of such an array of ill-defined concepts) occludes a whole range of considerations that might otherwise be crucial determinants in explaining the complexity of abusive parental behavior and its great variety of forms—even those, like the alleged MBPS, which occur specifically within the context of otherwise seeking medical care and hospital supervision for the child. Among these occluded elements, the most striking are perhaps the virtual exclusion of real socioeconomic conditions of the "MBPS mother," as well as any real understanding of the traditional and contemporary situation regarding the relations between women and the medical profession. These relations extend to the attitudes held toward women by the profession as well as to the effective delivery of health care services to women. Another element in the formulaic construction of the authors' etiology, which is of central concern, is their unreflective treatment of the ways popular images are communicated concerning the authority of the medical profession itself, the power and centrality of physicians, and the ways women are said to become "attached" to these presumably "powerful figures." The etiology is thus built up around the idealized role of the "loving, caregiving physician," who is held to be an all-powerful figure of affective fulfillment and personal salvation for what could only be termed an emotionally and intellectually eviscerated woman. It is on the basis of such a disproportionally structured dyad of abject dependency that the woman is said to offer up her child as a fetish, or, more plausibly, as a sacrifice, to the physician (obstetrician, gynecologist, pediatrician) as a (de-)sexualized token of her willing submission to his authority.

Granted, the foregoing account of Schreier and Libow's etiological argument is but an initial sketch, which we will elaborate in greater detail. But the centrality those authors attribute to their etiology oddly serves to deflect what seems to be the original aim of their book—that MBPS be understood, that its diagnosis and prognosis be clarified so that its victims can be treated and its occurrence prevented—in favor of advancing an extraordinary model of medical hegemony over women and their behavior. What results from the elevation of the medical model of MBPS advanced by Schreier and Libow is the effective, if unintended, devaluation of the women who reportedly suffer from the disorder. In consequence, the "MBPS mother" progressively becomes understood in more criminalized terms as the "perpetrator" or as the "suspect parent."

The child, likewise, is effectively reduced to the caricatured status of a fully defenseless "victim" of abusive MBPS behavior; the child becomes evermore "infantilized" in the course of their account. In the dynamics of what initially was a factitious disorder by proxy, wherein women sufferers were said to be fairly typical of the population at large and where children ranged from neonates to teenagers, these children now become almost exclusively referred to as "preverbal infants," who are incapable of articulating their needs, fears, or life-threatening dangers. Hence, in the evolution of Schreier and Libow's discussion (which parallels the historical discussion of adult Munchausen's and MBPS), what originally was understood as a deviancy of women's behavior, or even as an "uncommon disorder" in relation to real childhood disease, which might indeed result in induced or feigned illness, this unusual disorder now becomes rhetorically transformed into a nationwide criminal assault on helpless, inarticulate infants.

With the dangers of MBPS so remarkably overdramatized, and with the subtending social and economic realities of women so completely understated, Schreier and Libow urge the medical and legal systems to wage a regulatory war against these mothers—all of whom are possessed by a disorder that, in each case, is now affirmed to be potentially lethal. Given these stakes, Schreier and Libow call for the creation of local and regional "intervention teams," directed by fully informed MBPS specialists, composed of health care professionals and social service personnel, who will be empowered as "private parties" to conduct surreptitious surveillance of the MBPS "perpetrators," who will seek court-mandated custodial outplacement of the MBPS children. These teams will likewise seek to mandate psychiatric therapy for the MBPS mothers; they will explain the MBPS dynamics to the civil and criminal courts, to the prosecutors and defense counsel, in the course of determination. The authors finally propose the formation of a "national electronic network" for tracking mother/perpetrators.

Thus, by the end of *Hurting for Love*, the circle is effectively closed. Like witchcraft and hysteria before it, MBPS (and adult Munchausen's as well) emerges as a fully, though differently, constructed disorder, one testifying to a broad range of real and imagined social and institutional concerns, a disorder that constitutes a threat to the health and general well-being of society at large. Just as in the case of witchcraft and hysteria, however, one of the emerging objectives of the Schreier and Libow MBPS construction is the maintenance of a certain discursive and punitive power through social controls. With MBPS, one is confronted by a disorder that threatens the well-being of children and of family life in general, as well as the social and cultural values thereby entailed. Remarkably, since MBPS is a factitious disorder, it can be diagnosed only by a medical specialist who is professionally trained to do so. The mother, the child, the larger unit of family and friends are said to be simply incapable of even recognizing the disorder—as are other, less well informed members of the medical, social service, and legal professions. It is precisely because of their ignorance about this "much underdiagnosed disorder" that the imperative to diagnose and contain it be conducted from the informed standpoint of those specially trained individuals who are fully capable of understanding it. This position of active intervention, of course, is exclusively occupied by the authority of medical power, which is the compelling but unstated goal of the new MBPS orthodoxy.[3]

We conclude with a review of how the MBPS model has been extended in the recent literature—in broadening its appeal to the legal and law enforcement communities, in expanding the parameters of its dynamics and etiology, and by increasing the length of the reported history of the disorder. Use of expanded communication technology has provided the law enforcement community, for example, with a variety of resources in the use of websites. Much of this computer-generated MBPS material serves purposes similar to those earlier articulated within the professional literature: establishing the urgency, pervasiveness, and danger of this underreported, much misunderstood disorder. Following the old pattern, much of the new literature simply restates—ever more stridently—those characteristics now so firmly associated with the MBPS phenomenon. Schreier (1996), for example, not only reintroduces the standard mother–doctor dyad, but he now extends it to a much-expanded array of "powerful figures," including lawyers, school officials, sheriffs, judges, and child care workers, thereby broadening its etiology and social compass. Libow (1995), too, endeavors to broaden this compass in her recent work on a group of aging, early childhood sufferers of MBPS abuse. In reviewing self-reported cases of MBPS ranging in age from 33 to 71, she claims to have found ample and reliable evidence of its earlier prevalence. Of course, all those claims are seriously compromised by virtue of inadequate methodology, spurious

---

3. The misuse of medical power and authority has been the subject of much recent scholarship, particularly in the areas of mother–child relations, sexual politics, and the psychopathologizing of society in general and of women in particular. We are very much indebted to many of these important studies in the fields of psychology, psychiatry, sociology, and medicine. Among the authors whose work we should particultarly acknowledge are Paula Caplan (1989, 1994, 1995), Kate Millet (1991), Louise Armstrong (1993, 1994), Susan P. Penfold, Gilliam A. Walker (1983), and Phil Brown (1990).

reasoning, and insufficient documentation, to the extent where it remains unsubstantiated whether the disorder actually exists.

Existent or not, MBPS nonetheless played a tragic role in the real conviction of Mrs. Yvonne Eldridge. In view of the importance of the Eldridge case, and the way in which the case emerged, the way in which it was diagnosed, reported, and prosecuted—precisely according to the now orthodox MBPS "profile"—we have attempted to reconstruct its relevent elements. These include the particular circumstances of Mrs. Eldridge and her family, as they correspond to and coincide with the profile we have described. Mrs. Eldridge, medically trained by the San Francisco "Baby Moms" foster child program, cared for approximately 40 medically compromised children over a period of several years. She had a fairly extensive lay knowledge of medical terminology; there were foster children who died in her care; her husband was disabled by ALS, and thus could be considered "absent" according to the standard profile. The children were repeatedly hospitalized, Mrs. Eldridge was constantly calling her doctors, and all of these circumstances were compounded by the allegation that she had had a sexual conflict with one of her accusing doctors. And, as is always the case with MBPS "sufferers," she vehemently denied the diagnosis and charge.

Beyond a critical account of the MBPS profile haunting the case, we attempt to point out a number of factors affecting the trial results, particularly a continual series of misstatements, misrepresentations, and falsifications on the part of key prosecution witnesses. Many of these statements were allowed into testimony, both in the grand jury hearing and in the regular trial, because Mrs. Eldridge was at this point indigent and thus was assigned a single public defender who was clearly overwhelmed by a well-financed prosecution. Indeed, it was this inadequate representation that deprived her of her rights to a fair trial and, subsequently, resulted in the overturning of the initial guilty verdict and the issuance of a new trial.

PART ONE

THE SOCIAL-MEDICAL CONSTRUCTION OF DISORDERS: WITCHCRAFT, HYSTERIA, AND MBPS

<table>
<tr><td>

CHAPTER
ONE

</td><td>

WITCHCRAFT

THE CONSTRUCTION OF AN OLD DISORDER

</td></tr>
</table>

How meaningless would these expressions be, that the devils are destined for eternal judgment, that fire has been prepared for them, that they are now tormented and tortured by Christ's glory, if devils were nonexistent!

—*John Calvin*

THE POWER TO POSSESS

If disorders in which symptoms are induced or produced in a second person—that is, factitious disorders by proxy—are located in the agent by virtue of the diagnostician's scrutiny, this scrutiny having been based on effects (real or otherwise) alleged to be found in the victim, then a remarkable symmetry emerges in the comparison of Munchausen by Proxy Syndrome and the dynamics of witchcraft, as is currently understood. While MBPS and witchcraft would encompass a great variety of formations, historical contexts, and cases, both instances suppose a profile of typical symptoms that would permit any singular identification—an identification that, in both cases, supposes a double subject: an agent and a victim constitute this original dyadic relation. Typical of both general categories would be the inclusion of atypical symptoms, so as to permit degrees of classification, degrees of severity, culpability, victimization, intervention, and, indeed, punishment. Such a complexity already indicates the presence of classificatory schemata, agents of diagnosis, and institutions of authority and remediation.

From the very start, then, the "fact" of "factitious disorders" or, indeed, of "witchcraft" supposes an elaborated, articulated intellectual system of classification, of social and cultural institutions, that would concern themselves with the instances so revealed, as well as the agency of particular political institutions that would deal effectively with the cases so disclosed in order to protect a larger population. At each level of this engagement or intervention (alerting the public as to the dangers posed, the recognition and isolation of particular cases, rehabilitation, incarceration, prosecution of wrongdoing), criteria would forcibly be present for distinguishing the veracity of claims and counterclaims, the severity of instances, and which forces should be mobilized in redressing the perceived harm that the alleged "patient" or "witch" might visit on other individuals or on society itself.

In addition to there being a relation between agent and victim for both witchcraft and Munchausen by Proxy Syndrome, both are characterized by a wide variety of symptoms inflicted on the victim. In the case of witchcraft, the number of symptoms visited on the victim is practically unlimited, given the powers of the supernatural. With the Munchausen by Proxy Syndrome, there is also a great range of possible symptoms produced in the victim child, precisely because the number of ways by which one can abuse a child is so extensive. Finally, both the witch and the MBPS agent are themselves held to be distinguishable by a characteristic set of signs that are, in turn, recognized or interpreted by a third party.

In the remarkable, and ever-growing, list of psychological and physical signs and symptoms by which one can recognize that a child is being abused by a mother said to be suffering from MBPS, one can generally expect to discover some of the following "induced" in the victim: apnea, asthma, general respiratory distress, chest pains, cutaneous abscesses, delirium, diarrhea, feculant vomiting, fevers, hallucinations, insomnia, lethargy, nystagmus (jerking eye movements), personality change, behavioral disorders, hearing loss, seizures, stupor, unconsciousness, vaginal discharge, vomiting, weakness, weight loss. As for the list of signs or symptoms by which one could identify the supposed MBPS agent, typically the mother of the abused child, some of the more frequently adduced symptoms include the following: inappropriate affective behavior, an extreme, painful desire for love from a figure of powerful symbolic importance, compulsive lying, rigid adaptability, borderline personality disorder, histrionic and avoidant personalities, narcissism, erotomania. (In their "Bibliographic References to MBPS Signs and Symptoms," Schreier and Libow (1993a) list some 105 indicating signs for the syndrome.)

In a less clinical framework, when MBPS is brought to the attention of the health care profession, law enforcement agencies, and the general public—particularly, when potential child abuse is suspected—the warning signs for the victim typically include the following: unexplained and prolonged illness, medical problems that elude definitive diagnosis, incongruous symptoms, failure to respond to medical therapy without cause, signs and symptoms that disappear when away from the parent. The warning signs descriptive of the MBPS subject (the mother) are as follows: mothers who are not as concerned by the child's illness as the medical staff are but, and seemingly at the same time, who attempt to convince the staff that the child is more ill than the child seems to be; mothers who form unusually close relationships with the medical staff; families in which sudden, unexplained infant deaths have occurred; mothers familiar with medical vocabulary; mothers with previous medical experience; a parent who welcomes medical tests of the child, even if these prove to be painful; increased parental uneasiness as the child recovers (Boros and Brubaker, 1992, p. 20).

The common profile of the MBPS subject is of a young woman, a mother, who may be a single parent or who is involved in a dysfunctional relationship. Most of the female subjects are said to suffer from some form of "perversion" owing to a number of causes, many of which have to do with unsatisfactory affective and familial relations or childhood traumas. All these mothers are seen as abusive of their children (in many cases, severely injuring or even killing their own children), with the primary motive of drawing sympathy and attention to themselves. In this respect, the child becomes an instrumental fetish, sacrificed, as it were, in order for the mother to receive this longed-for, but heretofore unrequited, recognition, typically, according to one important interpretation in the field, from a "caring" physician (Schreier and Libow, 1993a, pp. 110–134 et passim).

Surely, the central axis of witchcraft likewise lay in the witch's power to possess and determine the lives of other people, particularly to create evil effects in ordinarily normal and oftentimes vulnerable individuals. Some of the signs and symptoms of the witch's power to possess others were causing strange behavior in children; causing convulsive swallowing, gagging, or a feeling of strangulation, which, in turn, sometimes caused the victims to fast for weeks at a time, as they were unable to take solid food; affecting the power of copulation in others, either by destroying the generative desires or by increasing them; causing abortions; killing infants in the mother's womb by mere exterior touch; killing men and animals; driving magistrates mad; causing various medical, meteorological and agricultural disorders, including disease, plague, and pestilence; devouring and eating infants, drinking the blood of infants; using drug powders, ointments, and venoms to bring about illness and sometimes death in others and; the use of fetishes, such as cats, small mice, rats, horns, insects.

As for the witches themselves, they were typically cast in the officially sanctioned religious literature as women who suffered from sexual perversions, usually those associated with extreme promiscuousness, erotomania, and various forms of sodomy, and who were almost always either unfaithful or estranged from their husbands (Kors and Peters, 1971, pp. 114–130). In popular folklore, they are often described as old, lame, bleary-eyed, pale, foul-smelling, with wrinkles, birthmarks, skin indentations, warts, boils, polymastia (more than two breasts). They often are pictured as lean, deformed, melancholic types, as well as being scolds, or doting, or simply mad (Notestein, 1911). But, in reality, all the women who were actually accused and tried as witches were drawn from the general population, and their physical and psychological constitutions were basically no different than those of any other women. The most recent scholarship suggests that approximately 80% of people accused of witchcraft were women, and, of those executed, the figure rises to some 85% (Barstow, 1994, pp. 15–29, 97–165). Indeed, the authors of the *Malleus Maleficarum (The Witches' Hammer)*—drawing from a compendium of sacred and secular sources, from early Old Testament sources, Classical Greek authors, the Church Fathers through St. Thomas Aquinas, and their own contemporaries—describe women with the power of possession almost exclusively in terms of their dispositional weaknesses, which incline them toward sexual perversity and thereby towards their distinctive heresy: witchcraft.[1]

> Others again have propounded other reasons why there are more superstitious women found than men. And the first is, that they are more credulous; and since the chief aim of the devil is to corrupt faith, therefore he rather attacks them. . . . The second reason is, that women are naturally more impressionable, and more ready to receive the influence of a disembodied spirit. . . . The third reason is that they have slippery tongues . . . and since they are weak, they find an easy and secret manner of vindicating themselves by witchcraft. . . .
>
> To conclude. All witchcraft comes from carnal lust, which is in women insatiable. . . . More such reasons could be brought forward, but to the understanding it is sufficiently clear that it is no matter for wonder that there are more women than men found infected with the heresy of witchcraft [Kors and Peters, 1971, pp. 120, 127].

In truth, then, a witch could be any woman who seemed to deviate from those norms dictated by the institutions of the times, regardless of her appearance. But, in the end, the principal condemning characteristic was the power of demonic possession attributed to her, that is, the power to induce evil and suffering in innocent victims.

Other striking examples of witchcraft's symptomatological symmetry with MBPS abound in the immense body of historical and documentary literature on witchcraft. One such example, because of its characteristic involvement of young children, is held by many scholars to be the most heinous demonic attack and the most famous "publicized possession occurring in Early America": the case of John Goodwin's four children (Booth, 1975, p. 21). Briefly, the children fell horribly ill, one following the other, in a relatively short period of time. The sequence of illness began with the eldest child, 13-year-old Martha, and then spread to all the other Goodwin children. The main distinguishing feature of the illness was the visitation of "strange fits." These fits rendered the children stiff and motionless, bringing about the

---

1. The *Malleus Maleficarum* was an encyclopedic manual written in 1486 by two Dominican Inquisitors, Heinrich Krämer and Jacob Sprenger, for the purpose of identifying and prosecuting witches. Prefaced by Pope Innocent VIII and approved by the Faculty of Theology of the University of Cologne, it was the principal manual for the prosecution of witchcraft cases for centuries, in both canon and civil courts. It is said that Sprenger himself executed some five hundred German witches in one year.

impression of their being "laid out dead." As the symptoms and signs increased, and as the disorders became more resistant to ordinary diagnosis, an eminent physician, Thomas Oakes, finally announced that the maladies had indeed been caused by "hellish witchcraft." The mother of a household servant of the Goodwin's was subsequently accused of having possessed the children, and, eventually, of witchcraft. Cotton Mather, a constant visitor to the Goodwin's household during the time of the children's crises, further strengthened the diagnosis of possession by claiming, on the basis of his own observations, that the children had undergone convulsive "distortions" and, further more, had the "preternatural strength" of the possessing demon (pp. 21–23).

HERESY-BECOMING-WITCHCRAFT

The continually repeated body of indications for witchcraft and demonic possession was, as with MBPS today, "revealed," verified, and perpetuated by the various institutions that controlled the social, political, economic, and discursive practices of the time. To deal effectively with the groups and individuals who bore these signs was, indeed, a means of protecting the very integrity, the sanctity, and the power of these institutions, particularly those associated with both church and state. The intensity with which witchcraft was prosecuted for several hundred years can perhaps best be understood, initially, by regarding it as the later efflorescence of the Christian church's (and the state's) concern to systematically eradicate heresy. From the earliest Patristic period in the West, the church employed its considerable energies to preserve its own unity, legitimacy, and authority in the face of enormous challenges posed by a variety of historically important and intellectually demanding heretical formations. From Albigensianism to Zoroastrian Manicheanism, the history of the Church can be dramatically charted precisely by the intensity of its attempts to eliminate the threat of heresy. All its resources—from its courts of canon law, its scriptural authority, its intellectual prelates and champions, its very political basis in European Christendom—were wielded in the firm determination to secure and defend the legitimacy of its doctrine and to maintain its institutional authority. The stakes, after all, were the very highest: eternal salvation for the believer; for the heretic, eternal damnation; for the church and state, absolute power. The heterodox position—or heresy itself—would exist as such only in its opposition to orthodoxy, that is, as its other, its nemesis, its constant threat. It was the preeminence of this concern that led Pope Alexander IV explicitly to equate witchcraft with heresy in his decretal letter to the Inquisition of 1258, *Quod super nonullis.*

One of the earliest, and most historically important, examples of heresy-becoming-witchcraft is to be found in the writings of Ralph of Coggeshall, an English Cistercian abbot. The case, detailed in his chronicle, which dates from the last quarter of the 12th century, is entitled "The Witch of Rheims" (Kors and Peters, 1971, pp. 44–47). It seems that, during the reign of Louis VII, the Archbishop of Rheims, together with several of his clergy and a young clerk (Master Gervais of Tilbury), was riding outside the city, when they came upon a young woman walking alone in a vineyard. Attracted by the young woman's striking beauty, Master Gervais approached her and, by his own testimony, "at length in courtly fashion made her a proposal of wanton love" (p. 45). The young woman, a peasant, refused his advances and responded, "with simple gesture and a certain gravity of speech: 'Good youth, the Lord does not desire me ever to be your friend or the friend of any man, for if ever I forsook my virginity and my body had once been defiled, I should most assuredly fall under eternal damnation without hope of recall'" (p. 45). To this seeming proclamation of Christian virtue and piety, Master Gervais "at once realized that she was one of that most impious sect of Publicans, who at that time were everywhere being sought out and destroyed, especially by Philip, count of Flanders, who was harassing them pitilessly with righteous cruelty" (p. 45).

Having spurned Master Gervais's advances, the girl was immediately seized by the Archbishop of Rheims and was brought before his archiepiscopal court, before his clergy, officials, and the local nobility (the Archbishop was himself the uncle of Philip of France), to be tried for heresy. She was questioned at length about scriptural matters but replied that she had not been well enough instructed in Biblical argument to respond in adequate detail to their charges, but that she did have an older friend who might help clarify her responses. The older woman was summoned to the court:

> Indeed, to the texts and narratives of both the Old and New Testaments which they put to her, she answered as easily, as much by memory, as though she had mastered a knowledge of all the Scriptures and had been

well trained in this kind of response, mixing the false with the true and mocking the true interpretation of our faith with a kind of perverted insight. Therefore, because it was impossible to recall the obstinate minds of both these persons from the error of their ways by threat or persuasion, or by any arguments or scriptural texts, they were placed in prison until the following day [p. 45].

The following day, after another inquisitorial session at the archiepiscopal court, the older woman

suddenly pulled a ball of thread from her heaving bosom and threw it out of a large window, but keeping the end of the thread in her hands; then in a loud voice, audible to all, she said "Catch!" At the word, she was lifted from the earth before everyone's eyes and followed the ball out of the window in rapid flight, sustained, we believe, by the ministry of the evil spirits who once caught Simon Magus up into the air [pp. 46–47].

As for the younger woman, who still refused Master Gervais's advances, she could not be reconciled by "the inducement of reason," nor would she accept the "promise of riches." Rather, she was promptly burned at the stake.

It would be difficult to imagine that a young peasant girl, walking through a vineyard by herself, could pose a threat to the institution of the church, much less to the nobility of France. Both in responding to Master Gervais that she might compromise her virtue and Christian piety by submitting to his proposal of "wanton love" and by having an older friend cite Scriptural precedent for the importance of chastity and modesty, she nonetheless posed a threat to the very determination of sanctity, virtue, and legality. If these peremptory values were not to be legitimated by the church and state, by what means could these institutions presume any claim to authority at all? By this simple personal act of virtue and modesty, that is, the rejection of Master Gervais, the entire foundation of church dogma and doctrine was threatened. The peasant girl thus embodied the foremost challenge to church authority and, in this respect, had to be dealt with as a deviant, as perverse and evil, possessed of the very metaphysical evil that had carried off Simon Magus, the Samaritan sorceror who attempted to buy the power of the Holy Spirit from the Apostles. The archiepiscopal court of inquisition found in what is arguably a simple case of lust precisely the fulfillment of its highest mission: namely, to reassert the power of the Church in determining the very basis of truth and falsity, virtue and sin, indeed, the metaphysical wellsprings of causality itself. Hence, the charge that the girl was in fact a "Publican," that is, a Paulician, a member of a minor Catharist faction derived from the nomadic followers of Bogomil the Bulgarian, a "purist" sect that had derived from earlier Gnostic and Manichean factions. At stake, then, for the institution of church and state is not the trifling and momentary pleasure of young Gervais, but rather the presence of evil loosed upon the universe, and, in turn, upon the Church and state. The threat of evil, in this case, could be effectively blocked; indeed it could be summarily eliminated precisely by the judgment of the archiepiscopal court, which ascertains the existence of the evil; by the authority of those who sit in judgment of the veracity of the claims; and by a penal system that justifies the execution of the subject possessed of and by this evil. All this—the detection, and, indeed, the creation and amelioration, of a "disorder"—is determined by, and within, the social, economic, political, and spiritual concerns of the church itself.

THE POLITICIZATION OF WITCHCRAFT

By the period of the Reformation, the concern with witchcraft became ever more generalized. Whereas in the earlier periods, witchcraft had been construed in the almost exclusively theological terms of heresy— buttressed by the orthodox ontology of Thomistic metaphysics and by a series of papal proclamations—the 15th and 16th centuries witnessed its emergence as one of a progressively more social and political concern. Both Luther and Calvin regarded devils and their powers of possession as "actualities" and thus in direct conflict with the daily conduct of Christian life. This doctrine, in turn, led to the widespread and aggressive prosecution of witches directly within the context of the common social, legal, and political institutions of the period. Whole populations, rather than canonical courts, were terrified by the prospect of evil and destruction, imminent and at hand, abroad in their very midst. In the earlier tradition, people could find solace in their faith through the protection of the church—as expressed in the teaching, for example, of Saint Anthony: "The devil can in no way enter the mind or body of any man, nor has the power to penetrate into the thoughts of anybody, unless such a person has first become destitute of all holy thoughts, and is quite bereft and denuded of

spiritual contemplation."[2] Such prophylactic faith had burst with the
Protestant Reformation's condemnation of the church itself, however.
Since, for the leaders of the Reformation, the Roman Catholic church
was visited by the apparition of Simon Magus—at least in the name of
simony (not to mention idolatry, spiritual laxity, dispensation of
indulgences, absolute papal authority, corruption, usury, commercial-
ism, and false sacraments)—it could no longer offer the institutional
protection it once could against the rampant evil. As Luther himself
remarked,

> for by this spiritual witchcraft that old serpent bewitcheth not men's senses,
> but their minds with false and wicked opinions; which opinions, they that
> are so bewitched, do take to be true and godly. Briefly, so great is the malice
> of this sorcerer the devil, and his desire to hurt, that not only he deceiveth
> those secure and proud spirits with his enchantments, but even those also
> which are professors of true Christianity, and well affected in religion [Kors
> and Peters, 1971, p. 197].

Despite the doctrinal diversity that was to emerge in the
Reformation, every sect maintained its concern with the heresy of
witchcraft. By the 16th century, it should be recalled, the judicial systems of the European states had undergone considerable consolidation
and reform, and in most instances, witchcraft had become subject to
these "newer forms" of civil prosecutions (Klaits, 1985, pp. 131–139).
While Charlemagne had long before issued edicts against witchcraft, the
16th century saw the passage of legislation—explicitly framed according to the Inquisitorial methods—that was designed, in large part, to
protect central authority itself from the powers of witchcraft. In 1541,
Henry VIII enacted legislation against witchcraft, which was initially
meant to support the church's prosecution of it, but the statutes were
strengthened in 1547 to permit a greater involvement of the state into
what were previously considered to be theological matters. By 1563, in
Elizabeth's reign, significant legislation was passed concerning witchcraft, enchantment, and sorcery, mandating the death penalty. The
major impetus for such dramatic legislation was occasioned by Queen
Mary's reestablishment of papal authority in England in 1555, together
with the repeal of Henry VI's antipapal legislation, the restoration of
ecclesiastical courts, and the new laws directed against heresy. These

---

2. Paraphrase of St. Anthony from Cassian's *Collations*, cited in *Malleus
Maleficarum* (Kors and Peters, p. 147).

developments, in turn, forced the departure to Europe of many of the English clergy in the period termed "the Marian exile." Having visited Zurich, Geneva, Prague, Basel, Frankfurt, and other places where the (largely Protestant) persecutions of witchcraft were vigorous and widespread, and, indeed, enjoying great celebrity, these Protestant clergy, fearing for the safety of the new monarch, returned in force and prominence to the now-Protestant realm of Elizabeth. It was widely supposed that the resident Catholic factions had taken league with witches and sorcerers for the purpose of eliminating Elizabeth. Conspiracies and plots against the sovereign seemed to be omnipresent, and it suited the understanding of the times that conjuration played a great part in these attempts. In 1558 several plots were uncovered against Elizabeth. Perhaps the most prominent was that led by Sir Anthony Fortescue, an eminent Catholic, who, with several confederates, was charged with casting the Queen's horoscope. It was claimed by two of the conspirators that a "wicked spirit" had assisted their predictions of Elizabeth's death and the resumption of the throne by Mary, Queen of Scots. The Roman Catholic ambassadors of France and Spain were also involved in the plot. Given the troubled times, the Anglican clergy would appeal to the monarch herself for her own protection against such evil schemes, fanciful or real. One such prominent clergyman was the Bishop of Salisbury, the Calvinist John Jewel. In a court sermon addressed to Elizabeth, he voiced his concerns about the danger and presence of witchcraft:

> This kind of people (I mean witches and sorcerers) within these few last years are marvellously increased within this your grace's realm. These eyes have seen most evident and manifest marks of their wickedness. Your grace's subjects pine away even unto death, their colour fadeth, their flesh rotteth, their speech is benumed, their senses are bereft. Wherefore your poor subjects' most humble petition unto your highness is, that the laws touching such malefactors may be put in due execution [Notestein, 1911, pp. 16–17].

Within three years' time the laws were passed, thus making the practice of witchcraft in England a secular crime. The Queen's councilors were alerted, justices of the peace and prominent citizens were informed by the privy council of any reported sorcerers or conjurers, and they were in turn instructed to submit any evidence they might encounter concerning such individuals. Shortly thereafter, and for a considerable period of time, the government engaged a network of detectives—

"witch detectors," or "witch finders"—to search out and prosecute conjurers and witches.

Elizabeth's successor, James I, had himself been the "victim" of a witches' plot against his life in 1590. It seems that one Dr. Fian, a Scottish schoolteacher, and Mrs. Gellie Duncan, a confessed witch, together with several (Catholic) confederates, had conspired with the devil to sink James's ship, which was returning him from Europe with his new Protestant bride, the Princess of Denmark. After an extensive period of torture, all the principals confessed to having made a pact with Satan himself, having conducted a black Sabbath, eaten dead babies, and orchestrated a violent storm intended to sink the ship, killing the king and his wife and thereby averting a Protestant line of succession for Scotland. The storm-tossed ship arrived in Leith, however, and the conspirators were ultimately exposed, tried, and burned at the stake. Such an event perhaps indulged James's interest in witchcraft, for, some seven years later, he wrote a lengthy treatise entitled *Daemonologie*, which detailed the nature and conduct of witches. The volume would recapitulate the most commonplace assertions about witchcraft, drawn in large part from the *Malleus Maleficarum*, and would serve as an intellectual and religious frame of reference for the extensive legislation he enacted against witchcraft in Scotland and, later, upon his accession to the throne, in England.

With the conjunction of both secular and religious concerns codified into statute law, the discovery and construction of witchcraft as a major "disorder"—one decidedly opposed to the established order—had assumed the status of indisputable "fact." One celebrated English magistrate, Sir Matthew Hale, would remark that he "did not in the least doubt there were witches; first, because the Scriptures affirmed it; secondly, because the wisdom of all nations, particularly our own, had provided laws against witchcraft, which implied their belief of such a crime" (Mackay, 1841, p. 519).

Virtually any sign, symptom, or accusation of witchcraft could easily be verified—principally by torturing the suspected witch, by establishing some congruence with previous cases, by offering leniency in exchange for incriminating testimony, or by merely by consulting the immense body of diagnostic material derived from the manuals. Since literature and the civil codes specified an enormity of figurations, deformations, symptoms, habits, inclinations, airs, behavior, and attitudes to be exhibited by or located on the person of the witch, and since the

witches themselves historically were accused of having fomented everything from affectations to assassinations (crop failures, droughts, fainting spells, infanticides), it remained only for the accused with to confess
the suspected act of evil-doing—extorted through torture and heresay
testimony (most often offered up by children, the superstitiously
inclined, or those to whom some benefit might accrue)—to achieve a
conviction.

Tests such as locating "the witch's spot" were also administered during this process to help validate these convictions. Tradition maintained
that there would be one place on the body of a witch that would be
insensitive to the pain of a pinprick. This belief gave rise to the profession of "common prickers," people who, with the help of "witch finders," would locate such a spot with uncanny regularity. Another
common test to establish the guilt of a witch was to bind her and to
lower her into the water. Since it was held that the natural element,
water, would reject the unnatural spirit of the witch, the witch would
perforce float. If the suspect sank, she was declared innocent (and, incidentally, dead), but if she happened to float, she would be found guilty
and then be executed.

> When they find that the Devil tells them false they reflect on him, and he (as
> 40 have confessed) adviseth them to swim and tells them they shall sink and
> be cleared that way, then when they be tried that way and float, they see the
> Devil deceives them again, and have so layed open his treacheries. . . .
>
> King James, in his *Demonology* sayeth, it is a certain rule, for (sayeth he)
> Witches deny their baptism when they Covenant with the Devil, water being
> the sole element thereof, and therefore sayeth he, when they be heaved into
> the water the water refuseth to receive them into her bosom, (they being
> such Miscreants to deny their baptism) and suffers them to float, as the
> Froth on the Sea, which the water will not receive, but casts it up and down;
> till it comes to the earthy element the shore, and there leaves it to consume
> [Hopkins, 1647, p. 6].

The regularity of the convictions and the unquestioned authority of
the system of prosecution tended to confirm the veracity of practically
any of the alleged "symptoms" that were regularly brought forth as evidence, many of them, needless to say, completely absurd. Under any
other circumstances, the claims made and the charges leveled against
witches would have been lamentably risible.

The tendency to confirm the typical symptoms and signs of witchcraft was especially evident in cases that involved children. The witch's

presence would often cause the child victim to fall into uncontrollable fits, which, in many instances, the child's siblings suffered as well. When such fits occurred in the physical absence of the witch, the child would usually claim that he or she had encountered an "image" of the witch, or the witch's "imp" (inhabiting flies, ants, moths, bees, cats, dogs, mice). If, in the absence of any convenient insects or such surrogates as the child's imagination could construe, the child continued to have fits, it was claimed that the odious power of the devil and his agents was all the more demonstrably at work.[3]

Perhaps owing in large part to a legitimate concern with the historical vulnerability of children—as well as with furthering the vested interests of church and state—much credence was given to the testimony of these children in the trial proceedings. Practically any claim, no matter how preposterous, was readily accepted as condemning evidence against the person charged with witchcraft. For example, in the celebrated Chelmsford witches trials, Agnes Waterhouse was burned, largely on the testimony offered by a 12-year-old neighbor, Agnes Brown. The child related to the court how Mother Waterhouse's cat (which, by earlier testimony, had already become a toad) visited her family's house in the form of an ugly black dog with horns and bearing the keys to the milkhouse in his mouth. The dog apparently frightened the child by jumping in the air and then sitting on a nettle. Nobody seemed surprised when the girl related how the dog talked to her, expressing his desire to have some butter. The girl declined to give the dog the butter, so the dog simply opened the lock to the milkhouse, ate some butter and cheese, and relocked the door. The next day the dog returned with the keys and reprimanded Miss Brown for speaking ill of him. The dog came back again with a bean pod in its mouth, and once again with a piece of bread in its mouth, this time asking the child to butter it for him. When the attorney summed up the case, Mother Waterhouse admitted that she prayed in Latin, not English. She readily confessed to having practiced witchcraft for 15 years and was burned.

In a later Chelmsford trial in 1579, Elleine Smith's young son delivered the damaging testimony that his mother kept three spirit imps—

---

3. The number of demons Satan had placed at the disposition of witches was calculated by Johannes Weyer (Wierus) at some 7,405,926. These were broken down into 72 battalions, each headed by a prince or captain. These demons or imps were difficult for the ordinary observer to discern because they could assume any shape they pleased.

"Great Dick" was kept in a wicker bottle, "Little Dick" in a leather flask, and "Willet" in a wool pack. A neighbor saw "a thyng like a black Dogge goe out of her doore." That was more than sufficient evidence for conviction. In yet another Chelmsford trial, in 1582, Ursley Kemp's eight-year-old son (a "base son" according to the examining justice) testified that his mother kept and fed four imps: Tyffin, Tittey, Piggen, and Jacket. In fact, Ursley Kemp had a white lamb, a grey cat, and a black cat—the ubiquitous toad was not far away, either. The son's testimony and the justice's promise of leniency led the Kemp woman to confess to witchcraft. Following the confession, it seems that the justice conveniently recanted his offer of leniency.

The ease with which such testimony was accepted—and confessions rendered—is alarming. Even some Elizabethan commentators expressed shock. Reginald Scot, whose *Discoverie of Witchcraft* was one of the earliest tracts against the whole charade of witchcraft, noted the typicality of the victims and of the testimony offered: "See whether the witnesses be not single, of what credit, sex, and age they are; namelie lewd miserable and envious poore people; most of them which speake to anie purpose being old women and children of the age of 4, 5, 6, 7, 8 or 9 yeares" (cited in Notestein, 1911, p. 46n). By contrast, the examining and presiding magistrates, justices, physicians, and members of the assize courts must have been daunting to the rural poor, the uneducated, and the confused. In the celebrated trial of Alice Samuels, in Warboys, Huntingdonshire, where Mother Samuels (an "old simple woman") was convicted of witchcraft for having induced "fits" in two children of the Throckmorton family, her judges and inquisitors numbered among the following: Sir Robert Throckmorton, Sir Henry Cromwell (grandfather of Oliver Cromwell), the Bishop of Lincoln, Justice Fenner of the king's court, a group of Cambridge scholars and Doctors of Divinity, and two additional theologians. Mother Samuels had claimed in her defense that the children, who often yelled vile imprecations at her, were simply "wanton." The court ruled otherwise: after a five-hour trial, Mother Samuels, together with her daughter and husband, was found guilty of witchcraft, and all three were condemned to be executed.

Given the extensive use of children's testimony—be it from their own children or from those of neighbors and other locals—and the fact that women were said to be almost exclusively the carriers of the signs and symptoms of possession, we can view the construction of witchcraft as a disorder that appears as a basic dyadic relation: victimization involving the aforesaid participants. Since this relation is itself structured by the subtending ideology of power (involving tortured confession, hearsay testimony and the like) it becomes complicated and oddly reversible. On one hand, the woman may "induce" symptoms of possession in the child; but, on the other, the child may well be "induced" to testify against the otherwise innocent woman and hence be itself the agent. In certain instances, the child may be itself identified as the demon or witch—in function of delusion, torture, testimony, or even playfulness[4]—just as the adult woman would commonly be.

This constructed relation of witchcraft becomes progressively inscribed within the framework of civil, religious, and secular authority. Once the suspected evil is established and codified as a danger, a threat, the various mechanisms of observation and power become progressively mobilized to thwart the malevolent evil at the merest suspicion of its appearance. This mobilization became dramatically evident when appeal for action, by church and state, was made to the new occupation of "witch finders." William Cecil, Lord Burghley, ever concerned with the security of Elizabeth's crown, had used his detective service extensively in the pursuit of conjurers, as did the Earl of Shrewsbury, who was charged with the confinement of Mary, Queen of Scots. While both Cecil and Shrewsbury were themselves on the Queen's privy council, their hired emissaries proved to be zealous in finding witches. Initially, many sorcerers charged with plotting against the crown were found close to London proper (and the privy council). But the politicization of witchcraft led to increased public pressure on local justices, magistrates, and assize judges to hang witches, even when no evidence of conspiracy was found. This served only to popularize and to demonize witches in the public mind. As Elizabeth's reign continued, the number of witch trials increased, and their locale spread far beyond the politically charged environs of London (and the watchful eyes of the privy council), to all counties and shires in the country. Magistrates and judges seeking preferments and, indeed, commissions for all the witches they could apprehend, eagerly prosecuted a growing number of witch-

---

4. In the Würtzburg witch trials, from 1627 to 1629, when 157 people were burned at the stake, a large number were children—executed, often enough, for mumbling well-known "enchantments" in public, or expressing their desire to exchange their souls for a regular meal or a pony (Mackay, 1841, pp. 531–533).

craft cases.[5] Witch seekers emerged with increasing frequency, usually from the ranks of the lesser Puritan clergy. They, too, were to receive great celebrity and profit from their work. John Darrel was a celebrated witch finder as was, even more notoriously, Matthew Hopkins, who graced himself with the title, "Witch-Finder General." In one year alone, Hopkins sent 60 people to the stake. His services were sought after throughout Essex, Norfolk, Huntingdon, and Suffolk, and he would charge 20 shillings per town (plus expenses) to review the inhabitants for any signs of witchcraft. He received an additional 20 shillings for any witch successfully prosecuted and executed.

The whole process of searching out witchcraft is of preeminent interest, since it lends congruency to the various agencies of authority, thereby reinforcing a common purpose (however disparate their initial aims were) and increasing public awareness and fear. With such an increase in public concern to prosecute witchcraft, the number of witches could but only increase, to assuage the public fear, but also ensuring that the authorities delegated to prosecute them would be further strengthened. With the relations of power so set, that is, the relations between the dominant and subordinate forces—the whole apparatus of witch hunting could be effectively engaged. Such action would stabilize the public's sense of well-being and lend greater reach to the agencies so charged to defend it. Thus empowered, the principal authorities would conduct their affairs in the relative absence of complex moral and legal consideration and explanation. As the French legal scholar Jean Bodin would remark in 1580:

> The trial of this offence must not be conducted like other crimes. Whoever adheres to the ordinary course of justice perverts the spirit of the law, both divine and human. He who is accused of sorcery should never be acquitted, unless the malice of the prosecutor be clearer than the sun; for it is so difficult to bring full proof of this secret crime, that out of a million of witches not one would be convicted if the usual course were followed [Mackay, 1841, p. 528].

The values of evil and good were at once clearly identified; the centrality of children and family were thereby reasserted; and the establish-

---

5. A celebrated justice of the time, Brian Darcy, would write, "There is a man of great cunning and knowledge come over lately unto our Queenes Maiestie, which hath advertised her what a companie and number of witches be within Englande: whereupon I and other of her Justices have received commission for the apprehending of as many as are within these limits" (quoted in Notestein, 1911, p. 46).

ment of what contravened the norms of social and moral propriety would be conveniently localized and literally demonized. In short, the authority of church and state administration could be reiterated and confirmed only through the successful prosecution of yet more witches. Indeed, if witches were entirely eliminated—as Calvin so astutely observed (Kors and Peters, 1971, p. 209)—these various agencies of church and state would risk losing a considerable part of their very raison d'être .

CONCLUSION

By the time the danger of witchcraft had been effectively thwarted, toward the beginning of the 18th century—the official charge of witchcraft itself had largely disappeared by then—this old constructed disorder had claimed the lives of approximately 100,000 victims (Barstow, 1994, p. 23)—mostly women, mostly poor, mostly from dire circumstances; oftentimes midwives, widows, women who were themselves victims of broken families, young mothers; overexcited or merely hapless children.[6] All bad swimmers, incapable of floating, insensitive to that one pinprick, or capable only of mumbling the words of The Lord's Prayer, or of saying it in Latin, often affecting black bonnets, owning cats, dogs, or toads, or having poor posture, warts, moles. All these individual "marks" were but the inventions of those interests and institutions, religious and secular, that sought to maintain their own authority, which, of course, was thought to be none other than the very stability and prosperity of the common weal.

Even with the emergence of relatively enlightened legislation in the 18th century, particularly, in advanced industrial countries, where the initial religious impetus for the prosecution of witchcraft became dissociated from the enactment of newly reformed civil law, there nonetheless remained a small fragment of the population that continued to be swayed by the traditional fascination with witchcraft. Such people, perhaps isolated from the growing economic prosperity produced by the industrial revolution and located in remote agrarian communities, were

---

6. It should be noted that some of the most cogent parallels drawn between the persecution of witches and the diagnoses of "women's disorders" appear in the work of Phyllis Chesler (1972) and Barbara Eherenreich and Deirdre English (1973).

still quite willing to invoke curses, incantations, maledictions, and spells upon their superstitious neighbors, who, in turn, would confirm their continued existence as witches. Possibly in reaction to the enormous change and complexity introduced by the economic development of the 18th and 19th centuries, along with the concomitant social dislocations and complexities of modern life, even today there are yet people who claim the mantle of witchcraft. The promise of preternatural powers, or indeed, what is often invoked as "natural" powers devolving to the possessors of such "truths" and "insights" as afforded by witchcraft cults, exorcism, herbalism, psychic powers, and fortune telling, is still witnessed in elements of popular culture, particularly in tabloid journalism and on late-night infomercials.

In the end, witchcraft would have served its purpose: it provided a legitimating activity, however ill conceived, for those who needed a subordinate other, an imminent but completely manageable danger, to oppose. It was, beyond legitimating, a means by which power, education, wealth, position, and expertise could be exercised with ease and relative impunity. No one—or hardly anyone—seriously challenged the actual hunting, the inquisition, the convictions and executions of witches, not to mention the logic and coherence of the very idea of witchcraft.[7] Indeed, the public applauded its prosecution. The construction of the "disorder" of witchcraft worked perfectly to vindicate the authority of those who were already in possession of it or, in other cases, of those who eagerly sought to attain it.

---

7. A notable exception was Reginald Scot, who, in his *The Discoverie of Witchcraft* (1584), questioned the legal and political aspects of witch hunting and the persecutions, as well as the credulity of the public in tolerating these (see Notestein, 1911). Most of the other criticisms against witchcraft and witch hunting stemmed from the emerging philosophical naturalism, materialism, and rational skepticism of the period. Certainly Thomas Hobbes, Benedict de Spinoza, and Pierre Bayle would number among the strongest of these enlightened voices.

CHAPTER TWO

HYSTERIA

THE CONSTRUCTION OF A NEWER DISORDER

> *What doctors could not cull from their experiments, which were still relatively primitive, they simply made up.*
>
> —*George Frederick Drinka*

THE MEDICAL MODEL

Long after the dark ages of witchcraft had receded, the 19th century witnessed a veritable efflorescence of disturbing disorders. Unlike witchcraft, which was established largely on the basis of public fear and the remediation of that fear, these new disorders were almost exclusively determined within the confines of the expanding modern science of medicine. Indeed, medical practitioners during this period were particularly concerned to distinguish themselves from the earlier, unscientific, superstitious tradition that was associated with such activities as alchemy, witchhunting, and the "curious sciences." They were so determined to portray themselves as rational and benign in their considered methodology that they formulated the cannons of medical practice according to the now fixed and universally acknowledged laws of modern natural science. The criteria of diagnosis,

anatomy, symptomatology, course of treatment, specification of etiology, and prognosis of disorders were all subject to experimental hypothesis and empirical verification. This rational method was a considerable
advance over previous notions of diagnosis and treatment—the century
saw dramatic progress in every branch and discipline—and it created an
articulated system involving specific methods, terminologies, and
approaches that, when invoked and scrupulously followed, appeared to
be objective and determinant. In other words, practically any disorder
that could be accommodated by the diagnostic, procedural, and termi-
nological canons of the discipline would perforce enjoy scientific
validation.

Owing to its place of prominence in the public mind, however, the
legitimation and authority belonging to the emerging science of medicine tended to confirm a broad variety of already existing social and cultural biases. What should have been free from these biases had, in many
instances, served to perpetuate and intensify them by adapting or incorporating the substance of these biases into the effective practice of the
scientific operations themselves. Thus, while the medical model can be
extremely useful in identifying diseases like syphilis or tuberculosis, it
can also be applied to other aspects of the human condition that are not
truly diseases at all. That is to say, the medical model can be applied,
inappropriately, to social conditions and to a wide range of human
behaviors.

A dramatic example of this unfortunate condition is to be found in
the medical theories of the American physician Samuel A. Cartwright.
Appointed by the Louisiana Medical Association in 1850 to examine "the
diseases and physical peculiarities of the Negro race," Dr. Cartwright
focused his research on a disturbing "behavioral abnormality," one peculiar to runaway slaves. Using biological, clinical, and even etymological
methods, Cartwright was able to determine that "the insane desire to
wander away from home" was caused by a dreaded disorder, "drapetomania" (from *drapetes*: Gk., "the fact of absconding"). Not only was he
able to diagnose this new disorder, but he also established an etiology,
prognosis, and cure for it. The cure for this "running away" disorder
involved a regimen of positive and negative reinforcements:

> If any one or more of them, at any time, are inclined to raise their heads to
> a level with their master or overseer, humanity and their own good requires
> that they should be punished until they fall into that submissive state which

was intended for them to occupy.... They have only to be kept in that state, and treated like children to prevent and cure them from running away [Chorover, 1974, p. 150].

Even if such precautions were taken, Dr. Cartwright claimed, a certain number of slaves were prone to cause disturbances and would attempt to run away yet again, precisely because they were subject to another abnormality, namely, an insensitivity to pain while being whipped. His diagnosis of this disorder focused on two distinctive features: "partial insensibility of the skin and great hebetude of the intellectual faculties"(p. 150). Ever rigorous in his pursuit of a complete cure, he established a common etiology for these two abnormalities, an "imperfect atmospherization or vitalization of the blood." He called this disorder "dysethesia." The treatment he prescribed for those who suffered the disorder consisted in a vigorous regimen of exercise, such that the patient's lungs could be stimulated and his blood purified, thereby revitalizing the subject and leading him away from "ignorance and barbarism." Dr. Cartwright would counsel the slave owner as to the proper course of treatment to be administered to the slave:

The liver, skin and kidneys should be stimulated to activity ... [to] assist in decarbonizing the blood. The best means to stimulate the skin is, first, to have the patient well washed with warm water and soap; then to anoint it all over with oil, and to slap the oil in with a broad leather strap; then to put the patient to some hard kind of work in the open air and sunshine that will compel him to expand his lungs, as chopping wood, splitting rails, or sawing with the cross-cut or whip saw [p. 151].

What is instructive, among other things, about dysethesia is that Dr. Cartwright was able to find what appeared to be a relatively sound basis for an otherwise completely absurd medical claim—a claim that was no more than a poorly disguised rationalization of slavery (see Gould, 1981, pp. 70–71). He accomplished this, in part, by drawing upon the systematic model of a developing medical science. Once their status as disorders was established on seemingly "scientific" grounds, drapetomania and dysesthesia could then assume a place along with other disorders. Their specific names, anatomical locations, prognoses, etiologies, symptomatologies, and treatments having been articulated, they could be compared, discussed, debated, read about, all within the framework of "medical science." Indeed, it was a medical society that commissioned the work, and a relatively responsible and well-known medical journal that published the results. Hence, even though the disorders were the completely absurd, self-serving inventions of a biased individual and his regional culture, they still enjoyed the status of being "real," of being scientifically feasible—so much so that the 1957 edition of *Dorland's Medical Dictionary* still defines drapetomania as "the insane desire to wander away from home" (Chorover, 1974, p. 150).[1]

THE ORIGINS AND EARLY CONSTRUCTION OF HYSTERIA

Although Cartwright's disorders were largely anecdotal in effect— noted, perhaps, by some curious readers of *Dorland's Medical Dictionary*—the construction of the disorder of hysterical neurosis or hysteria had wide-ranging and often dire consequences. Taken in a broad context, the popular history of the disorder can be traced back to ancient Greek and even Egyptian times.[2] In fact, along with melancholia, hysteria ranks among the first emotional and behavioral disorders that were determined to have an organic cause. The Greeks associated it with the uterus, thus the term hysteria, from the Greek *hystera*. Hippocrates himself believed that most "female problems" stemmed from the uterus, rather than, as in most cases, from the nerves and that, in these illnesses, the uterus moved literally through the body, wandering wildly from place to place, causing great disorder and disease. In certain cases, the upward movement of the uterus (the *hystera*) would cause great irritation and pain in the pelvis; in other cases, it moved directly into the throat, creating a sensation of strangulation caused by the imaginary sensation of a lump in the throat (*globus hystericus*);

1. Oddly enough, a variation of this disorder was still listed in *DSM-II* (American Psychiatric Association, 1968): Runaway Reaction of Children (or Adolescents)— 308.3 (not international). It should also be noted that the drapetomania entry has been deleted from the most recent edition of Dorland's dictionary.
2. See Decker (1991, p. 207). There is a strong revisionist argument made as to the historical continuity of hysteria by King (1993, pp. 3–90). She suggests that classical hysteria was in reality invented by physicians in the late middle ages and Renaissance and was subsequently legitimated in the writings of medical historians. King's account, of course, bears serious consequence for the traditional view that Hippocrates was the "father of hysteria" and that hysteria has more or less evolved continuously from ancient times to the present.

in still others, it might cause flushing, paralysis, seizures, violent headaches, or fits of sobbing.

By identifying and introducing a course of treatment for hysteria, Hippocrates in many respects followed a course approximately the one Cartwright later would follow in rationalizing slavery. He applied a set of characteristic procedures drawn from the medical science of the period to what really amounted, at that time, to an unfathomable mystery, namely, women's sexual behavior and the disorders seemingly specific to women. Given the economic and political suppression of women in ancient Greece, their lack of productive social interaction, their literal condemnation to the home and hearth—in short, a fully repressed status—there was an implicit need for a justification of their repression (Slater, 1968). This need became manifest in the wide cultural understanding of women as inferior human beings, not fully mature in their rational faculties or self-control. That women's repression erupted in occasional outbursts of unusual behavior merely confirmed their subjected status. Generally, this "excessive" behavior would be permitted to take place within the relatively secluded and removed Bacchic religious cults (Dionysian, Corybantic), or it would be managed according to a medical model, which would further confirm that these outbursts were organically determined and were localizable phenomena, subject to a physician's diagnosis. Thus, medically, hysteria was a rationalization of the symptoms that women's repression led to. Given the lot of women in ancient Greece, it was more likely that such behavior would be stigmatized by men and perhaps be less noticed by the women themselves, since they could hardly imagine a social position markedly different from the one they occupied. The errant behavior of the uterus, so singled out as the "cause" of hysteria, would thus be orchestrated with medical precision so as to relieve the hysterical symptoms. Since hysteria—for the Greeks, and for the next two millennia — was associated with virgins, widows, and spinsters, it was thought that the ministrations of the physician would repair the "drying out" of the uterus.

> A hysterical symptom, for a Greek woman, permitted a safe expression of certain unmet needs, and the relationship with the doctor allowed a form of gratification that would otherwise be forbidden. The doctor who treated such a woman was permitted certain muted sexual gratifications while simultaneously preserving culturally held beliefs that ignored female sexuality, unless it was aimed at producing heirs. Thus the hysterical symptom

and the doctor's treatment might serve a social-regulatory function [Simon, 1978, p. 242].

If the uterus was too dry, it would tend to float and wander about the woman's body in search of moisture, thereby causing great distress. Likewise, if the woman failed to menstruate, similar physical and mental symptoms would occur, including delusions (*paraphrosune*), depression, and madness (*mania*). Treatments typically involved bodily bandaging, to constrict the movement of the uterus; the oral administration of medicine and wine; fumigations of the nose, to force the uterus back down to its rightful place; or aromatic fumigations of the vagina, to induce the return of the uterus. In the end, Hippocrates would have the caring physician counsel marriage, remarriage, and intercourse to stem the hysterical symptoms (p. 243). Such counsel would indeed persist well into the 20th century.

Claiming the "wandering uterus" to be an absurd fiction, the Roman physician Galen presented a far more medically sophisticated, but no less incorrect, explanation for women's disorders—an explanation based not only on the retention of menstrual blood, but more important, on the effects of a spermlike substance secreted by the uterus. On examining one of his patients, a widow who was a postmenopausal "hysteric," he would declare:

> Following the warmth of the remedies and arising from the touch of the genital organs required by the treatment there followed twitchings accompanied at the same time by pain and pleasure after which she emitted turbid and abundant sperm. From that time on she was freed of all the evil she felt. From all this it seems to me that the retention of sperm impregnated with evil essences had—in causing damage throughout the body—a much greater power than that of the retention of the menses [Veith, 1965, p. 38].

For Galen's theory of humors, the whole problem of uncontrollable sobbing, headaches, decreased sexual drive, skin flushing, and the like was the result of the woman's inability to dispel this vaporous, spermlike substance from the uterus. Galen, like his Greek predecessors, also developed a cure for the disorder. Giving certain salts to the sufferer would drive the vapor into the pelvis and therefore relieve the suffering. More important, however, was his view that the women who were "receptive and eager [to receive] the advances of their husbands" would be less likely to be afflicted by hysteria in the first place. If the onset of hysteria was brought about by excessive retention of semen in the woman's uterus, Galen viewed abstinence in men, by analogy, to be the cause of male hysteria. Such an account would, in turn, seem to corroborate the general bias against women prevalent in Greek medicine and culture: here again it is the woman who perfectly accommodates the model of pathology for dysfunction, disease, and psychological disorder.[3] Further examination of the feminine hysterical model yields three classifications: a) women who lost consciousness and the ability to move and who presented a scarcely perceptible pulse; b) women who remained conscious and lucid but who tended to collapse from respiratory difficulties; and c) those who had contractures of the limbs. The common factor for all three classifications was "uterine affections."

VICTORIAN HYSTERIA: THE EMERGENCE OF THE MEDICAL MODEL

As odd as these ancient medical and moral models, taxonomies, etiologies, and treatments may seem, the humoral view of hysteria persisted well into the 18th century, and the theory that women's emotional and behavioral disorders were rooted in the uterus was still predominant in the medical science of the 19th century. Perhaps the most dramatic change in understanding hysteria occurred in the work of an English physician, Robert Brudenell Carter, (cited in Veith, 1965), who was significantly ahead of his time and for this reason did not attain the influence he rightly deserved. Articulating what was all along implicit in the tradition, Carter argued against the archaic humoral and explicitly "nerve"-centered biological medical model. He urged that the real etiology of hysteria was to be found in the patient's inability to deal with

---

3. One senses a certain bias against women even in Galen's description of his own mother, whom he compared to Socrates' wife, Xantippe, and to whom he ascribed "shameful passions." Indeed, he noted, "My mother . . . was so irascible that she would sometimes bite her serving-maids, and she was constantly shouting at my father and quarreling with him. . . . I observed that he was never depressed over any affliction, while my mother became annoyed at the merest bagatelle. You yourself doubtless know that boys imitate what they are fond of, and avoid what they do not like to see" (Veith, 1965, p. 33). It should be noted here, however, perhaps in Galen's defense, that Foucault, (1988) suggested that Galen may not have been so ill-disposed toward women, as he was ambivalent about the sexual pleasures in general (pp. 112–123).

emotional conflict, especially when confronted with oppressive social conditions. In such difficult situations, the patient would forcibly repress her emotions to such an extent that—as "ideo-motor acts"— they would provoke somatic effects typical of hysterical symptoms. Carter specified that these repressed emotions were of the "deeper" kind, such as sexual passion, but that they also included, hatred, envy, and other affects:

> It is reasonable to expect that an emotion, which is strongly felt by great numbers of people, but whose natural manifestations are constantly repressed in compliance with the usages of society, will be the one whose morbid effects are most frequently witnessed. This anticipation is abundantly borne out by facts; the sexual passion in women being that which most accurately fulfills the prescribed conditions, and whose injurious influence upon the organism is most common and familiar. Next after it in power, may be placed those emotions of a permanent character, which are usually concealed, because disgraceful or unamiable, as hatred or envy; after them others equally permanent, such as grief or care, but which, not being discreditable, are not so liable to be repressed [Veith, 1965, p. 201].

Despite the relatively enlightened psychodynamic model proposed by Carter, he nonetheless drew heavily on negative cultural stereotypes of women in framing his account. He would argue that women are especially subject to hysterical disorders because their emotional sensibilities are more refined than those of men and that they are less intellectually inclined to recognize and deal with their own problems. Thus, he remarked, "If the relative power of emotion against the sexes be compared . . . it is seen to be considerably greater in the woman than in the man, partly from that natural conformation which causes the former to feel, under circumstances where the latter thinks" (pp. 201–202). Variations in the tendencies to hysterical response were further explained by Carter as due to differences in the intensity of sexual drive and the increased social pressures on women to conceal their emotions. Thus, Carter's system was in large part based on his transference of social and cultural norms into the very construction of his model of hysteria. The three diagnostic classifications of hysteria he developed in his *On the Pathology and Treatment of Hysteria* encoded these biases. For example, he argued that a patient who would develop the *tertiary* form of hysteria was a woman who felt herself neglected and uncared for rather than one who was simply suffering from sexual frustration (which would be adduced in primary hysteria). This form of hysteria would be characterized by the production of simulated symptoms, so as "to make herself an object of great attention to all around her, and possibly, among others, to the individual who has been uppermost in her thoughts" (p. 203). Typically, these self-induced symptoms would include fainting, swooning, hemorrhaging, vomiting, coughing, aches, paralyses, neuralgias, and so on, symptoms that, for Carter, suggested great deceptiveness and guile on the part of the patient. Hysteria of the *primary* form was typically characterized by severe attacks or convulsive fits, which would be transient in nature. These fits would be emotionally induced by the patient, since there was no apparent organic disease or dysfunction present. If repeated by suggestion, convulsions would be characterized as *secondary* hysteria. Interestingly, Carter maintained that the secondary type of hysteric was particularly difficult to cure. If, after repeated counsel and moral therapy, the patient persisted in her illness, marriage should be advised as a cure.

What is clearly demonstrated by each of these three diagnostic categories—primary, secondary, and tertiary hysteria—however, is that the Victorian understanding of a weak and vulnerable femininity was inscribed, once again, as an occasion for the exercise of medical authority: first, hysteria was designated as a sexually or emotionally motivated psychosomatic disorder; second, as the compulsive repetition of the first; and, third, as a dissembling object of attention. In this respect, it may well be said that Carter's diagnostic classification is not a clear and objective account of a single medical disorder at all—hysteria—but rather, and again, a constructed set of related, but different, disorders, collectively designated by the term hysteria.

The tendency to designate collectively a whole set of disorders as hysteria is perhaps nowhere more evident than in the immense body of clinical work done by Jean-Martin Charcot (1890). Unlike Carter, who eventually turned to opthamological surgery, Charcot spent virtually his entire career in the study of neuropathology and neurology. He built a considerable reputation in these fields through his careful clinical descriptions of multiple sclerosis, amyotrophic lateral sclerosis, and the localization of lesions of the brain and spinal cord. Like Carter and Paul Briquet before him, Charcot also attributed a major significance to psychic trauma in the production of hysterical symptoms. But his strong formation within the French experimental tradition of medicine led him in the end to claim a generalized neurobiological model to explain the entire range of behaviors. For the specific hysterical behavior—

which he categorized according to two orders: the seizure proper and the various typical sets of symptoms ("stigmata") related to the presumptive underlying condition—he sought validation in the discovery of particular neurological lesions. When these could not be anatomically ascertained, he would posit what he termed "dynamic lesions" and an inherited "nerve weakness" to explain the specific etiology of the behavioral disorder.

The result of this approach was the formation of what might be very loosely termed a kind of "brain mythology."[4] Charcot would focus on describing and classifying an enormous number of specific and striking taxonomic details—hysterical symptoms exhibited by his patients while undergoing the paroxysms of fits, contractions, spells, and swoons—all the while postponing the experimental verification of an organically based disease. This theoretical construction could be dramatized to great effect in the amphitheater of the Salpêtrière Hospital in Paris, which became a veritable salon for the display of his patients. His lectures were conducted in the form of a summary of the case in question, followed by an extended demonstration of hysterical behavior by selected patients, who were usually placed in arresting hypnotic states by a team of assistants. Conflating the psychological symptoms of hysteria with the neurological model, Charcot could appeal to these most dramatic "psychological" experiments to confirm his theoretically postulated neurology.

He claimed that the hypnotic state, and the behavior exhibited therein, was precisely what was understood as hysteria. Of course, this claim would be according to his own initial classification of the symptoms: anesthesia, tremors, paralysis, contracture, swooning, tunnel vision, and the presence of "hysterogenic" zones of sensitivity. He additionally classified the seizures into four phases: the epileptoid phase (flailing and jerking motions); clownism (twisting, turning, grotesque feats of dexterity, including the celebrated "arc-en-cercle," an extreme bridging of the back, so as to balance on the heels and the back of the neck); passionate attitudes (a series of dramatically expressed mental states, including hallucinating images of snakes and monsters, and oftentimes manifest in the hysteric's pleading for kisses and sexual intimacies from the doctors); and the delirious phase (laughing, giggling,

---

4. For an extended historical discussion of the emergence and complexity of this type of pervasive myth, see especially Lothane (1992, pp. 464–465).

weeping, stupor). It has also been argued that the physicians themselves were hardly disengaged spectators of these erotically charged displays: on the contrary, it has been claimed that the erotic power relation between doctor and patient could well have been a major causal factor in precipitating these hysterical behaviors, especially the "passionate attitudes" (see Didi-Huberman, 1982). Charcot reasoned, simplistically, that, if all these behavioral effects could be caused by suggestion and by the touching of certain zones during the hypnotic trance, then the patient must have had a significantly weakened nervous system; that is, hysteria was caused by lesions and neurological dysfunctions.

Not only did Charcot's appear to be a remarkably self-referential system, but it was also effectively "validated" by the hysterics themselves, who participated in these hypnotic dramatizations: patients who, it could be argued,[5] oftentimes simply acted these phases and states out— having repeatedly done so before, having discussed them with other patients, having been posed in these states by the medical assistants (for the attending photographers), having been influenced by their proximity to hundreds of hysterics and epileptic patients as well. It is also important to realize that these hypnotized patients repeatedly performed their hysterical roles before such notable members of the audience as the Prime Minister of France, Léon Gambetta, and Guy de Maupassant, as well as a continuous train of Parisian and European doctors, dramatists, authors, intellectuals, actors, actresses, all of whom found the spectacle most fascinating.

One of the most striking features in Charcot's experimental appeal to hypnosis is that only "diagnosed" hysterics were used; hence the "patients" for the experiment, as well as the experiments themselves, could have no extentional value whatsoever. That clinically diagnosed hysterics could—even without the inducements of celebrity and reasonably decent creature comforts—display hysterical symptoms, repeatedly and under hypnosis, could at best support the claim that they were hysterics in the first place, and not, as Charcot had assumed, that a psychological model would be confirmed by, or explained by, a neurological model. Nor, for that matter, did the hypnosis lend any credence to

---

5. See Drinka (1984, pp. 73–107). This argument is one of the bases for Thomas Szasz's (1974, in particular, pp. 17–47) criticism of Charcot, who, he claimed, simply either invented his patients' symptoms or overlooked the possibility that they might have been invented by the patients themselves. Szasz based his claims, in part, on information drawn from the biography of Charcot by Guillain (1959).

the claim of the presence of "lesions," however "dynamic" the patients themselves might have been. The use of hypnotism in defense of the neurological model only served to prove that hysterics, when hypnotized, act like hysterics.

Like many 19th-century investigators of hysteria, Charcot demonstrated very little with regard to the existence and etiology of the disorder termed hysteria. In fact, he may well have occluded the existence of numerous other disorders, for example, organic illnesses and other psychological disorders, by imposing on his subject a presumably scientific and objective, radically closed model of hysteria. The majority of his patients were referred to him and had already been diagnosed by other physicians as hysterics. It has been repeatedly claimed that Charcot rarely bothered to administer a thorough physical examination upon the arrival of those patients at Salpêtrière. Some notable misdiagnoses by Charcot were his taking rheumatic or autoimmune illnesses, as well as cardiac illnesses, for hysteria, not to mention the many psychoneurotic and psychotic disorders that were diagnosed as neurologically based hysteria (Drinka, 1984, p. 102).

Despite the different models of hysteria employed by such figures as Carter and Charcot—psychodynamic and biological, respectively—they both agreed that some form of shock or trauma was initially involved in triggering the hysterical fits. For Charcot, the trauma would have disrupted an already enervated nervous system (genetically inherited or plagued by "dynamic lesions"); for Carter, it would have been precipitated by emotional stress and repression. Nonetheless, both individuals would invoke the same set of cultural biases that had plagued women from ancient times through the 20th century. The expressed indifference or opposition to these prevailing codes of propriety would in large part constitute the measure of hysterical depravity (sensual indulgence, moral obliquity, determined willfulness, egoism). Carter himself would invoke an ancient maxim against feminine sexuality, precisely in this respect: *Salacitas major, major ad hysteriam proclivitas* [The greater the salaciousness, the stronger the proclivity to hysteria] (Veith, 1965, p. 202). Like their earlier counterparts, both Carter and Charcot saw the remediation of these disorders through a moral/medical model of treatment, a model that would basically demand that the patient reenter the social and moral codes from which she had so obviously deviated. Hence, for both Carter and Charcot, treatment strove to emphasize the authority of the physician "to change the patient's moral environment" (p. 236).

This was such a compelling necessity for Carter that he went so far as to prescribe the

"wearing out the moral endurance of the patient, and . . . by taking from her all motives for deception," that is, by making the psychological costs of continued "illness" too great for the patient to persevere in such conduct. Its object was to remove the patient's underlying motives for remaining in a state of chronic, self-induced hysteria (namely, her morbid craving for sympathy and attention), not by attacking the inherent strength of the motive, but rather by frustrating every means which might be adopted for its gratification, or making such gratification available only at inordinate personal cost to the patient [Clark, 1981, p. 295].

While Charcot's interests in hysteria were principally clinical and diagnostic, his treatment was largely limited to symptomatic therapy. On one hand, he attempted to neutralize the original psychic trauma and go on to assure the patient of an eventual cure. On the other, he usually suggested removing the patient from her "moral environment," which meant her home and, that is, institutionalization. In many cases institutionalization proved helpful and led to an improvement. But, in the end, his treatment—or relative lack thereof—was due to a not unfamiliar bias. Hysterics were, after all, inferior people, who typically were subject to moral degeneration, owing to faulty heredity and, ultimately, faulty cerebrums. As Drinka (1984) remarked about Charcot's hysterical patients and his attitude toward them,

their neurological systems lived on the edge of dissolution. To Charcot, in the fight for the survival of the fittest, hysterics were creatures burdened with central nervous systems that could not withstand any variety of stress, psychic or physical. Furthermore, the majority of hysterics were women, creatures more emotional than men, with smaller brains and muscles. Some of the male hysterics were described as effeminate, and Charcot believed that those males who were not effeminate had usually inherited the taint from their fathers or their mothers [pp. 100–101].

The medical approach in determining the nature of hysteria in the 19th century largely paralleled the logic of Charcot's own investigations: symptoms were classified, cases were studied, behavior exhibited; but relatively little was done other than to confirm the presumed existence of a sort of deviant or aberrant behavior that was plainly obvious in the first place. These behaviors were, in turn, observed, reported, recorded, studied, discussed—to such an extent that a large and articulated body of presumably reliable medical data was generated and widely distributed. This dissemination, in turn, led to a generally accepted confirmation of the disorder by the profession. In reality, little was accomplished in terms of objectively establishing the existence of the disorder and thereby of treating it. Patients were more often than not regarded as the subjects of a burgeoning literature than as persons suffering from a specific disorder, that is, hysteria, whatever that was. Hence, the question of treatment and the position of the patient—again, the woman—simply fell to the most commonplace prejudices and biases, medical and cultural. The obliquity would be countered and treated through repeated consultation, by "rest" cures, by spa "vacations," as well as by temporary or long-term isolation in a growing number of public hospitals and charitable institutions or by authoritarian mandates to conform to the codes of acceptable moral behavior or be left in silence—or get married.

Pierre Janet, the author of the 19th century's perhaps most encyclopedic volume on hysteria, *The Mental State of Hystericals* (see Veith, 1965), was concerned to analyze the classifications and conventions associated with the description of hysterics. His clinical experience taught him that hysteria was far more limited in scope than his predecessors (notably, Charcot) maintained. Indeed, tradition had described hysteria according to such a myriad number of symptoms and formations that, for Janet, the whole account seemed implausible. Rather, Janet proposed a much more coherent, narrowed, and ordered system, one that could account for diverse manifestations, precisely by having what he termed an *idée fixe*—a central, obsessional notion—as the axis of each patient's disorder. In locating the singular features of what would be the traumatic core of the mental illness, Janet found that the hysteric's attentional field was considerably more focused and intensified than that of others, that this focus tended to incline the hysteric to egocentricity and, thereby, to inattention to other, everyday concerns. The intensity of the hysteric's states could thus be accounted for in terms that, for once, were not explicitly sexual; indeed, Janet determined that "the hystericals are, in general, not any more erotic than normal persons" (quoted in Veith, 1965, p. 251). Of the 120 patients Janet diagnosed in his massive study, sexuality had a prominent role in only four cases, and, even for them, he remarked, there was little strange or pathological. Sexuality, amorous relations, even erotic fantasies were perfectly normal for young people, after all.

Even though Janet, following Briquet, liberalized thinking about the role of sexuality in hysteria and limited the symptomatic formations of the disorder, he nonetheless remained convinced that, underlying a hysteric's various mental states, and even preceding the patient's initial psychic trauma, the etiology of hysteria once again indicated an organic pathology. The pathology was induced by a set of "provocative agents," a term Breuer and Freud (1893–95) would later use, in deference to Charcot. Most of those agents were of a physical nature and included chronic diseases, hemorrhages, typhoid fever, and a variety of diseases of the nervous system. Despite his extraordinary clinical acumen, in many respects Janet tended to mimic the reductionist physiological theories of Charcot. He set up a structural system for hysteria that began with an organic predisposition and was transformed into a psychological state of "mental weakness" by a traumatic set of "provocative agents." These provocations and dispositions would coalesce the disorder around the *idée fixe*, which, in turn, served as the organizing principle of the hysteric's formations. Janet further postulated that the *idée fixe* was itself an unconscious phenomenon, and extensive analysis was required to locate it and to establish its correlation to the original trauma. This approach would be necessary to begin to treat the hysterical "accident" and thereby to relieve the patient's symptoms. But all these stages associated with the analysis and treatment of the disorder were based on a series of assumptions that were hardly well-grounded. For example, if the claim for an organic basis of hysteria is incorrect—which is clearly a possibility, given the weakness of Charcot's evidence—what could be claimed for all of the subsequent stages? Would the very structure of the disorder remain unaffected? Or would the disorder of hysteria prove to be something else entirely—or, perhaps, several separate but related disorders?

The Invention of the Unconscious:
Hysteria as a Psychosexual Disorder

The same year that witnessed the publication of Janet's *The Mental State of Hysterials* would indeed find something quite similar but also entirely different. Josef Breuer and Sigmund Freud (1893) published their landmark analysis, "On the Psychical Mechanism of Hysterical

Phenomena: Preliminary Communication" and received immediate international attention.[6] Most striking, perhaps about the "Preliminary Communication" was that the difficult issue of organic pathology was, at least initially, avoided. Breuer and Freud focused on the symptomatological dynamics of hysteria, especially on the earlier partition of symptoms, which Charcot had characterized as the "third phase" of hysterical "crises," that is, "passionate attitudes."

> Our attempted explanation takes its start from the third of these phases, that of the "*attitudes passionelles*." Where this is present in a well-marked form, it exhibits the hallucinatory reproduction of a memory which was of importance in bringing about the onset of the hysteria—the memory either of a single major trauma (which we find *par excellence* in what is called traumatic hysteria) or of a series of interconnected part-traumas (such as underlie common hysteria) [p. 14].

The decision to begin the examination of hysteria from this particular focus was to shape the entirety of Freud's later theoretical enterprise. The analysis would begin from within a specified range of observed behavioral symptoms, but, more importantly, Breuer and Freud cast the terms of analysis according to the dynamics of memory and trauma. Doing so allowed them to overcome the specific difficulties that had plagued Charcot and Janet, namely, the organic and physiomotor determinations of hysteria. They accomplished this by simply reducing the etiology of each of these other phases to an ideopathological disturbance. For example, in cases where the phase of the "attitude passionelle" was not evident, when there were purely motor phenomena involved, this disturbance would be attributed to an underlying memory of a psychical trauma—a typical explanation, involving a young girl with epileptic seizures (the epileptoid phase), centered on an encounter she had with a vicious dog. The "passionelle" phase would be similarly determined, but complicated by the additional components of hallucinations, delusions, false images and memories. Breuer and Freud could thus state the hysterical "mechanism" concisely:

> The typical course of a severe case of hysteria is, as we know, as follows. To begin with, an ideational content is formed during hypnoid states; when this has increased to a sufficient extent, it gains control, during a period of

---

6. For a detailed and in-depth historical account of Breuer and Freud's work on the etiology of hysteria, see Sulloway (1979, pp. 22–100).

'acute hysteria', of the somatic innervation and of the patient's whole existence, and creates chronic symptoms and attacks; after this it clears up,
apart from certain residues. . . . An attack will occur spontaneously, just as
memories do in normal people; it is, however, possible to provoke one; just
as any memory can be aroused in accordance with the laws of association.
It can be provoked either by stimulation of a hysterogenic zone [a term
Freud employs, largely to show continuity with Charcot] or by a new experience which sets it going owing to a similarity with the pathogenic experience [p. 16].

The strength of their claim lies in the persistence of memory as an
abiding cause of the hysterical episodes. This persistent memory, in
turn, led to Breuer and Freud's claim that their method had "therapeutic advantages" over others, since these retained memories, and the
suffering they caused, could be abreacted (released) in normal consciousness and dealt with (and, thereby, dispensed with) on the level of
speech. The physician could then help the patient to remove the initial
traumatic memory through suggestion, associative integration of ideas,
and further psychoanalytic therapy. Effectively, this intervention would
mark the announcement of both "the Freudian (or "repressed") unconscious" and "the talking cure."

Following this path, Freud elaborated the entire corpus of his work,
which is, of course, legend. The few cases and examples of interest here
are those in which Freud applied these new insights to hysteria and in
which he nonetheless invoked some of the disturbing inconsistencies
and cultural biases that have for so long surrounded the disorder of
hysteria.

The fourth chapter of *Studies on Hysteria* (Breuer and Freud,
1893–95), "The Psychotherapy of Hysteria," consists, in part, of selected
case history summaries of Breuer and Freud's hysterical patients. It was
intended as a means of describing the ongoing evolution of psychoanalytic technique (Kerr, 1993, pp. 62–65). Ostensibly, the point Freud
wished to make in this chapter, through the synopses, is that hysteria is
not an "independent clinical entity," as such; that is, it occurs within a
much broader and more complex range of "neurotic" symptoms. Pure
forms of hysteria, like pure forms of obsessional neurosis, are very rare.
What seemed to complicate almost every case, Freud argued, was the
intrusion of some form of "sexual neurosis." Even in Breuer's case of
Anna O, documented earlier in the *Studies*, where there certainly
appeared to be an isolated, "classic" hysteria, Freud noted that Breuer

had never considered the case from the point of view of sexual neurosis, therefore rendering it useless in determining the hysteria. He then referred to one of his own contributions to the volume, Frau Emmy von N, and proceeded to reintroduce virtually all the biases traditionally associated with female sexuality in its relation to hysteria, but in a remarkably deceptive and self-ingratiating way:

> When I began to analyse the second patient, Frau Emmy von N, the expectation of a sexual neurosis being the basis of hysteria was fairly remote from my mind. I had come fresh from the school of Charcot, and I regarded the linking of hysteria with the topic of sexuality as a sort of insult—just as the women patients themselves do. When I go through my notes on this case today there seems to me no doubt at all that it must be looked at as a case of severe anxiety neurosis . . . which originated from sexual abstinence and had become combined with hysteria. Case 3, that of Miss Lucy R . . . had an unmistakable sexual aetiology. . . . The patient was an over-mature girl with a need to be loved, whose affections had been too hastily aroused through a misunderstanding. . . . Case 5, Katharina, was nothing less than a model of what I have described as "virginal anxiety" [Breuer and Freud, 1893–95, pp. 259–260].

On further reflection, then, sexual neurosis was at the core of virtually all female hysteria. When it was not obvious or appeared to be absent, there was some methodological anomaly at work: Breuer did not consider sexual neurosis in the case of Anna O; Freud himself overlooked or understated it in the four cases he reported in the *Studies*. But the connection between hysteria and sexual neurosis would have been much clearer if he had reported the "*twelve* cases [he had examined] whose analysis provides a confirmation of the psychical mechanism of hysterical phenomena put forward by us . . ." (p. 260). The stratagem is obvious. Freud wished to reintroduce the standard model of "female problems" in a new guise: sexual neurosis. Women are hysterics not because they have an organic predisposition or "loose" morals, but, rather, because, as women, they are subjected to various traumas, which, in turn, create the core for subsequent hysterical attacks. As sensitive creatures, they are subject to "virginal anxiety," or "the need to be loved," or they may have their affections "hastily aroused."

In the early writings on hysteria, Freud had focused on the importance of memory, trauma, and the therapeutic use of hypnosis to help diagnose his patients' disorders. By the time of his major case studies, he was equipped with a remarkably well-developed theoretical apparatus. During the intervening years, he had further elaborated the mechanics of the unconscious and repression, the dynamics of the dream-work, the theory of infantile sexuality, and the Oedipus drama. This eleboration would permit him to engage in a far more complex analysis of what he had examined early on in his professional career, namely, hysteria. In the Dora case, for example, he would explicitly identify neurosis in general with a sexual etiology, and hysteria in particular would be equated with the inability to deal successfully with the erotic drives on a conscious level. Dream analysis would yield an immense amount of material derived from childhood sexual traumas and from repressed wishes and desires in the unconscious minds of his patients. Particularly striking in the case studies, especially in the Dora case, is that, once a patient was initially diagnosed as a hysteric, there would be little content in her dream life at all, other than repressed, displaced, condensed, reversed, contradictory, or (to be generous) ambiguous sexual content.

Since the Freudian unconscious is the repository of every memory of the most apparently inconsequential event, emotion, occurrence, or, indeed, trauma—all subject to infinite transpositions and associations—it is altogether possible that, under analysis, a patient's dream content could well confirm the suspicion of the professionally trained physician that a sexual etiology is at the basis of the hysteria. In fact, Freud (1905) claimed that, given his analytic methods, others would quickly lend their assent:

> I handle unconscious ideas, unconscious trains of thought, and unconscious impulses as though they were no less valid and unimpeachable psychological data than conscious ones. But of this I am certain—that anyone who sets out to investigate the same region of phenomena and employs the same method will find himself compelled to take up the same position, however much philosophers may expostulate . . . [it] is the sexual function that I look upon as the foundation of hysteria and of the psycho-neuroses in general [pp. 82–83].

If one employed the same method as Freud to analyze the same phenomena he did, arguably, one *would* tend to arrive at the same conclusion, especially when the logic of the unconscious excludes negation. But this assent also derives from the patient under analysis:

> No one can undertake the treatment of a case of hysteria until he is convinced of the impossibility of avoiding the mention of sexual subjects. . . .

The patients themselves are easy to convince; and there are only too many opportunities of doing so in the course of the treatment. . . . There is never any danger of corrupting an inexperienced girl. For where there is no knowledge of sexual processes even in the unconscious, no hysterical symptom will arise; and where hysteria is found there can no longer be any question of 'innocence of mind' in the sense in which parents and educators use the phrase [p. 49].

Given this methodological paradigm, one could be fairly well assured of finding some sexual content in the mind of anyone who could communicate with another human being—or, in Dora's case, someone who could read an encyclopedia. Since there would be some content, so understood, in the unconscious, it would but remain for someone trained in this particular methodology to bring it forth. Hence, the Freudian model is so inclusive in its approach that literally nothing articulable can remain outside the associative or syntagmatic chain of sexual signification. By the same token, many of Freud's patients were themselves bathed in sexually charged surroundings and hence could, as he remarked, be easily convinced of the sexual etiology of their disturbances. Dora, for instance, had to fend off the sexual advances of her father's mistress' husband; the mother was obsessional and "frigid," and her whole family, she included, seemed to be afflicted with some form of venereal disease (pp. 75–76). The very mention of sex would no doubt set off a whole series of associations.

What, in fact, did Freud contribute to the identification, evaluation, clarification, and treatment of hysteria? He did shift the focus of analysis from an organic model of degeneration to one of a psychic determination. But, by narrowing hysteria to Charcot's "third phase," he effectively lent focus to, and thereby narrowed, the classification of hysteria under the then-popular "conversion" type, in which patients displayed dramatic somatic symptoms. As we indicated earlier, however, Charcot's partition of the various symptoms, his observations, and his various experiments were themselves seriously flawed. By transforming a part of Charcot's celebrated model into his own nascent view, and by specifying and insisting on its sexual etiology, Freud managed to legitimate his own view of hysteria. But he did this by, in part, accepting the underlying premises of Charcot's model, that is, the organic model, which was largely that of the tradition itself. Oddly, by his so narrowing the model of hysteria and by so emphasizing its psychosexual pathology, the ordinarily literate public no longer permitted itself to display such "psychosomatic" kinks as flailing their arms, kicking their legs, compulsively coughing, dragging their feet, swooning, and the like.

With its field of operation so narrowed, and with the inception of modern medical and neurological diagnostics, hysteria virtually disappeared by the early part of the 20th century as a diagnosable disease or blanket disorder. Freud was thus partially responsible for eradicating the disorder, which, it could be argued, was never specifically determined in the first place. By his raising the analysis of psychopathological disorders in general to a highly sophisticated and taxonomically precise science, particular symptoms could be addressed and treated through a scientifically cast nosology. This practice, in turn, led to more accurate—and in some cases, far more complex—sociological, neurological, and psychiatric evaluations. As a general category, hysteria was effectively defined right out of existence and was replaced by a multitude of trauma and stress disorders, phobias, dissociative and mood disorders, compulsions, psychological and psychophysiological syndromes of every stripe and hue. Other than in some rare cases of "conversion hysteria," hysteria is viewed today largely as a modifier. Indeed, this was a situation Pierre Janet foresaw with some trepidation: "The word 'hysteria' should be preserved although its primitive meaning is much changed. It would be very difficult to modify it nowadays, and truly, it has so great and beautiful history, that it would be painful to give it up" (quoted in Veith, 1965, p. 254).

THE IMMINENT END OF HYSTERIA

If the persecution of witchcraft found its initial impetus in the religious prosecution of heresy, so did the millennia-old determination to cure hysteria find an impetus in the desire to eliminate the aberrant, troublesome and divisive social behavior of women. The attempt to isolate and eliminate witches was further abetted by the political determination of the state to establish and maintain its own power and security. So did the medical profession—from Egyptian instruction, through Hippocrates, Galen, the Renaissance medical historians, and through the 19th- and 20th-century physicians, therapists, and clinics—seek to mollify the outbursts of nonconforming and emotionally threatening conduct of women. Both witchcraft and hysteria were characterized from earliest times as having a remarkable, and sometimes, interchangeable, sexual component—in their respective practice or dynamics. And both, it can now be understood, were themselves constructions by public institutions and opinion, whose interests (religious, social, economic, cultural, emotional) would be served by their systematic suppression. The early Church had to eliminate schisms and heresies to maintain its own authority, and this effort extended to the hunting of witches, who, it was feared, would deprive the faithful of eternity itself.

Like witchcraft, hysteria was seen to militate against the broader social interest. If the dominant social structure of archaic and even modern society generated a reduced social and cultural role for women, provided little outlet for feminine creativity—much less for aggression or erotic behavior—and was thus viewed as a superior form of organization, precisely by forbidding such behavior, it was perfectly reasonable to restrict and to convert that behavior into a norm of compliancy and dependency. The norms of social and sexual integration were derived from the traditional sources—precisely what made them norms—and toward the middle of the 19th century became the object of explicit scientific inquiry. For the professions of medicine and psychiatry, abnormal behavior could be specified, and material causes and determinations for this behavior could be located (through the medical model) in the areas of anatomy, physiology, endocrinology, neurology, diet, hygiene. Corrective steps could be taken to assure a medical diagnosis and cure, or failing that, to institutionalize certain persons (in a medical or penal setting) who failed to conform to acceptable norms of behavior. All these steps would be "scientifically" applied to a disorder that, ultimately, no one seemed to be able to locate, to observe correctly, to determine clinically, much less, to cure. That misdiagnosis was so common and that medical "treatments" for hysteria oftentimes got out of hand should, however, be understood in the light of both the inadequate knowledge of the time and the fact that, as a newly "rigorous" discipline, medicine was at the same time charged, both socially and scientifically, to accommodate itself to the cure of what it could not possibly understand. Unlike the earlier witchcraft, which was actively pursued for gain by all concerned parties—and which was fully "understood" by them—hysteria was thrust onto the developing medical profession as a problem it was hardly prepared to address, much less, remediate.

As the prognosis for witchcraft proved short-lived at the end of the 17th century, so would that of hysteria at the end of the 19th. Likewise, just as the institution of church and state would survive the demise of witchcraft, so would the prestige and authority of medicine survive the passing of hysteria.

CHAPTER THREE

MUNCHAUSEN BY PROXY

THE CONSTRUCTION
OF A NEW DISORDER

*Spitzer also had the results of a questionnaire
about masochism he had sent to APA members
interested in personality disorders. The poll,
however, had a rather imposing bias built into
it. The first question asked its readers, Do you
support including the masochistic disorder in
the DSM? If the answer was no, they were
instructed not to fill out the rest of the questionnaire. This method, Spitzer conceded,
managed to eliminate half of the people polled.*

—*Susan Faludi*

ANOMALIES IN THE MEDICAL-MENTAL MODEL OF HYSTERIA

Emil Kraepelin (1907) noted that the exact
pathology of hysteria was not yet clear. It was
indeed a congenital morbid mental state, one
characterized by a variety of physical symptoms.
Following Paul Julius Moebius, he claimed that
most of the symptoms were caused "by ideas,"
but, to add to the confusion, the entire condition
was complicated by the patients' general emotional disposition. Nonetheless, "the true nature of

the disease is still unknown [and] there is no known anatomical pathological basis for the disease" (p. 459). It had occurred to Kraepelin, and to many other physicians, however, that a large number of hysterics' symptoms may have, in fact, been simulated, if not merely exaggerated. Precisely because of this concern, he warned against the use of such therapies as hypnosis, since their employment tended to multiply symptoms in the patients, particularly those who were suggestive or overly sensitive in the first place—a peculiar trait of hysterics widely noted in the 19th century.

> Hypnotism is of limited value, because those susceptible to hypnotic suggestion are apt to be influenced by any powerful suggestion that happens to be presented. Furthermore, hypnotic experience brings about an undesirable dependency of the patient upon the physician, which makes impossible an effective subjugation of their own wills in the strife with the morbid influences. The greater the influence exerted, the more easily autosuggestions arise, and the quicker the efficacy of the hypnotic suggestion is nullified by other and opposing ideas. . . . In the treatment of the hysterical attacks, the patient can often be restored to clear consciousness by a brisk command, or, if this fails, by a dash of cold water upon the face, by the electric brush, or pressure over the ovaries or upon the hysterogenic zones [p. 474].

It might seem somewhat retrograde that Kraepelin instructed clinicians to compress the ovaries, to turn on the electric brush, or even to administer chloroform to hysterical patients. But he was concerned to raise the issue of what the 19th century called the role of "will" or "volition" in hysteria. His prescription of these abrupt "stimulants" was meant merely to "shock" patients back into a state of self-possession and self-control and away from the suggestions (becoming autosuggestions) that hypnosis (and other types of treatment) might induce. These concerns signaled a more difficult issue: the complicitious patient who induces her own "illness" raises the fundamental question as to what is really meant by the term "illness." Focusing on this issue would also serve to point out the obstinate presence of dependency, malingering, and hypochondriasis so often displayed by hysterics. Two subsequent—and determining—problems would emerge from this issue as well, namely, the disruptive relations that might ensue between patient and physician, individual and institution, as well as something internal to the authority of medicine itself: the disruption of the very model of illness by the introduction of "nonillness" into the medical model. Thus, on one hand, hysterics were notoriously difficult to deal with and to cure; on the other, the notion of mental illness itself was so confusing that one could hardly expect to find a cure.

Kraepelin's concerns about the completeness and validity of the medical model of hysteria at the beginning of the 20th century had already been anticipated earlier on in the 19th century. Physicians such as Sir Benjamin Brodie (1837), a noted orthopedic surgeon, devoted considerable time and effort to explain the perplexing presence of symptoms in certain of his patients whose illnesses should not have been characterized by, or even accompanied by, those symptoms. In many of his cases, he could find no organic cause at all for these frequently atypical symptoms. He generally termed these symptoms "local nervous affections" when no organic etiology could be ascertained for them.

> For a long time these cases occasioned me great perplexity, and it was not until after I had published the first edition of my *Treatise on the Diseases of the Joints*, that the occurrence of the case, which I am about to describe, first led me to suspect the real origin of the symptoms, which I had not comprehended formerly [p. 34].

After he completed his treatise, it occurred to Brodie that the troublesome symptoms he encountered were hysterical symptoms, "simulating diseases of the joints of the extremities" ("local hysterical affections"), and that, at least in part, they were attributable to "a moral cause having a depressing influence on the constitution." Brodie would, in turn, specify these "moral causes," largely in terms of temperament, character, willfulness—or conversely, the lack of will-power. Treatment would thus focus on redirecting these agencies, so as to remove the cause of the hysterical symptoms: "In like manner the agency of moral causes, especially of those which compel the patient to make much physical exertion, often leads to her recovery" (p. 42).

Whereas Carter (see Veith, 1965), for example, would seek a conventionally Victorian "moral" cause and cure for hysteria in women, Brodie's concerns lay elsewhere. He treated the "hysterical affections" and their moral causes principally as anomalies that affected the physician's ability to diagnose properly and treat certain common medical disorders. Indeed, Brodie (1837) viewed these hysterical symptoms as simulative affects that tended to confound common medical knowledge. He thus described and recorded these "affections" not so much in view of discovering the root causes of a disease called "hysteria," but, rather, to signal them as anomalous factors that complicated medical diagnosis in other fields; in his case, orthopedics. This diagnostic impetus to set the hysterical symptoms apart is evident in the following two cases, recounted in a series of lectures on "hysterical affections:"

> But sometimes it is otherwise, and they [affective symptoms] vanish all at once without any evident cause. For example: in the year 1834 I was consulted respecting a young lady labouring under a well marked hysterical affection, simulating disease of the hip joint. . . . Her symptoms had continued, nearly unaltered, for nearly two years, when one night, on turning herself in bed, she said that she had a feeling that something had given way in her hip, and from that moment she was quite well.
>
> Another young lady was brought to London for my opinion in October, 1833. She also was supposed to labour under a disease of the hip-joint. After a careful examination of her case, I was satisfied that it was one of hysterical affection, and that there was no actual disease of the joint [pp. 44–45].

In his concern to lend diagnostic precision to the examination of these atypical cases, Brodie revealed many of them to be what we would now call psychosomatic and stress-related disorders, and others were tied to a patient's perhaps understandable anxiety about persistent minor pain. As for the latter, he said,

> Close attention will discover in any, even in the most healthy organ, sensations which had been previously overlooked; and constant anxiety on the subject may magnify such sensations into pain. In these last-mentioned cases a strong assurance that no disease exists will make the patient happy, and remove the pain; but no such assurance will be adequate to the cure of a genuine hysterical affection [pp. 53–54].

The medical model would thus be equilibrated by dissociating the causes of these atypical symptoms from the specific disorder in question. They would not be simply assimilated into the disorder as accompanying "hysterical symptoms," nor would they be consigned to a medical model of "hysteria" proper. Regarding the latter, Brodie would come to stress the central role of the patient's will, the dissimulative and simulative inclination, for whatever gain or attention the patient might seek. His diagnostic skills were paramount here in his being able to ascertain proper physiological and neurological functioning and thereby establishing a reliable medical frame of reference for the exclusion of, and explanation for, hysteria:

Where there is paralysis, or a tendency to paralysis, it is quite different from what is observed in cases of pressure on the spinal cord or brain; and I may take this opportunity of observing, with respect to hysterical paralysis generally, that it has this peculiarity: *it is not that the muscles are incapable of obeying the act of volition, but that the function of volition is not exercised.* The accuracy of this observation will, if I am not much mistaken, be acknowledged by all those who are at the pains of studying these cases with the attention which they so well deserve; and the importance of it in medical and surgical practice is sufficiently obvious [p. 48].

RESTORING THE MEDICAL-MENTAL MODEL

Charcot (1890) was so impressed by the foregoing general diagnostic procedure that he proposed to call it "Brodie's sign"—in that it could definitively differentiate the hysterical formations from specific organic disorders. While, for Brodie (1837) the differentiation was largely a corrective, something to set disease apart from nondisease, it was precisely this same differentiation that would permit Charcot to render them parallel, thereby elevating hysteria to the full dimension of a medically diagnosed disease. Initially, in his lectures on hysterical affections, he warned his students that these symptoms were so disorienting to both patient and physician that they could well affect the entire diagnosis and course of treatment for hysteria. In fact, certain patients were so pained and obsessed by their symptoms that they eagerly submitted themselves to surgical operation for remediation of their condition. This hysterical obsession in the patient, *mania operativa passiva*, Charcot observed, often had the unpleasant consequence of inducing more than complicitous surgeons to operate on the poor victims—giving rise to a complementary disorder in the physician, which Charcot (1890) (following the American surgeon Louis Stromeyer) termed *mania operativa activa* (p. 373). Charcot gives a particularly shocking example of *mania operativa activa*, the case of a young girl who continually sought surgery to alleviate the pains in her knee joint. She was repeatedly rejected by surgeons but eventually found one who would operate. After the amputation of her leg, the postoperative examination revealed that, in fact, no physical pathology was visible—even granted her pain may well have been real.

Charcot's deep concern for the disquieting complication of hysterical symptoms, however, belonged to his broader interest in medically validating an organic basis for hysteria itself. Brodie's introduction of hysterical affections—which he could not trace to organic sources—seems to indicate a psychopathological or psychosomatic origin, or what Brodie himself called the volitional basis, for the existence of anomalous or atypical symptoms. Charcot (1890), however, claimed that the symptoms, the pain, the seizures, the paralysis, the whole hysterical disorder itself was not brought on by volitional weakness, by simulation or dissimulation, but was fully real by any measure of the term, even when the term itself was *sine materia*.

> The conclusions drawn from the results of the examination in question, gentlemen, are the following: 1) There does not exist, in the present subject, any traces of an organic affection of the joint. 2) This individual is very likely a simulator.
> But, following the preceding presentation, gentlemen, we evidently cannot subscribe to the latter conclusion.
> Most certainly, organic coxalgia does not exist in our patient, and this has been clearly established. But he does have a hysterical coxalgia, *sine materia*, you might say. But, whatever the *dynamics* might be, the illness is perfectly legitimate, perfectly real, and nothing, absolutely nothing, would allow us to accuse this man of being a simulator [p. 384].

This stress on the reality of the disorder, and on its parallel to an organic disorder, clearly indicated a move on Charcot's part toward establishing as organic what Brodie had found to be ideational. Charcot's patient, had no organic disorder, but this does not necessarily mean that the patient did not have a real disorder or that he was simulating a disorder. Rather, by stipulating that this disorder was "real," its etiology could ultimately—though somewhat obscurely—be equated with the organic, medical model so favored by Charcot. It's simple. The patient suffers from hysterical coxalgia, which differs from real coxalgia only in that it has a different etiology, prognosis ("a less somber one," according to Charcot), and regimen of treatment. In fact, he ended his lecture on hysterical affections with an invitation to deal with specific clinical cures for such affections.

Charcot would have been hard pressed to objectively establish his case for hysterical coxalgia, since there was really no basis for it within the traditional norms of clinical determination. But Freud quite easily avoided this nettlesome problem by introducing the domain of the

unconscious as a diagnostic tool.[1] In doing so, he would complete what
Charcot had attempted, namely, to reestablish the hysterical disorder
fully within the medical/psychiatric model and to give a clinical and
theoretical elaboration of it. What Brodie had torn asunder, Freud
would bring together. By the same token, Freud would dispense with
Brodie's problem entirely—that the hysterical symptoms were products
of a weak volition, a simulative intention, or a dissimulative "will"
(much less, that so many symptoms seemed to be completely anomalous). The solution was elegantly simple: transfer the errant "willfulness" of the dissembling hysteric away from that person's doubtless
irksome personality and character and locate its agency within the
unconscious. A new name and a new scene would now greet the "psychoneurotic disorder" of hysteria. The patient would effectively have no
conscious volition at all; rather, she would be unwittingly subject to the
deterministic ravages of the unconscious. The hysteric was not to be
blamed, but treated with all the medical acumen at the service of the
psychiatrist and psychoanalyst. Freud (1905) barely hid his disdain
for the "commonplace" misunderstandings surrounding this form of
psychoneurosis:

> The crudest and most common place views on the character of hysterical
> disorders—such as are to be heard from uneducated relatives or nurses—
> are in a certain sense right. It is true that the paralyzed and bedridden
> woman would spring to her feet if a fire were to break out in her room, and
> that the spoiled wife would forget all her suffering if her child were to fall
> dangerously ill or if some catastrophe were to threaten the family circum-
> stances. People who speak of the patients in this way are right except upon
> a single point: they overlook the psychological distinction between what is
> conscious and what is unconscious. This may be permissible where children
> are concerned, but with adults it is no longer possible. That is why all these

1. Here we refer to Freud's structural theory of the unconscious as a general and
broad explanation for virtually any psychopathology. In this respect, the structural
theory of the unconscious operates as an organizing principle, much like the medical model itself, through which difficult to discern behaviors simply may be
attributed to a specific causal-interpretive nexus. The structural theory should be
distinguished from the broader topographical model of the unconscious (Cs., Pcs.
and Ucs.), where the unconscious is, rather, held to be a region belonging to the
partition of psychical reality. In the latter respect, one can see the unconscious as
operating within the world of human consciousness, and as affecting certain
behavior, for example, defensive behavior, like lying, or protectiveness, denial,
without, for all that, being exclusively determinative of that behavior.

asservations that it is 'only a question of willing' and all the encouragements and abuse that are addressed to the patient are of no avail. An attempt must first be made by the roundabout methods of analysis to convince the patient herself of the existence in her of an intention to be ill. It is in combating the motives of illness that the weak point in every kind of therapeutic treatment of hysteria lies [p. 45].

Now, "without doubt," nonillness became firmly established within the domain of illness. What Brodie found perplexing, what Charcot had difficulty in establishing, Freud posited as a fundamental premise. Remarkably, he seems to have done so by following Charcot's own injunction to physicians against falling subject to *mania operativa activa*. If the patient "herself" is not entirely convinced about her own illness, it is precisely the task of the analyst to convince her that she is sick. Whatever symptom the patient might have, whether or not it can be empirically and clinically established, counts as a valid symptom of a psychoneurotic disorder. Charcot's "simulator"—given this approach —becomes Freud's very model of illness. With this conflation of non-illness with illness, the ideational with the physical, the etiology of hysteria becomes clear: For Freud (1905) it is always both psychical and physical: "In this connection we must recall the question which has so often been raised, whether the symptoms of hysteria are of psychical or of somatic origin. . . . As far as I can see, every hysterical symptom involves the participation of *both* sides" (p. 40). What makes this doctrine of "participation" particularly elegant is that the hysteric's body has an organic "potentiality" or "disposition" to receive these hysterical symptoms. When the symptoms are visibly displayed, the diagnosis can be rendered clearly: hysteria. How can the body actually participate in these psychic disturbances? Freud has a ready response: "It cannot occur without the presence of a certain degree of *somatic compliance* offered by some normal or pathological process in or connected with one of the bodily organs" (p. 40).[2]

When the "meaning" of these somatically compliant hysterical symptoms confounds the physician, Freud, unlike Brodie, again has a ready answer:

The hysterical symptom does not carry this meaning with it, but the meaning is lent to it, soldered to it, as it were; and in every instance the meaning

---

2. For an interesting account of Freud's notion of "somatic compliance," see Masson (1984, pp. 104–106).

can be a different one, according to the nature of the suppressed thoughts which are struggling for expression. However, there are a number of factors at work which tend to make less arbitrary the relations between the unconscious thoughts and the somatic processes that are at their disposal as a means of expression, and which tend to make those relations approximate to a few typical forms [pp. 40–41].

Anticipating the objection that this "new view" of somatic compliance might complicate the traditional problem of etiological determination, Freud remarkably claims that, quite to the contrary, it will diminish the whole issue. But how could that be? By viewing the hysterical symptoms as differentiating factors of hysteria!

I may remark that this new view has not only to some extent pushed the problem further back, but has also to some extent diminished it. We have no longer to deal with the *whole* problem, but only with the portion of it involving that particular characteristic of hysteria *which differentiates* it from other psychoneuroses. The mental events in all psychoneuroses proceed for a considerable distance along the same lines before any question arises of the 'somatic compliance' which may afford the unconscious mental processes a physical outlet. When this factor is not forthcoming, something other than a hysterical symptom will arise out of the total situation [p. 41].

The development of the theory of hysteria from Brodie through Charcot to Freud indicates a growing willingness to subsume a broad variety of behaviors, attitudes, character traits, and dispositions—willfulness, laziness, moodiness, contrariness, promiscuousness, loneliness—under the medical model of analysis; that is, the determination to understand an immense range of human behavior in function of organic and physiological categories of etiology, symptomatology, nosology, prognostics, and, eventually, remediation. After a trajectory of millennia, what was finally recognized as having little to do with illness at all, once again became reintegrated into medical discourse—initially, into the specific area of outpatient neurology that was concerned with nervous disorders generally, which in the first decades of the 20th century became reabsorbed into the area of psychiatry. This process of reintegration, however, was largely arbitrary and to a great extent was motivated by concerns that fell outside the theory and practice of medicine. In effect, it created a whole area of "psychophysical" medicine and therapy, which came to fruition in the 20th century, but the objectivity and veracity of whose claims—not to mention its humaneness—

remain, nonetheless, highly questionable. This contemporary situation has perhaps best been described by the noted critic of modern psychiatry, Thomas S. Szasz (1974):

> The notion of hysteria as a mental disease, the psychoanalytic theory of hysteria, and especially the idea of conversion have all become the symbols of psychoanalysis as a medical technique and profession. The psychoanalytic theory of hysteria, and of neurosis patterned after it, made it easy for physicians and others in the mental health professions to retain a seemingly homogeneous scheme of diseases. According to this medical model, diseases are either somatic or psychical; and so are treatments. Any psychological phenomenon may thus be regarded as a mental disease or psychopathology, and any psychological intervention a form of mental treatment or psychotherapy [pp. 78–79].

THE CRISIS IN MEDICAL AND ACADEMIC PSYCHIATRY

What Szasz referred to as a "homogeneous scheme of diseases" had enormously disruptive effects on the field of mental health in general and on psychiatry in particular. Because Freud's advance in positing a "solution" to the problem of bridging psychical and somatic disorders opened the field of psychiatric medicine to virtually unrestricted psychoanalytic intervention—through the treatment of behaviors as well as bodies—it tended to create a rift between psychoanalysis and medical and academic psychiatry. Originating with—but hardly restricted to—a "disagreement" between Freud and Eugen Bleuler in 1911 and continuing at least into the 1960s, this schism has run an extraordinarily tortuous, and remarkably complex, historical course.[3] It covers intrigues within the psychoanalytic movement itself, especially those initiated by psychiatrically trained members, as well as an intense competition among psychoanalysis proper, its many subgroups and countermovements, and the increasingly sophisticated methods of medical and academic psychiatry. Each discipline, each group, each cellular unit

---

3. For an informative, though largely Freudian-oriented, account of this split, see Alexander and Selesnick (1966, pp. 211–265). Another interesting acccount of this basic split, presented in terms of a conflict between "medical psychology" and "medical psychiatry," appears in Zilboorg and Henry (1941, 479–510). See also Kerr (1993, esp. pp. 280–284 and passim).

was engaged in a profound struggle to find and assure itself a place within the medicotherapeutic establishment. This struggle—combined, of course, with other forces—tended to produce an incredible array of new therapies and medical and quasi-medical techniques. In addition to classical psychoanalysis, we can count reflex therapy, reciprocal inhibition therapy, behavioristic psychotherapy, Jungian analysis, transactional analysis, primal scream therapy, rational-emotive therapy, bioenergetics, and so on. Contemporary medical psychiatry, not to be outdone, drew on modern scientific discoveries in allied fields, especially biochemistry, to expand and fragment into such diverse, therapeutically oriented forms as neuropsychiatry, psychopharmacological psychiatry, social psychiatry, and child psychiatry.

Beyond the obvious complications of competing with psychoanalysis, new psychologies, and new psychodynamic theories, there was another problem for psychiatry. Since somatic and psychical illness had been rendered homogeneous, behavior itself became the central, treatable feature of "mental illness." By the early 1950s, it was apparent that psychiatry was not doing a very good job of treating severe, debilitating behavioral disorders:

> Psychiatry's primary therapeutic orientation, based on psycho-dynamic theory, while enormously influential in intellectual and cultural circles for nearly a half-century, was hopelessly impotent in confronting what were being recognized as the public mental health needs of the nation. However effective individual, long-term, out-patient psychotherapy was with people with neuroses, psychiatry was ill equipped to handle the problems of those crowded into state mental institutions [Kirk and Kutchins, 1992, p. 18].

But only a decade later, however, psychiatry finally appeared to be overcoming its problem of "warehousing" mental patients. The recourse was to make use of increasingly sophisticated and effective medications then being developed by the pharmaceutical industry. These at least gave psychiatry a reliable medical technology, which could be advanced as an effective treatment for severe mental disorders. At the same time, the administration of these medications would also serve as a means of "humanizing" mental institutions by reducing their chronic populations through outpatient care and, at the same time, responding to the public shock expressed about overcrowded conditions. Reduction in the populations of public mental institutions was, moreover, welcomed by the various legislative assemblies, owing, at least in part, to the savings incurred by their tax-paying constituencies. Much of the obvious expense involved in maintaining large public mental institutions would now be transferred to other sectors, such as to private insurance, social services, and the patients' own families, with whom many of the formerly institutionalized mental patients would henceforth reside.

Unfortunately, the benefits of a widespread program of medication were relatively short lived. In the absence of truly adequate provision for "aftercare," the crowds in the mental institutions were simply shifted onto the streets of major cities, creating even greater problems for psychiatry. Indeed, present estimates suggest that between one third and one half of the homeless population suffered from severe mental illness. The public at large was now obliged to suffer this population's disturbing and achingly obvious presence. In time, it became generally recognized that psychiatry had failed to cure these newly medicated, and currently released, patients. Even the most optimistic evaluations concerning the effectiveness of medication ultimately worked against psychiatry. Psychiatry itself seems to have failed to conform to the public's high esteem of medical effectiveness. In the 1950s, the whole aura surrounding the new generation of "wonder drugs"—the entire family of antibiotics, the Salk vaccine, diptheria inoculations—never really extended to psychiatric medication.

ATTACKS FROM WITHIN: SZASZ AND LAING

Although psychiatry was reasonably well equipped to deal with criticisms of treatment and technique and was continually introducing reforms and progressive measures, by the 1960s it would come under a much more serious attack, one aimed at the very core of the discipline: the nature of mental illness itself. This criticism came not from the public but, rather, from a number of influential figures, several of whom were psychiatrists themselves. The most disruptive, and perhaps the most lasting, of these critiques came about as a result of Szasz's two important theoretical works, *The Myth of Mental Illness* (1974) and *The Manufacture of Madness* (1970). The former consists of an attack on the logic of the very concept of mental illness. The latter is an inquiry into and a critique of the operative notions guiding the social and political ideology of psychiatry. Although Szasz's attacks on psychiatry display a number of flaws—a fact profusely noted by his many critics (see, e.g.,

Sedgwick, 1982, pp. 149–184; Dain, 1994, pp. 415–444)—he still managed to raise a troubling question: what, if anything, is the precise field and object of psychiatry? He claimed that what had historically been termed mental disorders were not illnesses at all, but, rather, socially unacceptable behaviors. The only true mental illnesses, Szasz argued, are those disorders which can be definitely linked to underlying physiological dysfunction. All the rest are merely termed "mental illnesses," for either social or ethical reasons. This nominalization rendered the concept of mental illness a metaphor, a usage that can only figuratively describe human relations and conflicts in terms of physiological disorders. Destined to function in service of a metaphor, a myth, psychiatry—at least as far as Szasz was concerned—had no real claim to priority or authority in the medical treatment of mental disease. Indeed,

> Szasz's attack suggested that in identifying and treating the mentally ill, psychiatrists had more in common with ministers and police than with physicians. In making these accusations, he threatened the intellectual and political foundations of psychiatry as a profession [Kirk and Kutchins, 1992, p. 21].

Whereas Szasz's attack came largely from the political right, his position eventually devolving into a veritable celebration of medical free enterprise, R. D. Laing (1962) challenged the psychiatric profession and the concept of mental illness, at least, initially, from a distinctly Marxist position, supplemented by, it should be added, a fair smattering of Rousseauian idealism. Briefly stated, Laing argued that mental illness—particularly, the whole concept of schizophrenia—is merely a social construct, albeit one that can indeed become embodied in the patient. It is effectively "composed" outside of, and imposed on, what he considered to be a pristine, authentic inner self. For him, this self exists in a world in which it is constantly threatened by, and implicated with, a "false" outer self. This outer self consists of a vast set of different perspectives, educational backgrounds, economic statuses, ideologies, affiliations, familial situations, and the like. Ultimately, these codes are not really part of the fabric of humanity. Rather, they are "things" that tend to come between individuals, that occlude their true existences; at the same time they distort the uniqueness of interpersonal communication. The most powerful, and the earliest, restrictions on the expansion of this authentic Self, Laing argued, come from the family. He took the family to be a microsocial unit that stands in the way of the infant's ecstatic birthright. The family tends to impose rules and allegiances, many of which are arbitrary and oppressive. In certain cases, these family restrictions and injunctions can lead to an overwhelming state of "ontological insecurity" in one of its members, a state from which, in many instances, madness (i.e., complete abdication of Self or the breakdown of social conformity) is the only escape.

The questions of what eventually happens to the "mad" family member, how he is treated and categorized, what the terms of his diagnosis are, were also of great interest to Laing. From the very beginning of his work, he aimed these pointed questions directly at what he considered to be a medicobiologically biased psychiatric establishment, one that depended on the methods, classifications, and theories of natural science to address what really amounted to existential problems. For Laing, there could be no such thing as a "science of persons," that is, if one equates the idea of science with the positivism of natural science. Individual consciousness is structured in such a way that external observers can at best draw certain inferences from observed behaviors.

> It is impossible to derive the basic logic of a science of persons from the logic of non-personal sciences. No branch of natural science requires that we make the peculiar type of inferences that are required in a science of persons.
>
> One person investigating the experience of another can be directly aware only of his own experience of the other. He cannot have direct awareness of the other's experience of the 'same' world. He cannot see through the other's eyes and cannot hear through the other's ears. . . . The inferences that one makes about the other's experience from one's direct and immediate perceptions of the other person's actions are one class of acts of attribution. No other science can supply adequate criteria for the validity of such personal attributions [Laing, 1962, pp. 28–29].

The point Laing wishes to make with regard to modern psychiatry, then, is that its methods are fundamentally misdirected in the diagnosis, treatment, and remediation of "madness." Modern psychiatry, he argued, is still laboring under the delusion of Kraepelin's systematic symptomatology of mental disorders. The profession's approach to diagnostics, etiology, and treatment, following Kraepelin, is 1) to establish clinically and academically that a disease exists; 2) to gauge the severity and recurrence of its symptoms in an individual; 3) to determine the initial cause and the subsequent prognosis of the disease; and 4) to devise a course of treatment, a course that all too often ends in institutionalization. The point of departure for attributing mental illness in the first place, however, is the nosological classification itself, the recognition of the patient as an instance of a disease, and not, as Laing proposed, an observation and interpretation of the full spectrum of the subject's existential situation. Ultimately, the so-called science of psychiatry is incommensurable with its very subject matter, the human condition, for this cannot at the start be reduced to a set of supervenient objective categories. Psychiatry fails, according to Laing, because, among other things, it applies the methods of nonpersonal science to a "science of persons." Effectively, Laing's criticism forcefully addresses what is so problematic about the MBPS "profile": namely, that the MBPS disorder is specified in diagnostic terms and symptoms that, when examined independently of the life concerns of the "subject," seem universally damning. But when these nosological categories are viewed with attention to the individual's social, family, economic, and other environmental concerns, they can well be construed as symptoms of perfectly normal behavior. The disorder or illness, as nosologically categorized, practically defines the "subject" into existence.

THE SOLUTION: THE EMERGENCE OF A "RELIABLE" PSYCHIATRIC NOSOLOGY

The woes of 20th-century medical and academic psychiatry do not end with Laing's attack. There were numerous other disciplines and individuals who to some degree or other were critical of psychiatry. The sociological/philosophical critics particularly Erving Goffman (1961) and T. J. Scheff (1966) bear mentioning, as does the poststructural account of Michel Foucault (1965). It suffices here, however, to indicate the main trajectory of modern psychiatry's problems. Psychiatry, facing a many-pronged attack, from within and from without, appears to have failed to achieve the status of an objective science or even to have attained a monopoly on outpatient treatment. By the end of the 1960s, the profession was fragmented and discredited by a half-century-long struggle with a variety of competing and similar techniques and therapies. Psychiatry's presumption of the universal objectivity of a medical science was largely ineffective in competing with the Rolfers, transactionalists, behaviorists, phenomenologists, Zen Buddhists, clinical and psychiatric social workers, and the like—mainly because medical science had lost its authority and legitimacy when it came to the assessment and treatment of mental disorders. The license created by the bridging of the physical and mental, of the psychosomatic and the somatic, opened the field of mental illness to virtually any therapy and technique that was perceived as being relatively successful in practice and could meet the often lax standards of state licensing statutes. Psychiatry had no exclusive purchase on medicoscientific truth, nor could it incontrovertibly verify either the reliability or the validity of its own procedures and claims.

This problem of legitimacy and authority, however, was being worked on. The desperately hoped-for scientific objectivity in psychiatry was germinating in the form of a long-evolving standardized nosology. In 1913, the American Medico-Psychological Association (the forerunner of the American Psychiatric Association), at the suggestion of the census bureau (Kirk and Kutchins, 1992, p. 27), created a committee on statistics. The result, in 1918, was the publication of the first standard psychiatric nosology, the *Statistical Manual for the Use of Institutions for the Insane*. The manual came under immediate attack, primarily because it almost exclusively reflected the biases in diagnosis and treatment of institutionally oriented psychiatrists and physicians in collateral fields and was thus of little practical interest to outpatient psychiatrists and their patients. The project, however, persisted, and the manual went through 10 editions, demonstrating that the real need for a nosological manual was motivated perhaps as much by institutional, administrative, and governmental requirements, as by concerns of psychiatrists or their patients (p. 27).

Despite this initial limitation, the widespread experience of psychiatrists in treating the psychologically maimed soldiers of World War II led to a further development. This was the production of yet another nosology, the *Diagnostic and Statistical Manual: Mental Diseases (DSM-I)*. From all appearances, this 1952 version was better organized and more popularly relevant than the previous standard manual. It reflected marked social and political shifts in American psychiatry, particularly a notable movement away from the troublesome somatic tradition, being perhaps more oriented to Adolph Meyer's version of "psychodynamic and psychoanalytic perspectives," which, as we have seen, began to play a dominant role in the profession's attempt to resurrect itself in the mid-fifties (Kirk and Kutchins, 1992, p. 27). This shift could be explained, at least partly, as a response to the kinds of mental disorders that had affected soldiers returning from the war. Many of these disorders did not respond to either hospitalization or standard medications but, rather, were much more successfully treated on an outpatient basis, through psychodynamic therapies, and in home or community settings, such as regional health clinics. *DSM-I* was thus forced into the position of taking psychoneurotic and psychosocial disorders much more seriously: "Clinicians increasingly worked with noninstitutionalized populations and those suffering from less severe disorders, such as neuroses and personality disorders, rather than psychosis" (p. 27).

DSM-II (American Psychiatric Association, 1968) continued *DSM-I*'s emphasis on less severe behavioral disorders but greatly expanded the number of disease categories. It was precisely the expansion of these disease categories, and the lack of critical reflection on the part of their inventors, that created the grounds for the acceptance and, in some cases, the construction of a number of extremely questionable disorders. Like the constructors of hysteria before them, the diagnosticians conflated a flurry of social and political concerns, professional consensus, and cultural, racial, and gender biases with the somatic and ideational, to arrive at a dizzying array of hybrid disorders. The following is an interesting description of one of these hybrid "disorders:" "For example, one disorder, 'inadequate personality,' was defined as 'ineffectual responses to emotional, social, intellectual and physical demands . . . inadaptability, ineptness, poor judgment, social instability, and lack of physical and emotional stamina'" (p. 29).

While generally addressed to sociopathic and residual schizophrenic-type personalities, "inadequate personality," thus defined, could well apply to just about anyone in a stressful situation—including the clinicians who were, no doubt, hard pressed to classify it. And, certainly, this was not the least of the problematic disorder classifications. The classification of homosexuality, for example, as a mental disorder, which first appeared in *DSM-I* and continued in *DSM-II*, was even more revealing of the difficulty that psychiatric diagnosticians had in determining what constitutes a mental disease. The initial impetus for including homosexuality as a mental disease was no doubt psychiatry's marked shift away from somatic medicine to psychodynamic and behavioral theories. Freud (1923), as we know, used homosexual personality development as one of the two axes of the Oedipus complex. It therefore represented the central path to an unsuccessful attempt to resolve this complex and, as such, was a deviation from "normal" sexual development. Even given its mythic etiology, this form of sexual "deviation" seems to have been easily incorporated into the nomenclature and classificatory logic of both the *DSM-I* and the *DSM-II*. But its inclusion did not go unnoticed. Activists in the gay community, as well as a growing number of psychiatrists, psychologists, and psychoanalysts, seriously questioned whether being gay—which, after all, only describes a sexual orientation and a life style—could be considered a form of mental illness. The creators of the *DSM-II* set out to resolve this issue by modifying the classification of homosexuality.

The resolution devised by the APA and the writers of the revised version *DSM-II* is even more revealing of the sociopolitical forces involved in constructing mental disorders. In point of fact, psychiatry was faced with an enigma and a dilemma when it came to homosexuality. No one seemed to be able to come up with adequate empirical data to establish that it was a true disorder. Nor was anyone very clear as to its etiology. With no consensus on the "fact" of homosexuality's existence as a mental disease or on its specific etiology, and, consequently, little sense as to its treatment and remediation, psychiatry was faced with the disturbing circumstance of having no adequate theory of pathology to ground its claims and diagnoses. If homosexuality was indeed a disease, then psychiatry would have to explain why. The solution to the dilemma, however, proved to be relatively easy: make up an explanation. But make one up that is politically accommodating to all sides, or at least one that could occupy a political middle ground. This task fell to Robert L. Spitzer, a member of the APA committee on Nomenclature and Statistics. His paper, "Homosexuality as an Irregular Form of Sexual Development and Sexual Orientation as a Psychiatric Disorder," is nicely summarized by Kirk and Kutchins (1992):

> Spitzer's position paper . . . did not recommend the entire elimination of homosexuality from the manual. Although homosexuality per se was not enough to warrant a diagnosis, those who were troubled should be given a new diagnosis of Sexual Orientation Disturbance. Spitzer did not accept the position of the gay activists that homosexuality was a normal variant of sexual behavior. He proposed a middle ground between their position and the assertion that homosexuality was pathological.
>
> Spitzer's reasoning was as follows. In order to answer the question of whether homosexuality was an illness, he felt that it was necessary first to define mental disorder as a behavior that was accompanied by subjective distress or a general impairment of social effectiveness or functioning. Since some gays, such as those he met at the APA meeting, did not suffer from

subjective distress because of their sexual orientation and were obviously high functioning, they could not be considered mentally ill.

   On the other hand, he did not want to give them a stamp of normalcy. He decided that homosexuality was a form of irregular sexual behavior [p. 85].

The flaws in both the procedure and the position advanced by Spitzer are obvious—so obvious that many of the member committees of the APA, as well as independent psychiatrists and public organizations, strongly objected to this new classification, that is, of homosexuality as a form of "irregular sexual behavior," later termed Sexual Orientation Disturbance. But after several internal debates and panel votes within the APA hierarchy, Spitzer won the battle to include his altered vision of homosexuality in the *DSM-II.* His victory was indicative of several serious flaws in psychiatric nosology—flaws that contribute to the continued construction of mental disorders. To begin with, Spitzer and his collaborators had very little hard evidence on which to base the claim that homosexuality was a disturbance of sexual orientation, rather than a pathology. Virtually all the studies done on homosexuality lacked a sound scientific basis and were, for the most part, consensual speculations by psychiatrists. Second, Spitzer largely invented the legitimacy and authority behind his classification. For example, he couched the referendum vote on his proposed classification in such duplicitous language that it seemed appealing to everyone concerned: "the proposal was persuasive to both liberals who wanted to declassify homosexuality and to some conservatives who wanted to maintain the status quo and reestablish traditional authority of the organization" [p. 89]. A third, and determining factor, is that one individual, precisely by taking over the control of a decision-making process—one that should have involved a significant portion of the APA's membership—was able to generate a classification of his own devising. This was a classification that, by almost any standard, was both poorly conceived and lacked evidential support. Not unremarkably, since Spitzer was head of the Task Force on Nomenclature and Statistics, he was able to remodify his modification of his initially proposed homosexual "disorder," Sexual Orientation Disturbance. This time, it appeared in *DSM-III-R,* under the title Ego-Dystonic Homosexuality, which refers to those who are deeply troubled by their homosexuality. Of course, given the widespread social disdain for homosexuality in a homophobic culture, it *would* be difficult *not* to feel deeply troubled about being gay—a situation simply pathologized by Spitzer in turn.

Such machinations were not limited to the earlier editions of the *DSM*. Susan Faludi (1992) discusses a contemporary project, initiated by Spitzer, to add, in the *DSM-III*, three "new" disorders, specifically directed to women patients: Masochistic Personality Disorder, Premenstrual Dysphoric Disorder, and Paraphiliac Rapism Disorder. The first disorder was based on an analysis of eight of Spitzer's own colleagues' patients (none of whom had been asked by their psychiatrists if they had ever been battered—which might well be sufficient cause for their "docile" behavior); the second sidestepped the biomedical determinations of endocrinology altogether; and the third concerned a person's (presumably a man's) repeated fantasies of rape and sexual molestation (presumably of a woman or a child) and who then "repeatedly acts on these urges or is markedly distressed by them." Faludi notes that such a "disorder" would prove to be "a handy insanity plea for any rapist or child molester with an enterprising lawyer." Criticism was swiftly forthcoming from thousands of mental health practitioners, as soon as these new classifications were about to be passed by the APA panel on revising the *DSM*. So chastened, the APA's trustees changed the names of the disorders: Masochistic Personality Disorder would henceforth be termed Self-Defeating Personality Disorder, Premenstrual Dysphoric Disorder was renamed the Late Luteal-Phase Dysphoric Disorder, and the Paraphiliac Rapism designation would come to be known as Paraphiliac Coercive Disorder. Fortunately, the last disorder would be "shelved" for further study, but the Masochistic and Premenstrual Disorders were placed in the Appendix of the *DSM-III-R* (with the appropriate medical code numbers that are required for insurance compensation [see Faludi, 1992, pp. 356–362; see also Caplan, 1991, 1995]).

THE EMERGENCE OF MUNCHAUSEN BY PROXY SYNDROME

If the disorder of "homosexuality" could, in the course of three editions, drift from being a pathology to being a sexual orientation disturbance, and then to being a source of discomfort, what other miraculous transformations and manipulations might be found in the *DSM*—and what precision of diagnosis, dynamics, etiology, and treatment, in turn, could be expected of other disorders? The core category of disorders for MBPS, factitious disorders, would prove interesting in this regard.

Much like hysteria and homosexuality, factitious disorders tend to raise significant questions regarding their classification as mental diseases. The main source of confusion regarding this category of disorders is that "factitious" disorders as such do not actually exist in any one individual, but are adduced by observer/clinicians as existing in the subject. Thus, the only indications of their existence are certain real behaviors that, from the standpoint of the diagnosing clinician, are said to be the presentations of "false" or self-induced psychological or physical "symptoms." These are, in turn, often accompanied by a set of "typical" complaints or statements that are held to be common to the accounts given by the "sufferers" of these disorders. In the psychiatric diagnostic literature, factitious disorders are distinguished from malingering, in particular, by the observation that there is a total absence of external incentives for the behavior, such as, for example, economic gain or physical well-being. This distinction, on further reflection, however, is itself impossible to maintain, since what are called factitious behaviors, have at their source a wide variety of both external and internal motivations, incentives, and gains. Hence, the very notion of "factitious" disorders is itself factitious, since many of the behaviors alleged to be factitious are simply defenses and reactions to the ordinary stresses of everyday life, or to far more complex psychological conflicts. Perhaps it was because of the abstruseness of this very notion, as well as the lack of substantial evidence of the actual existence of factitious disorders as mental diseases, that caused the authors of both *DSM-I* and *DSM-II* not to mention them at all. After all, both versions were constructed on the basis of professional consensus and stressed clinical acceptance and professional compliance, the prospects of which would be considerably diminished in the face of an indeterminable "illness" (American Psychiatric Association, 1978).

These seemingly immense difficulties did not, however, deter the framers of *DSM-III* from creating a category called factitious disorders. They, unlike the more modest writers of *DSM-I* and *DSM-II*, were determined to create an exhaustive, reliable, and scientifically valid psychiatric nosology. Although, as we have amply demonstrated, there are many extraneous concerns involved in the construction of the various *DSM* classifications, perhaps the most revealing with regard to that of factitious disorders is the *DSM-III*'s stress on the role of the doctor/clinician/observer as virtually the sole determinant factor in revealing the course, and even the existence, of this set of disorders. While factitious disorders are said to be "not real, genuine, or natural," their symptoms are alleged to be "produced by the individual and are under his voluntary control" (p. 285). Remarkably, however, the patient's "voluntary control" is not under the patient's "voluntary control" at all. Hence—like Freud's stratagem of depositing the patient's "will" in the "unconscious"—the authors of *DSM-III* (American Psychiatric Association, 1978) would claim that "the sense of voluntary control is subjective and can only be inferred by an outside observer" (p. 285).

The claim that the physician alone has the power to ascertain the nature of the patient's own will—postulated as the cause of factitious disorders in the first place—would be supplemented by the so-called reliable diagnostic apparatus of the manual itself. But, given the immense political, economic, social, and institutional concerns affecting the deter-mination of each disorder, as well as the simply premature and largely inadequate character of the statistical and nosological operations used to create the manual, patients becomes subject to a double bind of author-ity, one they simply cannot counter (Kirk and Kutchins, 1992, pp. 31–45). A physician says a person is sick because the nosological data specify that he is sick, even without the patient's knowing it. In other words, the text of the *DSM-III*, which was constructed by and for physi-cians to legitimate their authority to determine the course, treatment, and very existence of illnesses, is the main determinant of those illnesses.

Szasz's (1974) early criticism of malingering as a mental illness cor-roborates this notion of medical power, though in a far more individu-alistic framework. He argues that the modern transformation of malingering (traditionally considered a nonillness) into a psychiatric ill-ness provided a perfect pretext for physicians to admonish "difficult" patients and to exercise punitive power over those people who happen to deceive them. In developing his own position, he cites a very inter-esting and relevant example of one such physician's punitive approach, an example drawn from John S. Chapman (1957), which, coincidentally, contains a description of someone who is thought to be "suffering" from Munchausen's syndrome:

> The case of a 39-year old merchant seaman is a remarkable example of hos-pital vagrancy and spurious hemoptysis. Similar patients in Britain have been said to have Munchausen's syndrome. . . . Such patients constitute an economic threat and an extreme nuisance to the hospital they choose to visit, for their deception invariably results in numerous diagnostic and ther-apeutic procedures. Publicizing their histories in journals, thereby alerting

the medical profession, seems the only effective way of coping with them. Appropriate disposition would be confinement in mental hospital. Such patients have enough social and mental quirks to merit permanent custodial care, otherwise their exploitation of medical facilities will go on indefinitely [p. 927].

In this excerpt, one sees a dramatic transformation of a "disorder" that was first identified several years earlier, in England, by Richard Asher (1951). Whereas Asher's patients posed themselves as irritants to the practice of medicine—Asher said of them that, whatever "kinks" were behind the behavior of these "Munchausen" simulators, they were harmless, but somewhat bothersome for hospital procedure—Chapman's patient in 1957, for all his "quirks," merited institutionalization precisely because the institutions of medicine seem hobbled by him. The determining feature of the fledgling, six-year-old Munchausen's disorder became the very defense, routine, and exercise of medical practice itself. Thus, the institution, it could be said, rendered this heretofore harmless behavior not only into a diagnosable mental illness, but also into one that could be dealt with only from within the medical model itself—by permanent confinement to a psychiatric hospital. The emergence of factitious disorders within the psychiatric lexicon—to be consolidated in the early drafts of *DSM-III*—would confirm the medical authority of behavioral analysis and diagnosis squarely within the profession and grace it with the power of treatment (not to mention confinement) and the not inconsiderable remuneration that might accrue to the members of the profession who alone were able to diagnose the disorder. The "objective" codification of the—even factitious—disorders would serve as norms or criteria of verification to "independent" scientific scrutiny and, incidentally, to a variety of other concerned institutions.

Arguably, the medicalization of Munchausen's syndrome amounted to little more than the absorption of symptoms previously alleged to be found in hypochondriacs, malingerers, and hysterics. As it has been said that the poor will always be with us, so, doubtless, shall the malingerers—or as Asher said, "hospital hoboes and vagrants." With the extension of Munchausen's syndrome to its so-called proxy form, however, there occurred a dramatic expansion of interested parties, players, and institutions. The dyadic relation of power between physician and Munchausen's patient became, with MBPS, extended to include the great public concerns of child abuse, the legal and judicial system, the whole social services apparatus, law enforcement agencies, and the complex interworking and consultation of all these agencies—in concert with, and orchestrated by, medical psychiatry—to isolate, treat, and remediate MBPS patients.

The first two documented cases of MBPS, those of young Kay and Charles, were reported by Meadow (1977). In the following extract, Meadow gives the case summary and introduction to his analysis:

> Some patients consistently produce false stories and fabricate evidence, so causing themselves needless hospital investigations and operations. Here are described parents who, by falsification, caused their children innumerable harmful hospital procedures—a sort of Munchausen's syndrome by proxy.
>
> *Introduction.* Doctors dealing with young children rely on the parents' recollection of the history. The doctor accepts that history, albeit sometimes with a pinch of salt, and it forms the cornerstone of subsequent investigation and management of the child.
>
> A case is reported in which over a period of six years, the parents systematically provided fictitious information about their child's symptoms, tampered with the urine specimens to produce false results and interfered with hospital observations. This caused the girl innumerable investigations and anesthetic, surgical, and radiological procedures in three different centres.
>
> The case is compared with another child who was intermittently given toxic doses of salt which again led to massive investigation in three different centres, and ended in death. The behaviour of the parents of these two cases was similar in many ways. Although in each case the end result for the child was "non-accidental injury," the long-running saga of hospital care was reminiscent of the Munchausen's syndrome, in these cases by proxy [p. 343].

Although his analysis of these troubling cases was extremely careful and circumspect, two features of his diagnosis are telling: the cases he treated were explicitly confined to a rigorous medical analysis. He detailed the frequency of pathogens introduced by the parents into the children's' urinary discharges (in Kay's case) or administered orally or rectally (for Charles), the detailed laboratory analysis of blood and urine samples, the chemical markers used to establish baseline and differential analysis. The second feature that stands out is at least some indication of interest in the broader family concerns of the two patients, the mothers' own health, the social circumstances of the respective families, and, especially, the marital problems both mothers seemed to have. If it were left at this point, perhaps the major axis for the diagnosis and treatment of MBPS might have been more on the order of a psychosocial disturbance, one that could well have been treated outside of the medical establishment proper. In fact, Meadow mentioned previous instances where young children had indeed been poisoned by their parents and this had simply been recognized as "an extended form of child abuse" (Rogers et al., 1976). Alternatively, he cites other instances where similar cases were understood to be the result of marital conflict and where the family and health situations were ultimately restored. This position is still characteristic of Meadow's (1995) view, some twenty years later:

> So in my book Munchausen's syndrome by proxy is a form of child abuse, rather than something that an adult who has perpetrated it suffers from. . . . I think it is much more to do with the sort of circumstances of the mother at the time. You know, if her life is good, with a good partner, or perhaps with a job, she copes with the child, whereas if things are tough, than this comes out [pp. 91, 99].

But Meadow's broader interests in the social and familial circumstances of the patients and parents proved to be somewhat incidental, given the direction and circumstances of contemporary medical psychiatry. Foremost for this branch of medicine was that the nonmedical elements of such cases should be absorbed into the medical model and that other disciplines, therapeutic approaches, social concerns, and the like be subordinated to the strictly medicopsychiatric determination of the disorder. Hence, whatever help various therapeutic approaches may have had, whatever intervention social service personnel could have effected, or family counseling might have brought about—all these would henceforth prove to be at best ancillary procedures, invoked as remedial aids to assist in the medically authorized treatment. In effect, medical authority was supplemented, and in turn strengthened, by the introduction of these various other important institutions and practices, precisely because of their disciplinary subordination to medicine. Indeed, not only would the disorder itself be treated primarily within the medical environment and absorbed into the diagnostic nosology of psychiatry, but its very existence and etiology as a disorder would be explained by a need of the patient's parent—the "real" subject of this disorder—to impress doctors and the patient's desire to get into a "supportive" medical environment.

Meadow (1977) focused on this curious desire for the parents of both his cases: "In these cases it was as if the parents were using the children to get themselves into the sheltered environment of a children's ward surrounded by friendly staff" (p. 345). Instead of focusing on other possible concerns—such as that "the mother of case 1 [Kay] may have been projecting her worries about her own urinary-tract problems in order to escape from worries about herself" or that the mother of case 2, Charles, had been earlier "labeled hysterical"; that she had an "undemonstrative husband, a shift worker who did not seem as intelligent as she"; and that during "one hospital admission had been thought to be interfering with the healing of a wound" (p. 345)—the principal interpretive axis of this newly coined disorder would evolve into an absurdly melodramatic call for "love" from the physician, an event we explore in greater detail in a subsequent chapter.

In retrospect, the construction of MBPS follows a pattern we have seen develop in both witchcraft and hysteria. In the former, a completely nonexistent "disorder" becomes inscribed in an elaborate set of social and cultural practices, subtended by religious and political concerns. Warnings were sounded and prohibitions invoked; diagnostic procedures were established and communicated through treatises and manuals. Widespread public concern was aroused through the dissemination of "confessions" and "trials," ultimately mobilizing entire populations to rise up in fear. Eventually, not only were witches "produced," but their existence became necessary for the very continuity of the institutions they ostensibly threatened in the first place.

As for hysteria, a similar construction occurred, but in this instance the force of authority or power was transferred to a medical model of authority. From the containment of women's behavior in antiquity—by medicine—through the immense number of hysterics in the 19th century, it seemed as if hysteria's existence validated medical diagnosis itself. It provided a framework and environment through which medicine (and, particularly, psychiatry and neurology) could reaffirm itself, could continue to develop its internal theoretical models of mental illness. The importance of hysteria was not so much that it was a "disease" that needed to be diagnosed and treated but, rather, that it served as a ubiquitous and malleable axis of analysis and, as such, provided a ready source of experimental subjects. In fact, just when it appeared to Brodie (1837) that hysteria was doomed to extinction, as an aberration of "willful behavior" (identified as unacceptable to social propriety), it reappeared with a vengeance in Charcot's salon and in the Freudian unconscious.

MBPS, having emerged from a two-and-a-half-page article in *The*

Lancet, enjoyed a similar, brilliant trajectory. As we have argued, this emergence was due largely to a series of historical, social, interdisciplinary, and institutional conversions, starting with Brodie's perplexity over "hysterical affections." Developing through Breuer and Freud's (1893) differentiation of hysteria from other forms of psychoneuroses on the basis of a particular theory of symptom formation and being sustained by Freud's subsequent conflation of psychical and physical etiology (where the dividing line between them could be determined only by the physician's psychological analysis), conditions were prepared for the emergence of disorders that could be identified only by those trained in psychodynamic techniques. (These techniques would eventually be fully absorbed by the medical model of psychiatry in the 20th century.)

With the field of psychodynamics now opened to neurology and psychiatry, it fell to the diagnosticians and clinicians to supply an accurate and reliable nosological basis for diagnosis, treatment, and remediation. This, in turn, provided a foundation of legitimacy for an immense taxonomy of previously indeterminate and difficult to diagnose cases. Factitious disorders fit perfectly within this newly constructed and elaborated system of classification. Such a system, which continues to be developed in the *DSM* series, would lend the appearance of reliability and validity to a new "disorder" whose etiology was unclear at best, that was referred to as a "kink" or "quirk" of behavior, and whose sufferers were likewise regarded as irksome "hospital hoboes." With this newly transferred reliability, and engendered by a psychiatric practice that had rescued itself from its critics, MBPS could now be put forward as a fully formed disorder, without the bothersome concerns as to whether the proposed etiologies, diagnoses, and treatments were at all reliable, correct, or even defensible. That such a disorder—which locates its primary contemporary axis on the desire of a mother to find affection from a medical doctor—should be linked, *ab initio,* to one of the most violent forms of sociopathology, child abuse, is telling indeed. Once this determination was affirmed by hundreds of academic papers and sanctioned by the legal and judicial offices of the state, its tenure was assured. No one questions the existence of MBPS as a disorder; rather, the issue now is how can the devastating effects of this illness be mitigated.

PART TWO

THE HISTORICAL-TEXTUAL CONSTRUCTION OF MUNCHAUSEN AND MBPS

CHAPTER FOUR | DOES MBPS HAVE TEXTUAL-HISTORICAL PRECEDENTS?

> *The APA panel's "data" rolled on, with a historical overview, written by Dr. Richard Simmons, president of the American Psychoanalytic Association, who argued that masochism must be a legitimate diagnosis because a 1950's European psychiatrist had described a depressive personality disorder "that had almost identical features."*
>
> —Susan Faludi

Writers dealing with difficult subjects and issues in a broad range of professional disciplines often cite textual and historical precedents for those subjects. The attempt to establish proof for an abstruse subject is in many instances supplemented by an appeal to the authority of a common tradition, which, it is thought, lends weight, substance, and continuity to the general thesis. This is, not uncharacteristically, often the case with those writing about the core category for MBPS, factitious disorders. It is largely taken for granted that these types of disorders have a long history in the medicoscientific tradition and that they thus form a discernible and continuous genealogical line, a line that, given certain detours, leads up to MBPS.

When Munchausen's syndrome was initially specified by Asher (1951), the very first line of his brief article introduced it as "a common syndrome which most doctors have seen" (p. 339). This statement was picked up again and quoted verbatim by Meadow (1977), when he called for a greater awareness of the syndrome (p. 345). Perhaps unbeknown to Meadow, Asher's (1951) account did in fact cause a spate of subsequent papers and letters to the editor, most of which "contained accounts of the severe form of the disorder in which there is a dramatic presentation of factitious physical symptoms and a history of multiple hospitalizations" (Sussman, 1989, p. 1136). Other examples of this tendency to associate factitious disorders with earlier and common instances (of a clinical, textual, and anecdotal nature) also appeared in later writings on the subject. Turner, Jacob, and Morrison (1984) mention the fact that "Gavin (1843) provided one of the earliest discussions of what is today referred to as chronic factitious disorder with physical symptoms." They go on to cite, in a perfectly continuous lineage, Karl Menninger's (1934) writings on "polysurgical addiction," and the work of Asher on the subject. Asher is lauded as the initiator of serious contemporary interest in these traditional patients: "It was only with Asher's introduction of the term *Munchausen's syndrome* to describe patients with factitious symptomatology that considerable professional interest in this area was generated" (pp. 332–333). In a more recent edition of one of the standard guides for the treatment of psychiatric disorders, we also find a reference to Gavin and the tradition: "The history of factitious disorders extends for centuries. Hector Gavin (1843) wrote a treatise on these disorders. Asher (1951) described patients who traveled widely, telling dramatic medical histories" (Eisendrath, 1989, p. 2160). Even Charcot is grafted onto this textual genealogy. His work on *mania operativa passiva* is cited as an early description of patients "who through self-inflicted injuries or bogus medical documents, attempted to gain hospitalization and treatment" (Boros and Brubaker, 1992, p. 16).

Given the continuity of the textual and reported clinical occurrence of factitious disorders, one might be led to believe that the genealogy leads ineluctably to MBPS. After all, earlier physicians described the disorder; diagnostic texts were generated; data were collected and classified; patterns of frequency were established, both through textual and clinical accounts; and, most significantly, virtually all subsequent authors who deal with the syndrome tend to return to these same initial sources. Indeed, by 1993, the major theoreticians and chroniclers of

MBPS, Schreier and Libow, could already accept as given the historical derivation of MBPS, as provided by the then substantial number of research articles—their references include some 445 items. Interestingly enough, they commence their book-length study without even mentioning such standard figures and textual sources (other than Asher and Meadow) as Gavin, Charcot, or, most notable for his absence, Freud. But, by then, such an immense textual apparatus would have already constituted an established canon, on the basis of which detailed clinical diagnosis—and its extension to collateral fields—could proceed without serious issue or impediment.

But the appearance of symptomatological and etiological continuity, of an established historical provenance, of an uninterrupted tradition within medical science for factitious disorders and their extensions, is largely that: an appearance. We argue that the main motivating concerns, the principal epistemic orientations, within the literature on factitious disorders—Munchausen's syndrome and, by extension, MBPS—are quite discontinuous and not really about factitious illness as a discrete medical or psychological phenomenon at all. Rather, what characterizes the earlier historical antecedents, as well as the more recent work in the field, are concerns that can be roughly divided into two interrelated categories: 1) the practical, personal, and supplemental and 2) the punitive and surveillant.

In critically reading the works within this so-called tradition, one realizes that the actual subject of the texts is not so much medicine, medical science, diagnosis, or treatment as factitious disorders per se, but rather an entire set of narratives and techniques for alternately treating, managing, exposing, preventing, punishing, and suppressing a whole series of "simulative" and "transgressive" acts and conditions. In the earlier "tradition," particularly in the contributions of George Cheyne (1733) and Hector Gavin (1838), the motivations for these works were eminently practical, punitive, and personal: intense nationalism, the maintenance of professional (i.e., medical) demeanor and reputation, concerns with cost-conscious industrial productivity, the efficient use and effective punishment of personnel in the military services, the restoration of proper morality and behavior within the social order, and so on. Other early figures who described what might be broadly considered factitious disorders, Brodie (1837) and Charcot (1890), were primarily concerned with maintaining economic efficiencies in the dispensation of hospital and clinical care, to prevent unneeded medical and surgical procedures, to identify correctly real but anomalous symptoms, as well as, in certain cases, to insure that no undue compensation claims were made by undeserving patients (against deserving insurance companies) (see Drinka, 1984, pp. 108–122). Even the works describing "factitiousness" that appeared to center on its discrete medical and psychological implications, particularly those of Freud and some of his followers, were to a great extent motivated by the more or less practical concerns of supplementing and, in the end, justifying, elaborate preexisting theoretical models.

In short, the impetus to signal out and diagnose factitious disorders was a largely practical matter, one governed by financial concerns, social control, the coherence of medical models, and questions of legal and professional responsibility and status. The composition, strategies, and basic structure of the early, as well as some later, texts in the tradition would thus be directed toward the necessary maintenance of a particular power relation between groups or individuals (patients, factory workers, soldiers, sailors, railroad passengers, nurses, neurotics) and those in positions of authority and responsibility—with a specific focus on the various ways in which this relation could be transgressed. Typical of this concern is the sentiment expressed in the subtitle of Gavin's principal work: *On the Feigned and Factitious Diseases—of Soldiers and Seamen, on the Means Used to Simulate or Produce Them, and on the Best Modes of Discovering Impostors.* Hence, the repeated invectives against malingerers, hypochondriacs, hysterics, extortionists, fakirs, idlers, loafers, simulators, impostors, bunko men, charlatans, grifters, ne'er-do-wells, fakes, quacks, crocks, neurotics, mountebanks, shirkers, deceivers of every pale and hue. What was characteristic of the so-called "tradition," then, was not the medicoscientific establishment of a set of discrete factitious "illnesses," or "disorders" at all (much less, their diagnosis, etiology, and treatment) but, rather, a discontinuous, broad set of concerns ranging from disclosing and punishing simple cases of fraud and deception to supplementing complex theoretical systems.

THE END(S) OF FACTITIOUSNESS: CHEYNE AND GAVIN

George Cheyne (1671–1743) was an English physician who, unlike most physicians, had first-hand experience of virtually all the "diseases" he chronicled (he was beset by extreme nervousness, hypochondriasis, and weighed, depending on the particular account, somewhere between 300 to well over 400 pounds). He was one of the earliest to systematically record and specifically address illnesses that had been considered to be either hypochondriacal or factitious in nature. The greatest part of this record appears in his most famous work, *The English Malady* (Cheyne, 1733), in which he characterized these seemingly organically baseless diseases as "hypochondriacal and hysterical distempers." Remarkably, he had self-diagnosed many of these diseases in his earlier years, and, he reckoned, they were the result of his own proclivity for "thick and dark-colored blood." Cheyne, bleeding himself, as he did his patients, discovered that his blood was one "impenetrable Mass of Glew" (Baur, 1988, p. 173). Since excessively thick blood, even in an age in which humors carried relatively specific etiologies, did not tell Cheyne very much, his various symptoms seemed vague and constantly changing. In fact, he lived in what amounted to a veritable hell, finally reaching a "perpetual Anxiety and Inquietude, [with] no Sleep or Appetite . . . a constant Colick, and an ill Taste and Savour in my Mouth and Stomach . . . a melancholy Fright and Pannick, where my Reason was no use to me" (p. 173).

Cheyne's initial reaction to all this, however, was quite interesting. Rather than seeing these symptoms as medically curious and, thus, as a means to productive research, he saw them, for the most part, as a nuisance and as a source of embarrassment to his professional demeanor: "All this time, I attended . . . the Business of my Profession. . . , but in such a wretched, dying Condition as was evident to all that saw me" (p. 173). After all, how could a doctor maintain his reputation among his peers and his patients if he was grossly overweight, constantly beset by "distempers," and quite unable to treat himself? As a result, Cheyne embarked on a curative odyssey, which led him to follow the professional advice of no less than six London doctors. He modified their prescriptions, placed himself on a strict lactovegetarian diet, and, after several difficult years, shed an enormous amount of weight, not to mention innumerable symptoms. Feeling that he had restored himself to a previous level of professional competence, Cheyne wrote that he was in excellent health and spirits with "as much Activity and Cheerfulness, with the full, free and perfect Use of my faculties . . . and going about the Business of my Profession . . ." (p. 174).

Cheyne's keen interest in restoring his own professional competence and demeanor was perhaps outweighed only by his obsession with the declining and fundamentally endangered English character. Virtually his entire *oeuvre*, which was substantial, reflected this obsession. But his most famous work, *The English Malady*, is a veritable casebook on the disturbing propensity of the genteel English for extreme and debilitating nervousness. Cheyne associated this nervousness with the richness of English life and culture and with the nation's immense success as a nascent industrial and colonial power. More specifically, he attributed it to a distinct difference in the habits, and thus the nervous constitutions, of the English upper and lower classes. Whereas the lower classes were relatively healthy, owing to their being physically robust in their life styles, not terribly bright, and sparse in their customary dining habits (no doubt because of relative penury), the genteel classes were prone to eating spicy, upsetting, and rich foods, being painfully sensitive, and indulging in carnal, orgiastic bouts of drinking and high living. Such a regimen would render upper class individuals, particularly young ladies and sensitive gentlemen, virtual invalids, possessed of a significant number of "hysterical or hypochondriacal distempers," some of which had historically been seen as being "crank" or "quack" complaints or, in certain cases, as resulting from witchcraft, enchantment, or sorcery, that is, in more contemporary terms, somewhat "factitious" in nature (Veith, 1965, p. 31).

Although Cheyne made some limited contributions to the corpus of medical knowledge—most notably, his development of an early psychiatric epidemiology (see Porter, 1991, pp. xli–xlii)—his real genius lay in his aggressive and brilliant manipulation of what had formally been considered extraneous to serious medicine, namely, hysterical or hypochondriacal complaints. Rather than taking complaints of nervousness, despair, "lowness," "heaviness of spirits," and the like as merely the "grousing" of cranks—or worse, witches—he treated them as serious medical conditions and elevated them to diagnosable afflictions that could affect the noblest of characters. Interestingly, he saw them as organically based disorders that he alone, as a fellow sufferer, was qualified to treat successfully. As regards the inherent nobility of the sufferers of hysterical and hypochondriacal distempers, he wrote:

> Now since this present Age has made Efforts to go beyond former Times, in all the Arts of *Ingenuity, Invention, Study, Learning,* and all the contemplative and sedentary Professions (I speak only here of our own Nation, our

own Times, and of the better Sort, whose chief Employments and Studies these are), the Organs of these Faculties being thereby worn and spoil'd, must affect and deaden the whole *System*, and lay a Foundation for the Diseases of Lowness and Weakness. Add to this, that those who are likeliest to excel and apply in the Manner, are most capable, and most in hazard of following that Way of Life which I have mention'd, as the likeliest to produce these diseases [p. 54].

And, elsewhere:

Notwithstanding all this, the Disease is as much a bodily distemper (as I have demonstrated) as the Small-Pox or Fevers; and the Truth is, it seldom and I think never happens or can happen, to any but those of the liveliest and quickest natural Parts, whose Faculties are the brightest and most Spiritual and whose Genius is most keen and penetrating, and particularly where there is the most delicate Sensation and Taste, both of Pleasure and Pain. So equally are the good and bad Things in this mortal State distributed! For I seldom ever observ'd a heavy, dull, earthy, clod-pated Clown, much troubled with nervous Disorders . . . [p. 262].

One of the main textual strategies of *The English Malady*, then, is to reassure the "sufferer" of hypochondriacal and hysterical distempers that he or she was indeed afflicted with a real disorder and that this "malady" was curable. This assurance, in turn, had the effect of bringing what was at best considered hypochondriacal in nature, and, at worst, sheer demonic possession, into the discourse and the practical applications of medicine, treatment, and diagnosis. But, on further scrutiny, the text itself has little to do with medicine proper, nor is it principally directed toward establishing some universally applicable medical treatment and cure: "Cheyne was no anatomist, experimentalist, or microscopist, and did not advance a detailed micro-physiology of the nervous fibers" (Porter, 1991, p. xxi). Instead, by designating the malady a class disorder, Cheyne (1733) oriented the "disease" to social success and status, thus maintaining the historical distinction between classes.

In a brilliant reversal of power relations, Cheyne appeared to subordinate the upper class English, only to demonstrate that they were in the end superior. These people were *really* sick, and they were sick only because they were the most sensitive, artistic, and learned of the English—and, no doubt, the rest of Europe—as well as the most morally worthy. Witness some examples of Cheyne's ingratiating opening descriptions of his case history subjects: "A Tender young

Gentleman, of great Worth and Ingenuity . . . ; A dignified Clergyman, of great Learning and Worth, well known by his excellent works, had naturally a great deal of Fire and Spirit . . ." (p. 295). The healthy (i.e., the poor) were prone to good health because they were just too dull to indulge in excess (not to mention, incapable of paying for it). And the rich and high placed were sick because they were so sensitive, so ingenious, so industrious that they were victims of their own "spirit and fire," victims of their own involuntary destructive tendencies. The hypochondriacal, the hysterical, and the factitious—i.e., disorders held to be entirely mental—were all signs of some organic disease that originated in weakened nerve "fibers" and that, ultimately, indicated success, distinction, and worthiness. Thus, one of the earliest systematic treatments of disorders that were considered to be factitious (if we take factitious, in this early historical context, to mean simply invented or purely mental) was centered largely on nonmedical concerns that focused on class, moral disintegration and recovery, professional self-image, justification for the status quo, nationalism, and so on.

In the slightly more than 100-year period between the publication of Cheyne's (1733) *The English Malady* and Gavin's (1838) *On the Feigned and Factitious Diseases,* British medicine, at least in its official governmental capacity, became considerably less tolerant of disorders that appeared to be simulated or fabricated. This lack of tolerance was due in large part to the challenging new personnel demands brought about by the continued expansion of British military power in the late 18th and early 19th centuries; it simply became necessary to maintain careful control over any potentially disruptive behaviors that might adversely affect the optimal performance of military duties. Likewise, for the civilian population, great attention was given to the organization, normalization, and routinization of labor practices in the expanding economy of industrial mass production, mining, shipping, and service industries such as banking and insurance. Behaviors thought to be disruptive to these sectors (which would then prove to be unproductive and inefficient), such as factitiousness, hypochondria, malingering, quackery, skulking, and dissimulation of any kind, were now fair targets for exposure and, in many cases, severe punishment.

Gavin's (1838) *On the Feigned and Factitious Diseases* is, without doubt, the official bible, the nascent *DSM,* of this newly punitive medical era. Originally delivered in 1835–36 as a "Prize Essay" to the Professor of Military Surgery in the University of Edinburgh, it was eventually published, in condensed form, by the Edinburgh University Press in 1838. The original text opened with a detailed listing of some 70 "feigned or factitious" diseases, including such exotic entries as: *erreur de sentiment*, *epistaxis*, *claudicatio*, *distortio*, *mutitas*, *nyctalopia*, *veternus*, and *insania moralis*. All of these diseases, however, were treated as diseases only insofar as they were simulations, that is, the function of certain forms of imposture in the military. In effect, they were not "real" diseases to be treated by medical officers, but rather subtle forms of fakery to be exposed by them. The subsequent format and thematic composition of the text is thus directed almost exclusively toward systematically routing out these various breaches of military order in the form of feigned "diseases" and imposing sufficient restrictions or, if necessary, punishment on their perpetrators. This intent becomes obvious from the very outset, when Gavin lists the four categorical headings under which these "alleged corporeal disabilities" might take place:

> 1st, Feigned diseases, strictly so called, or those which are altogether fictitious.
>
> 2d, Exaggerated diseases, or those which, existing in some form or degree, are pretended by the patient, or with his concurrence.
>
> 3d, Factitious diseases, or those which are wholly produced by the patient, or with his concurrence.
>
> 4th, Aggravated diseases, or those which originated without the patient's concurrence, but which were afterwards increased by his use of artificial means [p. 1].

Gavin begins his treatise with a veritable manifesto as to the motives subtending these factitious or feigned disorders: the desire to be discharged from service, to obtain a pension, to avoid duty, to avoid transfer, to seek transfer, to obtain a hospital stay, to avoid corporal punishment, to enjoin compassion, and to seek revenge. Medical officers are charged with preventing these abuses, for the protection of the services against these impositions, for optimizing the performance of military discipline, and, not least, to protect the national treasury from being "burthened by men quite unworthy of its advantages" in the form of compensation for alleged damages and for undeserved pensions. It is clear at the very outset of the text that the duties of the medical officers are at least twofold: to render medical attention to those worthy of it and to police the system against those who might abuse it. Not only do these two forms of professional discipline combine in daily practice for the medical officers of the armed services, but each discipline articulates the range and content of the other.

Medicine, in the service of detecting fraudulent abuse on the part of the simulator, assumes a focus and intensity not previously experienced, surely not in its civilian employment. Its taxonomy is constructed not in view of broad medical diagnosis, which would seek to ascertain the etiology and treatment of a wide range of illnesses (even among a rather narrow population of patients), but, rather, to determine which diseases are most commonly "feigned or simulated." The effective policing of these patients results in the establishment of a broad series of tests, experiments, and observational procedures, which thereby determines the nature of medical practices in the services. A good doctor in this respect often becomes one who is capable of "detecting" a disease that is factitious or feigned, rather than one whose principal interests are with the more broadly construed concerns of public health, prevention, and treatment. Hence, the medical formation of physicians in the army and navy must be in large measure directed to the concerns of "deception," so often practiced by what Gavin calls the "malingerers" (usually an army usage) and "skulkers" (typically a navy usage).

> Some diseases or disabilities are much more easily feigned than others; and in such, the imposture is often more difficult to detect. In those diseases, the symptoms of which are naturally obscure, or variable and uncertain, much care should be taken not to be mislead; for every man engaged in practice knows, that there are some diseases which there is no change of pulse, or alteration of the natural color or temperature of the skin, or any evident derangement of its functions, to indicate their existence. There are also diseases whose symptoms may be imitated by the effects produced by certain drugs, or by the use of certain external applications. An intimate knowledge of the anatomy, physiology, and pathology of the human body, and of the effects of the articles of the *materia medica*, is consequently essential to the medical practitioner, to enable him in such cases to obviate false conclusions and detect imposture [pp. 5–6].

Or again, on the same topic:

> "It is obvious," says Dr. Cheyne, "that the more we know of disease by reading and observation, the more patience and temper we possess, the more successful shall we be in the detection of imposture." And I cannot but concur with him in believing that the wiles of soldiers in hospital will be more certainly discovered by those who have an accurate knowledge of disease, obtained from clinical observation, and pathological writings of authority, than by those possessing natural sagacity in the highest degree, if unassisted by a habit of carefully contemplating and studying disease. . . . every instance in which fictitious or fabricated disease escapes detection and pun-

ishment, becomes not merely a reward granted for fraud, but a premium held out to future imposition [p. 7].

With the accumulated knowledge of a medical science—whose primary concern was to heal the sick—now converted into a method of detection and punishment, Gavin was free to extend his discipline of medicine to the service of military discipline generally. The exercise of such a medically informed discipline on the members of the armed services would effectively confirm, if not impose, an entire set of values that reflected interests other than purely medical ones. The perfection of the military corps, for example, Gavin judges to be inversely proportional to the number of malingerers and skulkers. Thus, he remarked:

In the present period of highly improved discipline of the British army, probably there are not two malingerers for ten who were to be found in the military hospitals thirty years ago. As the discipline of a corps approaches to perfection, so do instances of simulated disease become less and less frequent [p. 8].

Gavin's hypothesis extends to ferreting out these malingerers, inimical to the corps' perfection; and, surprisingly enough, he finds that the large number of simulators derive from ethnic minorities and the working classes. Indeed his gradations of the value of various regiments and the individuals composing them seem to reflect the cultural biases prevalent among the English upper classes:

The Irish are the most numerous and expert at counterfeiting disease. The lowland Scotchman comes next to the Irishman, and what he wants in address he makes up in obstinacy. Malingering seems to be least of all the vice of the English soldier [p. 8].

Such sentiments were widespread. Indeed, perhaps the most famous English historian of the age, Thomas B. Macaulay (1906), voiced quite similar views regarding the natural inequality of the native peoples:

There could not be equality between men who lived in houses and men who lived in sties; between men who were fed on bread and men who were fed on potatoes; between the men who spoke the noble tongue of great philosophers and poets and men who, with perverted pride, boasted that they could not writhe their mouths into chattering such a jargon as that in which the *Advancement of Learning* and the *Paradise Lost* were written [p. 603].

Having drafted medicine into the service of discipline and forensics, Gavin (1838) insistently maintained its authority (pp. 6–10), even if this be ever further removed from the objective conditions of political, historical, and economic reality. If, in the interests of an expanding British colonial empire, the army was in need of a growing number of recruits—in India, the West Indies, Asia, North Africa, the Mid-East—it was only reasonable to expect that the principal source of these recruits would not be the upper classes, which routinely provided officers for the distinguished Cavalry and Highland Infantry regiments, but, rather, those peoples displaced from their lands, with no income, often no food, and few prospects of gainful employment at all, other than service in the military. And who would these people be? Precisely the victims of the Enclosure Acts, people driven out of the Highlands and into the slums of Glasgow; precisely the victims of the Irish land seizures, overpopulation, and the soon-to-come potato famines. Gavin is clear to note that these soldiers often had little professional interest in dying for the glory of England in the East and West Indies. He neglects to note, however, that the populations of malingerers were higher 30 years earlier most likely because—other than their being Irish or Lowland Scots—they, not unreasonably, hoped to avoid death or serious injury in the middle of the Napoleonic Wars. When he compares his analysis of British military malingerers with those of other armies, he likewise finds that, during the period of 1800 to 1810, there was a dramatic increase of malingering among French soldiers. It seems not to have occurred to him that a soldier—a French conscript, at that—might prefer to induce a "factitious ulcer," or "feigned ophthalmia," or "feigned myopia," rather than enjoy the pleasures of an extended campaign under Napoleon. It should be recalled just how brutal these times were. On Napoleon's Russian campaign, for example, his army numbered some 422,000 men when it departed from the Polish-Russian border; upon his retreat from Moscow, no more than 10,000 soldiers returned (Tufte, 1983, p. 40). With a survival rate of slightly more than 2%, one might question the sanity of those willing to serve.

> In the department of the Seine, of every 1000 conscripts who were exempted from service in consequence of disabilities, from the year 1800 to 1810, fifty eight were excused in consequence of being near-sighted. Never were there in France so many myopes as during the conscription laws. Formerly, of 100 young men, scarcely five were found to wear concave glasses—then, at least 20 [Gavin, 1838, p. 41].

Beside applying rigorous medical knowledge to ferreting out impostors and simulators, Gavin argued that treatment and medication should be administered to the "patient" if the physician himself was not entirely sure he was dealing with a case of imposture. Thus, if the proposed "patient" was, in fact, sick, he would be properly treated, and the physician would have fulfilled his professional responsibility. If the "patient" was, however, a simulator, the treatment and medication would be uncomfortable enough—sometimes painful—to force the patient to admit to his imposture. Likewise, by having exposed the fact of the patient's simulation, the physician would have fulfilled his responsibility, precisely and unintentionally, by simulating a cure for the nonexistent illness. Thus, the physician who was initially unable to detect simulation ultimately did so through his own simulation. He practiced a cure for what was only factitious. A particularly difficult disease to confirm was rheumatism, which, incidentally, was "the disease most generally feigned by soldiers, and that it is of all affections the most difficult of detection" (p. 104). Gavin encouraged physicians to proceed with the standard treatment for rheumatism, precisely to yield its nonexistence:

> The treatment applicable to chronic rheumatism will, if persevered in, sometimes remove the simulated disease;—local bleeding by cupping, issues [the induced release of various bodily fluids], tartar emetic ointment, low diet, purgatives, emetics in the evening, antimonial diaphoretics, and *electricity* [p. 107].

The real problem, of course, lies in making the initial determination as to illness or simulation prior to being driven to treat the simulated illness "as if" it were real. Here Gavin emerges as a master compiler of detection schemes to be used in uncovering imposture. With full medical and military authority to make these determinations, the physician often exercised this authority in a manner that rendered it indistinguishable from torture. Pressed evermore into the role of exposing fraud, uncovering imposture, dealing with insubordination, revealing dereliction of duty, the physician risked distancing himself from what were, after all, his principal concerns: the administration of medicine, the cure of illness, the humane care of the sick. Gavin repeatedly remarks that, if a military physician is quite sure he has ascertained a case of fraud or simulation but has not been able to prove it beyond all doubt, corporal measures should be called for to force the admission of guilt and that the physician should defer to the authority of the commanding officer to inflict such punishment. This deference would preserve, at least in theory, the separability of medical from punitive authority and thereby maintain the ethical responsibility of the physician and the legitimacy of the discipline of medicine. In practice, however, things were different.

Within the proper domain of the medical determination of illness or simulation, the diagnosis itself would draw on a litany of practices, many of which simply amounted to forced confession, stark terror, or even torture. In the case of a suspected simulator who persistently complained of cephalalgia, given "the distant prospect of success, and the scorn of his comrades," Gavin enjoins the physician to follow Waldschmidt's suggestion: he should allow the patient to overhear a discussion concerning the benefits of employing "the trepan"—that is, to drill a few holes in his skull. The use of coercion, torture, and terror is particularly obvious when Gavin speaks of revealing factitious epilepsy. Since many soldiers feign epilepsy, and in doing so, are fully aware that epileptics are often insensitive to pain in the accession of the seizure, Gavin is perhaps at his most extreme here in recommending means of detection: insert pins and needles under the skin to provoke the revealing sensations of pain in the patient. If this tack is not successful, which is often the case, recourse must be taken to other provocations:

If any evidence of feeling can be excited by stimulants, it may be inferred that the disease is feigned. The agents commonly employed for this purpose are numerous, but two are chiefly had recourse to—viz. the access of a strong light to the eye, and the application of the vapour of hartshorn. . . [or] . . . sulphurous acid to the nose. The first of these tests is not satisfactory. . . . The second is also inconclusive. . . . Blowing Scotch snuff up the nostrils is said to be an effectual means of rousing suppressed sensations. Common salt placed in the mouth has been recommended; the impostor generally shows his sense of taste perfect by endeavouring to spit it out. . . . Marshall has several times succeeded in putting an end to a paroxysm, by applying to the side of the patient the end of a flannel bandage dipped in boiling water. The actual cautery may be *proposed* in the hearing of, or exhibited to the patient, or even applied to his back. . . . Glowing coals and hot sealing wax put on the hand or forehead of the impostor will draw from him expressions of pain. Individuals have been roused from a feigned paroxysm by dropping into the eye a few drops of alcohol . . . or a minim of the oil of turpentine may be employed . . . [or] . . . a pod of Cayenne pepper to be put into the eye . . . [or] . . . unexpectedly firing a musket near the patient, pricking with a sharp-pointed instrument, applying pressure to the praecordia, so as to interrupt respiration . . . throwing a bucket of water on the head at the commencement of the accession. . . . A tremendous fit was once put to a stop by order being given, in the impostor's hearing, to introduce a red-hot ramrod into his anus. [Another simulator] . . . was betrayed by jumping up and asking pardon, on hearing the surgeon ask for the instruments necessary for castration . . . [pp. 89–93].

Integral to the examination and detection of simulated illnesses is the use of observation, surveillance, and trickery. Gavin insists that the suspected impostor has to be "isolated, and watched unknown." When the impostor thinks he is observed, he will stage fits; when not, he won't. This approach is essential to the general practice of discovering imposture:

For the most part, nothing but the closest observation, constant and long watching, favoured by concurring circumstances, are likely to be successful in detecting impostors. An intimate knowledge of the duties, habits, good and bad qualities, of soldiers and sailors, will contribute considerably to prevent us being misled by their attempts to deceive. But this is a species of information which can only be acquired by living among them—more particularly by being on board ship with them [pp. 11–12].

Surveillance and provocation are often combined in rather unusual experiments designed to determine simulation, and to force the impostor to "give in":

Probably the following plan is as good as any, where the paralysis is confined to one of the superior extremities;—namely, to bind the sound arm to the side, and place the individual in an empty chamber, in which there is a shelf with bread and water on it at such a height that he can only reach them by extending his arm to the full extent. This will be a good means, at any rate, of making the impostor *give in* [p. 102].

In the case of feigned epilepsy, which, as Gavin noted, is particularly difficult to uncover, he proposes a peculiar variant of the old "hotfoot" trick:

He [De Haen] recommends the remedy used in Paris to a mendicant there, who often fell into fits. Being usually laid on a bed of straw through compassion; when next attacked, the four corners were set on fire, which caused him to spring up and flee [p. 94].

In cases of partial paralgia (paralysis of a limb), frequently feigned by soldiers, Gavin recommends the application of burning plasters,

flagellation, and the traditional "water cure," which consists in throwing the suspected simulator into a body of deep water, where he will
be "obliged to strike out with both arms to save his life" (p. 102).

As one might easily imagine, this nearly seamless union of medicine
and military discipline had a number of negative side effects. A principal effect was that medicine, in its desire to maintain discipline and control and to eradicate imposture in the military, opened up theretofore
unknown access to private spaces, including the human body itself. In
the course of discovering imposture, the medical officer, with the assent
of command authority, was able to keep close watch on the most private
quarters of the "simulator," indeed, invade the very privacy of his body,
his most secret places. Gavin cites the case of a man who feigned
chronic vomiting with the absurd aim of vomiting the enemas regularly
given to him. Granted that this was a physiological impossibility, it was
nonetheless necessary to demonstrate the imposture to the authorities
and to reprove the man himself: to expose the fraud, the physicians
administered color-coded enemas to the unwitting simulator, such that
the vomited ejecta could be demonstrably shown not to be the color of
the initial enema: "it was necessary to overcome the simulator. This they
did by injecting an enema, the colour of which was unknown to the
patient, and which consequently he could not prepare" (p. 26).
Medicine had surrendered its historical license and its access to the
human body, with its private spaces, to the military. The military, in
turn, granted medicine the authority to impose and justify its diagnoses,
biases, and experiments—in effect, to find a field for the virtually unfet-
tered application of its power. Each power formation informed the
other. Each contributed to the other's legitimacy. In explaining some of
the responsibilities of the medical officer, Gavin provides a striking
example of this subtle interaction:

> When the surgeon is convinced that the complaint is unreal, the case ought
> to be reported to the commanding officer, with the grounds for his opinion.
> But he may also propose any measures which his knowledge and experience
> entitle him to recommend as likely to lead to detection, and put a stop to
> the practices of the culprit. If the commanding officer authorises him to use
> personal restraint and punishment, these may then be had recourse to . . .
> [p. 27].

Also issuing from the union of military discipline and medicine in
Gavin's text is the virtually complete disregard of human motives, per-

logical conditions. Similarly, Lamphere's psychiatric profile as motivation for his behavior went, by and large, unnoticed, save to use his previously diagnosed neuroses and psychoses as evidence of his danger to the medical profession.

Clearly, the patient had some palpable mental problems: he was alternately diagnosed as paranoid, paranoid-schizophrenic, psychopathic, sociopathic, passive-aggressive personality, among others. There is certainly some ground for drug dependency or addiction, as Lamphere seemed virtually to inhale immense doses of Demerol at every stop on his so-called peregrinations. He also attempted suicide at least three times. But Chapman, much like Asher before him, reduced all these environmental, social, economic, medical, and psychological indicators to a "pattern" of deceit and imposture. The "fact" that Lamphere—a deceiver, an impostor, a nuisance—suffered from Munchausen's was already established by the "fact" that he fit perfectly into the pattern. It is thus not remarkable that, throughout his letters and his article, Chapman did not even hint at a single treatment for his "peregrinating problem patient"—this notwithstanding that he had an extensive and immensely detailed history of the patient. Nor, for that matter, did he provide any significant diagnostic or etiological insights into the case. What is remarkable, though, is that Lamphere was the only "identified" case of Munchausen's to appear in the United States literature at the time. He was the sole representative of this growing scourge.

Another fascinating piece of Munchausen's literature to arrive on the scene at this time is a paper by two British doctors, Edwin Clarke and S. C. Melnick, entitled "The Munchausen Syndrome or the Problem of Hospital Hoboes." The paper is particularly interesting in that it tends to follow exactly the pattern set by the aforementioned earlier studies. Opening with the now common urgent warning against those offensive Munchausen's sufferers, it suggests, this time—perhaps somewhat overzealously—that such patients threaten the very axioms of medical analysis. Their alleged simulation undermines the very possibility of ascertaining the "truth and falsity" of physicians' diagnoses: hence, the legitimacy of clinical medicine itself is at stake. As the authors remark, "If the physician should ever cast doubts on the veracity of [patients'] statements the whole structure of clinical medicine would be undermined" (p. 6). They continue in this mode, extending the now compulsory credit to Asher as the founder and namer of the syndrome. They also credit his extraordinary detective work in routing out these nuisances and drains on medical time and money: "They may now be detected more rapidly and studied more carefully, for knowledge of their existence and the clinical pictures which they may present vastly repays the physician and the hospitals in time and expense saved" (p. 6).

The first of three case studies focuses on a woman, an "obese railway worker," who certainly appears to have been a classic Munchausen's sufferer. She had an immense number of admissions to an immense number of different types of medical institutions, for an equally immense number of complaints. Some of her admissions were to hospital casualty departments; some to specialized divisions, like psychiatric wards. In the instance Clarke and Melnick describe, she complained of abdominal pain, loss of consciousness, rapidly increased obesity, blackouts, headache, and a vast number of other ailments connected to several previous operations that had been performed on her. The patient also demonstrated the requisite "criminal" and unsavory background, having undergone in a period of four years "two illegitimate pregnancies, two attacks of venereal disease (probably gonorrhea) and served no less than six prison sentences for theft and prostitution." She also had the temerity to "leave her home and husband, never to return" (p. 7).

Perhaps most interesting about this patient, other than her uncanny resemblance to "classic" Munchausen's, is the sheer number of actual medical procedures that were performed on her before it was alleged that she had been merely fabricating all these dire symptoms. She received six laparotomies, an appendectomy, and a total hysterectomy, and, the authors note, "additional surgical procedures have also been carried out." Following this period of repeated surgical procedures, she was involuntarily admitted on several occasions to mental hospitals, where she was diagnosed as suicidal, psychopathic, and depressive. Aggressive psychiatric interventions were performed at these hospitals, including electroshock therapy. Her psychometrics were not promising either. Her tests showed that, although she was a person of average intelligence, she was extremely egocentric, emotionally immature, narcissistic, and exhibitionistic and lacked insight into her motives and behavior. The writers concede that, in view of this litany of medical and psychiatric procedures, "some of her admissions to mental hospitals may have been genuine in view of her known mental instability" (p. 7). But this appraisal is quickly dismissed, since, the authors argue, "her behavior on the whole has been most unusual" (p. 7). The final determination for a more profound disorder, however, lay in the genes: "the patient's psychopathy is familial for, as well as her mother and father, her eighteen year old son cannot keep a job and has recently appeared in court charged with homosexual practices" (p. 7).

At this point, it seems almost superfluous to cite the flaws and oversights in Clarke and Melnick's view of this "typical example" of a Munchausen patient. Essentially, they argued that a woman with innumerable, clinically established disorders, both mental and physical, and a patently miserable social and economic existence is a Munchausen sufferer because she appears at hospitals with great frequency, therefore duplicating a pattern set forth in a brief, seriously flawed article by Asher. One might well ask: why don't Clarke and Melnick diagnose her as a psychopath, a pervert, a narcissist, an exhibitionist, a depressive, or, alternately, as a person suffering from operable (her hysterectomy) gynecological disorders, or from a variety of (operated on) vascular conditions? Why, moreover, don't they realize that the extensive skein of what might—or might not—appear to be misdiagnoses, mismanagement, malpractice, or unnecessary operations could be a major contributing factor in this "typical" patient's case? Their response, it seems, would be precisely because all these disorders, conditions, mistakes, and procedures—real or not—taken as a whole, simply result in the determination of one central condition: Munchausen's syndrome. An uncannily neat organizing principle.

Further predication for the claim of Munchausen's is, of course, based on the nuisance factor, on the punitive dimension of the cases presented. Clarke and Melnick (1958) devote a large portion of their lengthy comments to establishing this factor. A number of the comments bear repeating. In one instance, the authors invoke what amounts to an interesting insight: that the National Health Service in Great Britain might itself be one of the contributing causes of Munchausen's. But, curiously, rather than seeing this as a social dimension of the "disease," they request further research to establish proof of "another evil of a state system of medicine" (p. 9). They also make a curious distinction here between "true" Munchausen patients and those who may need some hospital care. True patients, according to the authors, need absolutely no medical assistance or care. From the various case histories (both presented here and elsewhere),it seems that this pure version of Munchausen patients is indeed a rarity. The now standard dislogistic litany, of course, continues in the commentary section of Clarke and Melnick's article: Munchausen's patients (either true or false ones) are referred to as hoboes or psychopaths. But what is most striking here is the appearance of a faint wisp of paranoia on the part of the writers themselves. In reiterating a scheme that might help to defeat these wily patients, they write,

> a suggestion made by Birch may help, for a while at least, to deal with this tendency; if the patient is told that he has Munchausen's syndrome and if he announces this at the next hospital, he will be detected at once. As with hoboes and other nomads, however, a secret system of communication between them may exist and news of the nomenclature would soon spread [p. 11].

In other words, should a Munchausen "hobo" tap into the universal hobo information bulletin board, he might find the coded injunction posted *not* to tell the next attending physician that he was suffering from Munchausen's, but to say that he was suffering from something else and perhaps needed yet another laparotomy, appendectomy, or perhaps some Demerol.

Another Munchausen's article is the psychodynamically oriented contribution by Cramer et al. (1971)[3]

Their text has several interesting points, not the least of which is the reappearance of the now "famous case of Munchausen's syndrome," Leo Lamphere, this time 14 years older and still in search of "psychiatric help."

Chapman (1957) had completed his analysis of this "problem patient" with the prescient remark that, "presumably, this remarkable man even now is causing havoc in an emergency room or ward of some large eastern hospital" (p. 930). True to form, Lamphere belatedly resurfaced, this time in New York, at Bellevue Hospital. It seems that he was initially admitted to another hospital, where he was diagnosed as having an "abscess of the thigh, bilateral venous insufficiency of the legs . . . serious pathological abnormalities of both legs with ulceration" (p. 574). He was transferred to Bellevue when he was recognized to be the celebrated Lamphere, and also because he had expressed a "desire" for psychiatric help. After some initial remarks about the patient, which conform exactly to the earlier account given by Chapman—Lamphere

---

3. What appears to be the most complete Munchausen bibliography to date—that attached to Schreier and Libow's (1993a) *Hurting for Love*—indicates that there was very little written on the subject during the 60s. Most entries during this period are on subjects related to the syndrome, for example, pseudologica fantastica.

had "mercurial" moods, he often expressed "childish sullen pouting and incessant nagging for care and medication," he "brought out rage" (p. 574) in the hospital staff members and so on—Cramer and his colleagues, (1971) commenced a psychiatric examination that revealed striking new information. After Lamphere had wandered about the country seeking help "for 16 years," after he had been treated in innumerable hospitals and clinics, the New York physicians finally ascertained some specific details about his childhood. Lamphere had been abandoned by his parents at the age of six months and had been institutionalized in an orphanage. He had a twin brother who, at the age of 13, was sent to "an institution for mental defectives." According to the case history, Leo so missed his brother that he sought admission there as well. After admission, however, they both were repeatedly beaten by the staff and were continually refused medical attention for the pain and injuries suffered in the beatings. Later, Leo was transferred to a state school, where he "spoke glowingly" about the physician who was the director, who trusted him, and who, presumably, was also willing to treat him.

Another point to emerge from the later case history, which perhaps has some bearing on the titanic struggle between Lamphere and Chapman, was Lamphere's claim that Chapman had made homosexual advances toward him, and "became angry when he would not respond to his advances" (Cramer et al., 1971, p. 575). It was further revealed that, as a young man, Lamphere had been operated on for the removal of a ruptured appendix, with a subsequent operation for abscess formations, but that he felt he was well-treated at the time. A later operation in, 1947, a bilateral vein ligation and stripping, was less successful. He was operated on in a Public Health Service clinic and was discharged the next day. The following day he was readmitted because his "legs became enormously edematous," and he was treated with Demerol for pain for a period of some seven months. He also underwent a bilateral lumbar sympathectomy. He remarked to the interviewer, perhaps with some justification, "This started me, and I've hated doctors and hospitals ever since. . . . They always talk about surgery, I figure they're going to send me out the next day" (p. 575). The final disposition of the case was considerably less dramatic: "He was described as a paranoid personality, warding off feelings of panic and depression; there were no signs of schizophrenia, but the possibility of concealed psychosis could not be ruled out . . ." (p. 575).

The three other case studies in the analysis offered by Cramer et al. seem to have had no less valid physical and mental complaints than those of Lamphere. In the first case, a 33-year-old staff nurse was determined to be a Munchausen's sufferer on the basis of a suspicion (never established by biopsy) that she injected paraffin subcutaneously to form lesions on her calves. She had been admitted to the hospital initially as suffering from "painful swellings on her right shoulder, with a temperature of 103 degrees, and she appeared to be acutely ill" (p. 573). On further investigation it was disclosed that the patient was the daughter of "a wealthy physician," that she claimed to have "witnessed the killing of her mother by the Germans when she was 10 years old" (p. 573) and that she was upset when her father remarried shortly thereafter. She had emigrated (from some unspecified country) to Canada with her fiancé, a physician, who broke off the engagement. She subsequently married a medical student whom she helped put through medical school, but her husband was unfaithful, and the marriage ended in divorce. When the patient was incapacitated by her illness, a housekeeper she had engaged "reported that the patient asked her to hold her hand and feed and cuddle her as her mother once did" (p. 573). The physicians who treated her during this period administered Demerol and large doses of barbiturates. The diagnosis offered by a psychiatrist—after an episode "was felt to be a simulated seizure"—was long-term schizophrenia. She was given Thorazine and discharged.

One of the remaining two case history subjects was a 39-year-old nurse who was admitted 17 times in the course of 13 years for acute alcohol intoxication but was seen to fit the Munchausen profile because she requested special medication and "was extremely provocative and hostile to the staff" (p. 574) as well as having had upward of 150 admissions to hospitals in the period of some 20 years. Her father had abandoned her at the age of three, when she was then placed in foster care. Her mother was psychotic. All her Bellevue admissions were related to Demerol and barbiturate overdoses. Consonant with this history of addiction is that virtually all these admissions involved some intensely painful disorder, such as acute abdominal pain, renal colic, hemolytic anemia, fainting spells, epilepsy, or hemiparesis. These conditions would at least indicate that the need for drugs to relieve the pain of afflictions was met with by their prompt and repeated administration, as well as with several operations.

The fourth case concerns a 31-year-old male nurse who was admitted for what appeared to be a duodenal ulcer. When the diagnosis proved negative, he "made a pathetic confession to an attending nurse" (p. 575), namely, that he been admitted to several hospitals "under the pretense of feigned illnesses" (p. 575). This acknowledgment led to his transfer to the psychiatric ward for two months, where "through the manipulation of different physicians, he obtained all sorts of medications . . . and almost succeeded in being operated upon, on two occasions" (p. 575). The case history established that his parents had been separated when he was three years old, and at the age of 9 and he was sent off to a military boarding school where he seemed to have considerable behavioral problems. His medical history is strewn with difficulties: he had "marked learning difficulties . . . a double herniorraphy at age 1, asthma until 14, tonsillectomy at 9, was 'scraped' again at 14, and suffered a head trauma at 12 with a suspicion of seizures for which he was treated . . ." (p. 575). After his parents' separation, his mother had as her lover the surgeon who later performed the tonsillectomy. Although the boy initially admired the surgeon, after he found a condom in the bathroom, "he developed an intense hatred of him and had fantasies of stabbing him" (p. 575). He was sure the surgeon "would kill him during the operation in retaliation for his murderous wishes" (p. 575). Shortly afterward, his mother died, and he began working as a practical nurse. At the age of 21 he contracted pneumonia and, after his release, began feigning symptoms of pneumonia—and other disorders—so as to be readmitted elsewhere. Additionally, he had his appendix removed and subsequently had plastic surgery six times to remove the scar. Cramer et al. reported that the patient "knew that these operations were painful and useless, [but] . . . was sure that no physician would refuse to operate, as he paid high fees . . ." (p. 575). The writers also indicate that he had several hospitalizations for suicide attempts and for psychotic, agitated states, as well as being diagnosed as having "a schizophrenic reaction." Given his extreme medical history and an immensely troubling personal and family life, the centrality of factiousness in his case seems overstated. His motives for seeking medical attention could well have resulted from many factors.

In their broader analysis of the Munchausen's syndrome, based on these four case studies, Cramer et al. claimed that, since many of the symptoms and the behavior exhibited by the patients may have been the result of "blending of characteristics belonging to hysteria and malingering," it is appropriate to focus the analysis on "intrapsychical" causes. Conceding that the patients in question suffered "severe pathological disturbance" in the first place and that "all of our patients certainly malingered, inasmuch as they employed conscious simulation," the authors likewise admit that the question of "secondary gain" would procure "advantages derived from symptoms in the environment. . . [and this is the] result of conscious manipulations" (p. 576). Ultimately, however, such tactics—to procure secondary gain—would tend to deny the role of "unconscious motivation," precisely what Cramer et al. wished to establish. This is, of course, the determination we earlier examined, that is, to find a larger, more theoretically complex basis to explain these various factitious and Munchausen-like behaviors. With such an insistence on the inner psychodynamic formation of the "disorder," the merely "environmental" or empirical concerns, such as trauma, drug dependency, alcoholism, real—as opposed to fantasized—abandonment, shelter, and attention could be reasonably side stepped on the way to establishing a convenient dynamics of explanation. In this instance, the dynamics would be located in the Freudian account of transference, in the sexualized patient–physician relation, itself derived from unresolved oedipal conflicts.[4] "In their adult lives these patients constantly seek a close relationship to physicians, either by working with them—as nurses—or by seeking treatment . . . [he] appeals . . . to the physician's role-assigned qualities of nurturance and omnipotence" (p. 576).

Unlike Asher, Chapman, and other earlier authors, Cramer et al. are careful not to directly admonish the patients or to attack them in some punitive sense. They are careful not to moralize, but they do erect precisely the same relationship of dominance and subordination that is all too common to this literature. In their case, the subordination is of the patient to the physician, who serves as the symbolic center of oedipal triangulation: "The relationship with the physician is a reenactment of the relationships with the parents. This is made possible because physicians became objects with whom vicissitudes of object relationships at different stages of development—oedipal and preoedipal—are being acted out" (p. 576).

With this psychodynamic foundation in place, two elements are immediately guaranteed. First, all "typical" Munchausen behavior, however unpleasant or trying it may be, is secured within the domain of the unconscious. Every motivation, every strategy, and tactic is now gov-

---

4. Indeed, one might add, these transferences may not be so much from parent to doctor, as from doctor to doctor—since, in all these cases, the patients had already undergone a series of bad relations with numerous physicians.

erned by intrapsychic forces beyond the patient's control and under-standing. Second, the physician or psychiatrist is fully exculpated from any role in the syndrome itself—which might lead to a charge of insti-gation, misdiagnosis, or malpractice—"by projecting [aggression] upon the physician who is seen as a careless, rejecting, and sadistic agent—[these are] all accusations that reflect the patient's resentment against the disappointing and punishing parent" (p. 577). The doctor's presence in treating the syndrome is thus a purely symbolic one. Hence, he is always the unconscious target, the unconscious object of desire, of nur-turing dependency, deceit, or aggression, depending on the specific object role he assumes in the relationship, and according to the partic-ular symbolic stage of development. But he is always the doctor. Understood within the transference relation, the patient is either aggres-sive or passive, punitive or dependent with regard to the physician as symbolic parent. The transference relation is thus posited as a universal receptacle for the entire range of Munchausen behavior, thereby con-firming the totalizing completeness—and theoretical security—of a rather simplified Freudian model. No one escapes:

> At first, what the patient seeks is the re-establishment of a state of comfort and dependency where the hospital setting and the physician plays a care-taking, maternal role. . . . On a higher level of development, our female patients experience physicians as ideal heterosexual objects whom they pur-sue and then resent for rejecting them; our male patients see the physician as a punitive father to whom they submit, seeking a regressive, more pro-tective, and homosexual relationship [p. 577].

Like all the previous writers on the subject, Cramer et al. do not tell us a great deal about Munchausen's syndrome as a self-standing disor-der. What they do accomplish is to draw the discussion, explicitly fol-lowing Menninger, back to the closed Freudian apparatus, once again posing patients in a defensive stance, "seducing," "deceiving," and "imposing" themselves on physicians, but now for purely unconscious motives. These motives, deeply buried in the unconscious, are read by the physician as "patient imposture," as "an attempt to fight severe feel-ings of inferiority," of "low self-esteem," of "rage," "of disappointment," "rejection," "anger"—all directed "against the physician." All this is imputed to the patients' unconscious, in this case, four patients who, by any estimate, had severely debilitating, environmentally caused psycho-logical and physical impairments in the first place. Although the authors do not appeal to alert front gate porters, or demand the formation of data banks, or, like Chapman, enjoin the tattooing of medical records on such subjects, to prevent the contagion of this disruptive disorder, they do strongly suggest that "one should refer these patients to inpatient psychiatric services. . . . to avoid unnecessary medical and surgical intervention and the possibly disastrous effects of a prompt discharge" (p. 578). Yet another recourse to a largely punitive solution.

Given the implausible, and often conflicting, range of diagnostic explanations, the limited number of case studies on which the syndrome gets constructed, and the varying apparent motives of the physicians and institutions themselves, it might be expected that the drama of Munchausen's syndrome would eventually disappear from public attention. But the revival of the syndrome in another guise—Munchausen by Proxy Syndrome—would make such predictions premature. The very instability of the original syndrome, its critical mass, as it were, would eventually lead to its own dissociation into a variety of component symptoms, symptoms that came to be associated with other, more precisely diagnosed disorders and illnesses. These symptoms ranged from somatoform and associative disorders through drug dependency, to various neurotic manifestations, recurrent states of depression, and even the more common set of environmentally induced behaviors. Nonetheless, two factors emerged to ensure Munchausen's perpetuation. On one hand, the extensive discussion and correspondence concerning the practical "difficulties" of dealing with often truculent Munchausen patients led to an increased awareness of the physician–patient relation, especially among psychodynamically oriented practitioners. This increased awareness, among other factors, resulted in a large number of professional journal articles devoted to troublesome patients (see Lipsitt, 1970; Martin, 1975, pp. 196–204; Groves, 1978, pp. 883–887). The attitudes of physicians expressed in the literature range, understandably, from thoughtful concern and tolerance toward these patients to disdain for them. The second factor contributing to the perpetuation of Munchausen's, in the form of a new syndrome, was the increase in awareness of child abuse. The propensity of Munchausen sufferers to abuse medical facilities, institutions, and physicians (and, indeed, themselves) and to tell tall tales seemed now to extend to the manipulative use of these very same agencies, but in the service of what appeared to be a new form of child abuse.

It would be these two axes—the psychodynamically conceived physician–patient relation and the increasing awareness of child abuse—

around which the new permutation of Munchausen's syndrome will revolve. Rather than having peregrinating patients as the focus of the syndrome, MBPS will be located in the person of the child's mother— or, far less frequently, the father or "caregiver"—who allegedly induces illness in the child. This configuration of the syndrome was first described in Meadow's (1977) brief article. Of the two-and-a-half pages of that article fully two thirds are devoted to a extremely detailed, albeit, brief, account of the case histories, diagnostic tests, and treatments of two young patients, three-year-old Kay (13 paragraphs), and 14-month-old Charles (5 paragraphs). Although there was strong evidence of child abuse in both cases, determined at one juncture by a police forensic unit, what is striking in this first instance of MBPS as described by Meadow is the prevalence of a conflictual relationship between patient and physician, but here, played out over an extended period of time, using the child as the agency of this conflict. The conflict assumes a sort of doubly frustrating structure of deceit for the physician: at once, the mother is alleged to present false witness about the child by giving an altered medical history and falsifying or simulating symptoms of illness in the child. But, at the same time, the physician is confronted by the presence of a child who appears to be ill, although the illness is strikingly difficult to ascertain owing to a confusion of real and simulated symptoms. In this case, the threat to the medical model—including the threat to the physician–patient relationship—goes far beyond the unwarranted use of hospital facilities, personnel, the physicians' time and workload, and the like by a handful of deceitful patients. Rather, what is at stake is the very basis on which the practice of medicine itself is normally conducted. The relation between patient and physician is disrupted by the intrusion of a traditionally trusted family member who cannot be trusted, who is alleged to be the perpetrator of the very disorder that confounds the physician. Meadow demonstrated his frustration concerning this kind of relation when he wrote,

> During the investigation of both these children, we came to know the mothers well. They were very pleasant people to deal with, cooperative, and appreciative of good medical care, which encouraged us to try all the harder. Some mothers who choose to stay in hospital with their child remain on the ward slightly uneasy, overtly bored, or aggressive. These two flourished there as if they belonged, and thrived on the attention that staff gave to them. It is ironic to conjecture that the cause of both these children's problems would have been discovered much sooner in the old days of restricted visiting hours and the absence of facilities for mothers to live in hospital with a

sick child. It is also possible that, without the excellent facilities and the attentive and friendly staff, the repetitive admissions might not have happened [p. 344].

One can palpably feel Meadow's sense of frustration, despair, and betrayal in dealing with such cases. The entire world of his most sincere concerns, his professional and personal objectives, seems to be inverted, set aside, and for no reason whatever. The trust underlying the physician–patient relationship, the generosity and good will of the staff, the excellence of the facilities, of the very institution, all this is willfully negated by the scheming parent, and for what appears to be no purpose, no good end, other than a kind of perverse self-satisfaction. His sense of betrayal extends to the admission that it might be better to dispense with recent advances in hospital care, to avert the tragic deception played upon him, upon the profession itself.

Even faced with this frustration, exacerbated by the eventual death of young Charles, Meadow, like Asher and Chapman before him, really fails to advance any substantive diagnosis, etiology, or treatment for the new Munchausen by Proxy Syndrome. Rather, he identified the syndrome in exactly the same way previous writers had, that is, by way of the fabulations, impostures, and deceit presented by certain types of patients. His MBPS mothers are compared to other adult Munchausen patients because they tell stories that "are both dramatic and untruthful." Moreover, like his predecessors, he does not seriously consider the medical background, the familial dynamics, or the environmental conditions of either of his two mothers, although he does hint at these factors' playing a role in the etiology of the "disorder." His mothers demonstrate difficulties and medical histories similar to those cited in much of the Munchausen literature. There was real indication of a variety of dire medical, familial, and social problems: marital strife, spousal abuse, drug addiction. What Meadow effectively did was to take two perplexing cases of alleged child abuse, interweave them with the preexisting Munchausen "lore"—its set of profiles, predetermining categories, apparent lack of etiological specificity, and so on (and the seemingly prescribed attitudes this "lore" typically gives rise to in the physician)—and arrive at a variant of the syndrome. Confronted with the new mutation, Meadow and other physicians would not unexpectedly express disdain, distrust, and skepticism toward the mother or caregiver of the young victim. By this very measure, they would encourage vigilance on the part of physicians, increased surveillance of patients and parents, exclusion of family from the wards, and the participation of police in forensic analysis. All this would coalesce in the "name" of a newly discovered syndrome: MBPS.

If MBPS is advanced as a variant of adult Munchausen's syndrome, its very designation testifies to the apparent validity of the initial syndrome. At least, this appears to be the case, and, indeed, seems to close the chapter on Munchausen's, effectively confirming it as a viable and valuable diagnosis in the psychiatric nosology. But, as we have argued, this is hardly the case at all. For a disorder such as tuberculosis, for example, there is a complex and varied literature, involving innumerable facets of the disease (etiology, histopathology, epidemiology, and prevention). The literature itself is at least about a "core" disease, tuberculosis. The literature is guaranteed its minimal identity and coherence—however diverse the particular theoretical accounts, experiments, and case histories might be—by reference to a specifiable object field of illness. For adult Munchausen's, MBPS, and factitious disorders, however, this specifiable object field is replaced by a series of discursive narratives about it, narratives that concern such widely disparate topics as surveillance, transgression, policing, doctor–patient relations, psychoanalytic theory, nationalism, racism, gender, class, punishment, dissimulation, deceit, personal conflict, overeating, socialized medicine, and economics, etc.[5]

Not only are these purported syndromes effectively replaced by this multiplicity of discourses, but the warrant for this equation is typically an appeal to the tradition that ostensibly discussed them in the first place. What we find to be particularly problematic about this situation, however, is that the warrant is fully specious. Not a single text in the tradition establishes the existence of factitious disorders, adult Munchausen's Syndrome, or MBPS in the first place. There is nothing

---

5. One might well make the claim that, for practically any of these texts about "Munchausen sufferers," and the varied concerns they raise, the analysis could equally hold for quite different types of illnesses or disorders. For example, most of the backgrounds and histories of these patients demonstrate a strong indication of addictive personality disorders and substance abuse. The common dispensing of drugs such as morphine, Demerol, and barbiturates thus serves as an inducement for these patients repeatedly to seek readmission and to create fabulations to obtain them or disturbances when they are refused them. In this regard, many of the articles and correspondence, ostensibly on Munchausen's Syndrome, could well be taken up in entirely different areas of concern and treatment, particularly those related to drug dependency and substance abuse in general.

determined in the tradition to ground the initial reference; hence, there can be no warrant for more recent writers in the field to claim a continuity of diagnosis for these illnesses, precisely because there is nothing to warrant. The return to the tradition only finds the loose, discontinuous set of floating narratives, narratives generated by a multitude of concerns: Cheyne's (1733) elitist nationalism, Gavin's (1838) determination to improve the quality of military service, Brodie's (1837) and Charcot's (1890) attempts to establish an organic pathology for anomalous symptoms, Freud's (1894, 1915, 1926a) and Menninger's (1934) totalizing rococo of the psyche, Asher's (1951) wish for tranquillity on the ward, Chapman's (1957) disgust with the obstreperous wrestler, and in the end—of this venerable tradition—Meadow's (1977) justifiable concern to prevent child abuse. The variety of concerns and the discourses that express them, even taken collectively, would hardly constitute the most minimal unity. In this sense, not even a part–whole relation of symptoms and case histories would establish either the existence or the identity of a syndrome. Unlike the tale of the six blind men and the elephant, who related testimony so varied that only the Rajah could unite their separate accounts, here we have an entirely different situation. There is no elephant at all, only the shadow of the omnipresent story teller himself, Baron von Munchausen.

CHAPTER FIVE

THE LANGUAGE AND ILL-LOGIC OF MBPS

To define is to deform.

—*Arthur Danto*

THE PROBLEM OF DEFINITION: WHERE THE SYNDROMES ROAM

That the terms Munchausen's and Munchausen by Proxy are followed by the term syndrome seems remarkably apropos. Indeed, if one looks closely at the specific characteristics of both versions of the disorder, it appears that, by definition, Munchausen is most definitely a syndrome. This definition, as it is applied within the psychiatric nomenclature, is relatively consistent. In their standard *Psychiatric Dictionary*, for example, Hinsie and Cambell (1996) define syndrome as a "group or set of concurrent symptoms which together are indicative of a disease" (p. 706). In a similar, but expanded and somewhat more stipulative definition, Donna A. Rosenberg (1987) proposes that "a syndrome may be defined as a cluster of symptoms and/or signs which are circumstantially related. In general, a syndrome, in contrast to a disease, may have multiple or different etiologies . . ." (p. 548). What could be a more "concurrent," "clustered," or "circumstantially related" set of symptoms or signs than those identified and proposed by the various observers of Munchausen's and MBPS? According to virtually all the reports, those patients have a continuing, long-term association with medical facilities, staffs, hospitals, and physicians; they fabricate and invent many, if not all, of their symptoms; they often induce symptoms (in themselves and sometimes in others) so as to be admitted into some medical facility; they are almost always troublesome to and strident toward medical personnel; they have some previous knowledge of medicine and medical procedures; they deceive doctors; and on and on. The case-to-case repetitiveness of these common signs and symptoms—their conformity to the very definition of the term syndrome—seems perfectly to validate and establish the existence of both syndromes. Or does it?

Before critically evaluating the problems involved in defining and classifying Munchausen's itself as a syndrome, we must at first focus on the whole conception of a syndrome in general. From the standpoint of technical definition, one might characterize the general medicopsychiatric definition of the term syndrome as being far too broad and, more important, given to a considerable amount of vagueness. The constant in this definition is that the condition—a syndrome—is designated by the fact that some "set" or "cluster" of symptoms or signs exists and that there is a distinct relationship or concurrence between these signs or symptoms, which, somehow, indicates the existence of a disorder or disease. In practical terms, this definition may serve as a suitable way of organizing symptoms until better knowledge arises. Thus, it would serve as an "operational definition," one lacking a definitive understanding of the underlying mechanisms and causes. But, nonetheless, the definition as a whole fails to take into account two crucial metadefinitional points: 1) that such a definition could just as well be applied to any number of seemingly related medical/psychiatric phenomena that do not constitute a syndrome at all, or, in certain cases, even a real condition; 2) that often a so-called objective observer (usually, a physician diagnostician) is the determining source of any "relationship" between the symptoms in the first place, that is, the relationship or concurrence exists only when it is determined as such.

Regarding the first point, we could find a perfect example in the aforementioned "dreaded diseases" discovered by the venerable Dr.

Cartwright (Chorover, 1974), "drapetomania" and "dysesthesia." Although Cartwright did not apply the term syndrome to the various phenomena he discovered in search of "the diseases and physical peculiarities of the Negro race"—perhaps because the term had a more technical and limited meaning at the time—he did discover a considerable number of signs and symptoms that seemed to indicate a very definite relation of concurrence. Many slaves had a strong desire to run away from their masters—a "sign" that almost any physician of the deep South during the height of slavery would most certainly have confirmed. Slaves showed a considerable dullness or "hebetude of their intellectual faculties," which could be verified by the most exacting "scientific data." Biological determinists, like Samuel George Morton, had already "established" this by extensive experimentation with craniometry (cranial measurements for comparative brain size) (see Gould, 1981, pp. 50–72). The skin of slaves was, no doubt, insensitive—perhaps owing to constant exposure to the sun or to repeated beatings—which was a sure sign of imperfect atmospherization or vitalization of the blood, and so on. Taken together, these signs could easily form a syndrome, perhaps "drapetomanic-dysesthesia syndrome," or even, "Cartwright's syndrome." After all, a reliable physician observed and recorded the signs; he wrote about them in a respected, scientific medical journal; and he could have found significant supporting evidence for many of his claims in the "science" of the day, particularly, craniometry. And, perhaps most important, there is virtually an absolute concurrence between these reported signs and symptoms, as well as confirmation of the syndrome from his immediate peers.

Although the general claim would most likely be that the medicopsychiatric determination of a "syndrome" is effectively based on a long-term consensus of collected observations and clinical experimentation, the second point—observer determination—still presents certain difficulties. Those involved in science itself, as well as those who critically evaluate scientific method and concept formation have been particularly concerned with the question of observation in the first place and, more specifically, of an observer. The question, however, tends to vary with the type of science involved. In physics, for example, the observer is often conceived of as nothing more or less than a variable in a complex theory, since the physical sciences take into account a number of relatively objective phenomena—space, time, motion, velocity—which fall outside the determination of some subjective observer. But this does not mean that the observer serves a completely neutral function in physical theory. Newton, invoking his classical model of physics, with its immense stress on absolute time, argued that there were a number of "preferred observers" in the universe, that is, a set of observers for whom "all of the laws of Nature look simpler" (Barrow, 1991, p. 58). Einstein, conversely, building his theory of relativity on the premise that there were no preferred observers in the universe, ultimately proposed that the observable laws of physics are linked to the same invariant relationships: "In Einstein's world, there is no special class of observers for whom, by virtue of their motion and time-keeping arrangements, laws of Nature look especially simple" (pp. 58–59).

In the human and social sciences, however, an observer takes on much greater significance. Unlike in the physical and mathematical sciences, observers in these disciplines—particularly in the life and behavioral sciences, like medicine and psychology—are usually compelled to draw major inferences about their subject matter and their subjects; human beings do not function under invariant laws, nor are they always, or ever, amenable to objective analysis. Unfortunately, many of these inferences are colored by certain a priori biases inherent in both the observers and their social and cultural contexts. In 19th century anthropometrics, for example, the culturally shared context was that white males were superior to women, Asians, Indians, and blacks. Virtually all the data gathered in the anthropometric and biologically deterministic sciences devoted to determining the comparative intelligence and worth of these racial and sexual types were thus either fudged, finagled, mishandled, or altered in some way to reflect this precise order of ranking. This situation was further exacerbated, as Stephen Jay Gould (1981) pointed out, by the fact that these biases were often reconfirmed in both the popular and the professional literature of the period (p. 82). Commenting on an anthropometric study of the comparative size of the genu and splenium (the front and back part of the corpus callosum of the brain) of Caucasians and blacks, Gould wrote:

> Prior prejudice, not copious numerical documentation, dictates conclusions. We can scarcely doubt that Bean's statement about black bumptiousness reflected a prior belief that he set out to objectify, not an induction from the data about backs and fronts of brains. And the special pleading that yielded black inferiority from equality of brain size is ludicrous outside a shared context of a priori belief in the inferiority of blacks . . . Craniometry was not just a plaything of academicians, a subject confined to

technical journals. Conclusions flooded the popular press. Once entrenched, they often embarked on a life of their own, endlessly copied from secondary source to secondary source, refractory to disproof because no one examined the fragility of primary documentation [p. 82].

There are numerous other accounts of the enormous problems encountered in observation, inference, and deduction in the human sciences. For instance, Laing's (1962) and Szasz's (1974) works contain excellent critical evaluations of the biases entrenched in observer-generated approaches to human subjects and the problematic theories that ensue from such approaches. Many of Freud's feminist critics, particularly Nancy Chodorow (1989) and Luce Irigaray (1985), question the deep biases at the root of his observation of women, particularly regarding his oedipal and preoedipal characterizations. Similarly, Adolph Grünbaum (1984) took Freud to task for his inexact scientific method regarding certain key inferences, conclusions, and observations. Suffice to say at this point, however, the function of an observer as a major determining factor in the existence of a psychological syndrome—the source of its genesis—is rife with potential biases, mistakes, miscalculations, and misreadings, particularly in the case of Munchausen's fragile beginnings.

Munchausen's syndrome is initially introduced by a single observer as a fait accompli by a single observer. Asher (1951) says that it is a "common syndrome which most doctors have seen" (p. 339). The very first line of the first article on the subject simply declares that it a syndrome. It is assumed, moreover, that this is a syndrome on which professionals would readily agree. Munchausen's is, then, a syndrome collectively conceived in the mind of a single observer. Like Athena born from the forehead of Zeus, the syndrome will commence its storied history fully formed at the outset. Granted, Asher presents the Munchausen's syndrome on the basis of three case histories to which he devotes some three columns. As we have noted, the wide variety of signs and symptoms brought forth in these three case histories could well indicate any number of other, and totally unrelated, illnesses and disorders, or a number of totally different trajectories for the various possible etiologies. Asher, for example, proposes that some of the concurrent symptoms and signs of Munchausen sufferers are drug addiction, repeated hospitalizations, an unwarranted dependency on hospital facilities, aggressive behavior toward doctors and medical staff, and the simulation and fabrication of symptoms.

Given the observer's standpoint and his a priori declarations of the syndrome, these indications all appear to be constitutive of Munchausen's syndrome. But they could just as well be indicators of substance dependency and abuse itself, misread by the observer. Rather than drug dependency's being one of the symptoms or signs of Munchausen's syndrome, it could well be a cause of them. Hence, the etiology of two of Asher's three patients' disorders might well be something entirely different from what Asher postulated, namely, "a psychological kink which produces the disease" (p. 341). As such, the symptoms and signs of Munchausen's do not fit even the most basic requirements of concurrence needed to fulfill the definition of a syndrome. Their concurrence may, in fact, be the indication of an entirely different disorder. The same dynamics could apply to a large number of the cases we examined earlier, with respect to a host of environmentally induced factors, as well as a number of dramatic, preexisting physical and psychological causes.

Within two weeks of its birth, Dr. J. E. H. Stretton effectively baptized the syndrome, again, in the very first sentence of his letter to *The Lancet*: "Dr. Asher is to be congratulated on his timely description and apt christening of this curious syndrome" (p. 414). The second sentence amounts to a collective confirmation of the syndrome as a disease: "Few hospital medical officers are unfamiliar with it, and with the extent to which its sufferers (for surely it is a disease) waste our already overtaxed hospital resources" (p. 474). The case history Stretton advances— already an "atypical" case, because "the patient did not take his own discharge" (p. 474)—is of a gentleman who sought entry to St. Giles's Hospital, complaining of "epigastric pain." The patient had four surgical scars on the abdomen which testified to earlier operations "on the stomach, gallbladder, and right inguinal hernia" (p. 474). Initially suspected of having a perforated peptic ulcer, the patient was examined, successfully treated by continuous gastric suction, and then released. Later on the same day, the patient sought an examination at Dulwich Hospital, again for abdominal pain. The admissions nurse, however, noted the earlier admissions certificate from St. Giles's Hospital in the patient's pocket. She called St. Giles's Hospital for confirmation, and the patient left, this time, more typically, taking his own discharge. This single "atypical" case, based in part on anecdotal evidence and on earlier hospital records, now serves as a reconfirmation of the syndrome, that "surely it is a disease." It thus lends legitimacy to the growing body of concurrent signs and symptoms. Moved to song, Stretton concludes his brief letter on a light note: "I wonder who's treating him now" (p. 474).

Another contribution to the swift, two-week consolidation of Munchausen's syndrome as a recognized medical disorder was advanced by W. M. Priest (1951), who, remarkably, drew "a good example of this syndrome" from his memory of a patient who "haunted London hospitals" from the period 1929–34, nearly 20 years earlier (p. 474). This ship's steward was first admitted to University College Hospital with the suspicion of amebic hepatitis, but after he threw a sputum mug, the attending physician, F. J. Poynton, promptly discontinued his pathological examination and summarily discharged the patient. In a later admission to St. Mary Abbots Hospital for a similar, tentative diagnosis, the patient was again discharged, this time for throwing food. Priest ends his note to *The Lancet* with the refrain—in close harmony with Stretton—"I wonder if he is doing it still" (p. 474).

Subsequent literature is so casually accepting of the syndrome that it effectively dispenses with any critical evaluation at all of the diagnostic process, professional methodology, and scientific objectivity in the formation of a medically or psychologically conceived Munchausen's syndrome. The initial observer, Asher (1951), simply asserted the principal characteristic symptoms and gave the profession a means by which to associate these symptoms in a relationship of concurrence, that is, that they are bound together in a pattern of simulation and deceptiveness so as typically to frustrate the examining physician. On the basis of this reassuring pattern of concurrence, there is never any question as to whether Munchausen is in fact a syndrome. Rather, attention is focused on whether or not there are sufficient typical—or atypical—signs and symptoms to designate the observed case in question as characteristically Munchausen's. Ultimately, what characterizes Munchausen's as a syndrome is the subjectively determined set of symptoms and signs advanced by one observer, Asher, and "confirmed" by several members of the profession within two weeks of the initial "baptism." It is the credulity of subsequent writers in the field and their readiness to employ the new-born taxonomies to clarify the often complex and anomalous symptoms found in certain difficult patients that will extend the questionable existence and coherence of Munchausen's as a syndrome to its literal progeny, MBPS.

In the first extensive review of the professional literature on Munchausen by proxy, Rosenberg (1987) sought to "help characterize the syndrome better," to "help understand the etiologies," to promote "early diagnosis" of the syndrome, and to "help treat and prevent" (p. 551) it. Toward these ends, Rosenberg begins her analysis with a stipulative definition of what constitutes a syndrome as such and then goes on to specify how this would apply to MBPS:

> In Munchausen's syndrome by proxy the following constitute the syndrome cluster:
> 1. Illness in a child which is simulated (faked) and/or produced by a parent or someone who is in loco parentis ; and
> 2. Presentation of the child for medical assessment and care, usually persistently, often resulting in multiple medical procedures; and
> 3. Denial of knowledge by the perpetrator as to the etiology of the child's illness; and
> 4. Acute symptoms and signs of the child abate when the child is separated from the perpetrator [pp. 548–549].

While clearly well intentioned and concisely stated, it is the very breadth of the definition and the attempt to extend it to cover a whole range of disparate signs and symptoms that effectively undermine the value of the definition itself. Such an attempt also demonstrates the extraordinary difficulty of trying to account definitively for MBPS as a disorder, that is, to survey precisely the range and complexity of signs and symptoms included in the syndrome—which often overlap with symptomatic characterizations of other disorders—and having to rely on the weakness of much of the evidence being reviewed. Clearly, the initial definition structures and predetermines what will be admitted as plausible evidence. In her review of what had already become a vast literature, drawn from a Medline computer search and a personal review of the principal journals dealing with childhood diseases and child abuse, Rosenberg reduces the number of cases to those which accord with her stipulative definition of MBPS. Out of 98 articles, she accepts eligible cases from 53 as well as a case study of her own. This material yields 117 separate case studies, not counting repeat cases in the journals.

After rejecting nearly half of the potential case studies for inclusion in her review—because of their lack of conformity to her own definition, or for lack of specific information about the patients themselves—she begins her analysis with a description of "the victims." Curiously, for someone who begins a definitive analysis of the syndrome, and who excludes a large part of the extant case histories owing to their lack of specificity, almost half the cases she draws on do not mention the age of the patient at the time of diagnosis, and almost one in ten fails to mention the sex of the child. Even more remarkably, after having defined the syndrome according to four typical "syndrome clusters," the principal one of which states that the child has an illness that is "simulated (faked) and/or produced by a parent," Rosenberg states that "information on simulation or production of illness was available for 72 cases" (p. 552). So, out of 117 preselected cases of what is supposed to concern the production or simulation of factitious disorders in someone else, fully 45 cases failed to give information concerning the simulation and/or production of illness.

This lack of information, moreover, leads to what certainly appears to be a methodological error on Rosenberg's part. She does not eliminate these cases from her sample. Instead, she uses the full sample to draw inferences about various other related phenomena. For example, both long- and short-term morbidity are predicated on the production of pain and/or illness in the full sample of 117 cases. But, given the unusable 45 cases, the figures provided for short-term (100%) and long-term (8%) morbidity rates of the victims, as well as the initial definition of MBPS morbidity itself, must be fundamentally qualified (pp. 552–554). Despite the absence of this relevant information concerning simulated or produced illnesses, Rosenberg goes on further to state that "of the 117 children, 10 died, giving a mortality rate of 9%" (p. 552). She lists the cause of death for each child, but what warrant is there for attributing all, or any, of these deaths to MBPS? Indeed, she seems to recognize this difficulty when she states that

> Sometimes when these infants die, the presumptive cause of death is sudden infant death syndrome (SIDS), but no autopsy is done. Inasmuch as it is frequently impossible to distinguish between SIDS and other causes of death without doing an autopsy, it is essential that an autopsy be performed upon all infants whose deaths are not entirely explained [pp. 556–557].

So there seems to be no sure warrant to attribute all these deaths to MBPS. Some could have been SIDS deaths, or indeed they might have been occasioned by any number of entirely different causes—even overmedicalization cannot be excluded—particularly given the complexities in determining infant death in general.[1] Out of this group, not a single

---

1. Even though autopsies are regularly conducted, however, there is little hope of quickly establishing a differential diagnosis. One of Britain's principal authorities

mother admitted to homicide, although one was convicted of murder.

As for the perpetrators of MBPS, all 97 were ascertained to be mothers (98% biological mothers, 2% adoptive mothers). Rosenberg notes that "in 1.5% of the cases there was evidence of paternal collusion secondarily" (p. 555). Their occupations seem to reflect those of women generally during the period of time in which the cases were reported. It should be added, however, that even though 40% of the "perpetrators'" occupations were listed as "unknown," it was claimed that fully 10% of the mothers themselves had adult Munchausen's syndrome—something that would seem to be far more difficult to ascertain than their occupational status. Out of the initial 117 cases, fully 60% gave no indication whatsoever as to the mother's statements concerning admission to or denial of the characteristic MBPS-type deception. Some did admit to deception (15% admitted completely, 7% did so "partially"—whatever that means) and 18% denied any participation at all. The "overwhelming number of mothers" were characterized as "having an affable and friendly demeanor and being socially adept" (p. 555). Yet a few were described as having some psychiatric or psychologic disorders. This characterization extended to some three given cases (again, out of 97 mothers).

Even given this paucity of pathological data and a considerable number of reports testifying to positive character traits, Rosenberg still speculates that the overall behavior of these mothers is "biologically abnormal." Indeed, she remarks, "Despite the fact that the mothers who perpetrate MBPS are frequently described as 'normal' psychiatrically, this is obviously not the case" (p. 557). With but three of the 97 mothers said to be suffering some form of psychiatric or psychologic disorder and admitting that "there is a dearth of information about the perpetrators" (p. 557) to begin with, Rosenberg buttresses her specula-

---

on SIDS and its legal implications has remarked on just this difficulty: "It is essential to point out that in every series of children presenting as cot deaths that I or others have examined, an adequate explanation for death has not been found in even one quarter of the cases, even after the question of filicide has been fully explored. To suggest that perhaps between one in five or 10 deaths in children currently attributed to SIDS may be an unnatural death does not imply that all unexpected deaths need to come under active suspicion. . . . A primary forensic approach to these deaths would, I believe, not be helpful at present. The majority of these deaths are, in my experience, multifactorial, and require the full experience of pediatric pathologists working together with some type of clinical social scientists" (Emery, 1993, p. 1099).

tions about the severe psychopathology of these women with the unusual claim that they have an "occult psychopathology" and that they are "highly sophisticated at deception" (p. 560). Hence, she recommends that there should be "court-ordered, long-term psychiatric/psychologic evaluation" (p. 560), long enough, one presumes, to fully expose the supposed occulted pathology to the light of day.

If the first claim of Rosenberg's extensive review was to better characterize MBPS definitively as a syndrome, one can hardly find much consolation from her results. On one hand, it is difficult to separate MBPS from other disorders: it is easily confused with "intentional poisoning, infanticide, pathological doctor-shopping, extreme parental anxiety, or parental thought disorder" (p. 551). Why should they be so confused? Because "the underlying psychopathology overlaps" (p. 551). Yet in this extensive review we are informed that fully 3% of the "perpetrators" were diagnosed as having any psychopathology at all (in one of these cases, the mother was described as being "probably psychotic" and in another as being "a gross hysterical psychopath"). Of course, 97% of the mothers may well have had an "occult" form, yet to be revealed.

As for the second claim of the review, namely, that we might better understand the etiologies involved in MBPS perpetrators, we are presented with a claim of such lamentable generality that it could apply to virtually any number of "disorders" in the *DSM*: "Their behavior may have its origins in their own early developmental histories, characterized by lack of care or indifference to pain and suffering, or perhaps there was an element of early learning where one was only nurtured in the context of disease" (p. 558). The result of such a nonexclusionary claim is equally hapless: "Inasmuch as the manifestations of MBPS vary, the roots of this behavior likely vary somewhat from perpetrator to perpetrator" (p. 558). Given that the syndrome has not been particularly clarified and that there are as many etiologies as there are "perpetrators," the third stated objective would similarly be difficult to fulfill, namely, that one could expect much help in "early diagnosis" of the disorder. As for the final claim, that MBPS might be better treated and, indeed, prevented, Rosenberg seems, at the end of her analysis, hampered by the "dearth of information" (p. 557) involved: "Almost nothing is known about effective treatment of the family when MBPS is occurring. This vacancy of knowledge is undoubtedly related to the poor understanding we have of the roots of MBPS" (p. 558).

Obviously, one may ask what unites the morass of conflicting information, multiple etiologies, incomplete case studies and histories, huge gaps in relevant information, no long-term analyses of either "perpetrators" or "victims," and a disparate array of symptoms and signs into a valid and diagnosable disorder in the first place? The answer to this question, at least in the present case, remains much as it did for the "father" of Munchausen's syndrome nearly 40 years earlier: define it as a syndrome. For Rosenberg, however, unlike Asher (1951), the definition was extended and manipulated to include whatever might be reasonably excluded from a precise definition of a disorder. After all, 60% of the alleged perpetrators gave no indication at all of their possible deceptiveness. Yet, the element of deceptiveness, which, after all, is likely common to all child abuse, had been crucial to Rosenberg's definition and discussion, as it has since the disorder emerged in its original form. Likewise, for her study, fully 45 case studies failed to give any indication of simulation or production of illness.

If only three cases out of 97 demonstrated degrees of "diagnosed psychopathology," one must ask what it means to be a disorder in the first place. Indeed, there is a remarkable degree of equivocation here, precisely where one would wish for clarity. On one hand, Rosenberg (1987) introduces MBPS as a variant of Munchausen's syndrome, which she acknowledges to be a "psychiatric disorder." Indeed, she strongly denies that the perpetrators of MBPS are psychiatrically normal. Alternatively, MBPS is termed "a form of child abuse." Likewise, it is called a "type of aberrant adult behavior" and, at least for Rosenberg, given that all the case subjects she reviews are themselves mothers, it is also referred to as "aberrant maternal behavior."

Whatever the equivocations might be, they are all "clustered" together to constitute the "definition" of a syndrome, but one that is so significantly broader than the usual conception as to accommodate virtually any anomalous, indeterminate, and even unstated, unascertained sign or symptom. Here the function of the observer (or reviewer) extends well beyond the earlier role set by Asher (1951). In this case, the observer serves not only as the organizing principle of describing signs and symptoms in the hospital or clinical situation, and observing and recording them for the professional literature. The observer also now serves as a principle of ordination, one that functions to legislate, regulate, stipulate, order, include, exclude, decree, and proclaim a veritable panoply of marks and traces to be a single, definable, and treatable syndrome—an undeniable and portentous syndrome at that. In fact, one of the principal problems Rosenberg (1987) advances in the treatment of MBPS is the difficulty physicians themselves have in accepting the reality of this factitious syndrome—and hence, the potential damage they do, however unwittingly. "Recognition of one's own denial as a contributing factor in one's opinion is often the first step in ameliorating this understandable situation" (p. 560). To deny the existence of the syndrome only contributes to its perniciousness. In her recommendations, Rosenberg warns that "disbelief and anger at the diagnosis [of MBPS] are often present among the medical and nursing staff" (p. 559). Hence, they too have to confront their own denial. As for the mothers' denial, her recommendation is brief and to the point: "Out-of-home placement of the child is prudent, especially when the mother denies the veracity of the diagnosis" (p. 560). Confronted with the likelihood of such denial, Rosenberg suggests that the physician "check out the mother's history of witnesses to illness in the child. This may entail calling babysitters, relatives, store clerks, etc." (p. 550). And should the courts be in denial as to the specific objectivity of the diagnosis, she again counsels the physician "to go to court. . . . Give attorneys, social workers and judges articles on MBPS" (p. 559).

THE QUESTION OF RECURSIVITY

> *An equivalent of Munchausen By Proxy is seen by veterinarians in which a person, usually middle-aged, fabricates medical signs and symptoms in a pet.*
>
> —Marc D. Feldman, M.D.,
> —Charles V. Ford, M.D.,
> with Toni Reinhold

What is particularly striking about the logical and taxonomic construction of MBPS is the repetitive and recursive nature of the information used to describe the disorder, that is, the uniformity of the textual apparatus generated by the disorder. Once the key terms, categories, phrases, role dynamics and the like have been established and codified by the textual apparatus—specifically, once they have been published, distributed, and taken up by a professional audience—the serial chain of MBPS literature takes on a life of its own, effectively operating as a principle of legitimation and confirmation. While the syndrome is alleged to have a general core of typical characteristics, these are by no means always empirically evident or confirmed by subsequent verification. Rather, cases are routinely referred back to the previous literature for validation (literature that is often characterized by a self-legitimating "scientific" rhetoric), and an accreted stratum of vocabulary and terminology evolves to govern the analysis of each subsequent case in turn. While such an occurrence is not unusual in the evolution of a discipline or a diagnostic procedure, with MBPS, the frequency of "typical" signs, symptoms, motivations, gender identity, and lack of social and economic specification possessed by the various patients is striking. The repetitiveness of the vocabulary is so remarkable that its very use seems to pass as validation for the existence of the disorder, the independent reality of which, all the same, remains itself seriously in question. In short, the massive proliferation of recursive literature and its largely uncritical acceptance occludes the fact that the disorder has been at best inadequately diagnosed and, at worst, largely simulated by a few members of the medical profession.

Strangely enough, even this obvious lack of sufficient explanation and diagnosis is itself a major element in the literature: health care professionals are enjoined, from the very first published mention of the syndrome down to the single most recent publication, to classify the disorder better, to ascertain the earliest possible diagnosis, to inform others in turn about the dangers the syndrome poses to children and families. Indeed, the dangers extend to the social order itself—consider the widespread popular and professional association of MBPS with the recent increase in reported child abuse cases, and with the emergence of Sudden Infant Death Syndrome as a significant cause of infant mortality. What is itself absent from our awareness of MBPS—namely, a specific, plausible diagnosis!—becomes a means of perpetuating research into the nature, etiology, characterization, treatment, and cure of this disorder.

The very locus of the disorder remains, even now, remarkably opaque. Hence, the diagnosis can be "confirmed" only when someone is actually seen, directly or on videotape, to inflict symptoms on the "victim" or when medical test samples are determined to be altered chemically, or by the addition of foreign matter. But in each case, whether it be an attempted suffocation of a child, a lesion inflicted, or a "doctored" urine sample, one should arguably claim that the event was a case of child abuse, willful endangerment, malicious mischief, or fraud. Where is the "syndrome" to be located, however? With this opacity squarely at the center of the syndrome, the syndrome itself can be maintained and perpetuated only by a chorus of repeated injunctions: that it be diagnosed, that etiologies be determined, and that subsequent treatment be effectively prosecuted. With the separation of these observed and confirmed "events" from a reasonably obvious cause or predisposition, it remains only to mystify the behavior, pathology, psycho- and family dynamics into a *suppositum*—a supposed unifying ground or isolable cause—and to then designate it as the core of a syndrome. The attempt is made, in turn, to try to locate it: somewhere or in someone. But, in a manner of speaking, one could claim that the syndrome is fully maintained by the apparatus that articulates it, precisely in the *absence* of locating what the apparatus was meant to serve, to diagnose, in the first place. Almost on the model of sin or guilt, the causes are to be found everywhere and nowhere. Everyone (especially, the woman) is potentially subject to it, every child is a potential victim, every therapist, attending physician, pediatrician, health care worker, nurse, social case worker, administrator, judge is charged to expose it, and is subject to be deceived by it—unless, however, they possess the armament of the literature about it to save everyone else from its scourge.

The most obvious examples of textual recursivity are plainly stated as a genre of research: surveys, surveys of the literature concerning a particular topic or even surveys of professionals' knowledge about the topic in question. Surveys, to be comprehensive, often include surveys of surveys, the latter, of course, being surveys of the literature and of the accreted information pertaining to the initial subject matter in question. Surveys bring professionals in the field up to date on the most recent literature, and, by unifying available knowledge in the field, they serve as focal points for subsequent research, diagnosis, and treatment. In the absence of a discernible and verifiable referent, however, a survey tends to become a discourse-operator, one that perpetuates and extends a collective body of opinion, a set of largely empirically unsubstantiated claims, anecdotal information, personal reflections, institutional biases, personal and professional fears and concerns, all in the service of the most esteemed professional objectives.

One such survey, in the area of MBPS research, is that authored by Keith L. Kaufman and his colleagues (1989). The survey concerned the relative familiarity of professionals (in the fields of medical and community programs, children's' services, as well as law enforcement agencies) with MBPS. Following a two-day conference on child abuse at Columbus Children's Hospital, the participants were polled as to their own demographic backgrounds and were presented with a definition of the Munchausen by Proxy Syndrome on the questionnaire, as part of the conference's evaluation process. The definition of MBPS was the following: "The fabrication of a child's medical history and/or medical symptoms by a parent with the intent of securing *unnecessary* medical evaluations, procedures and hospitalizations" (p. 143). The participants were then specifically questioned in four areas: 1) if they had heard of MBPS; 2) if yes, from what source? 3) if there were cases where they seriously suspected MBPS in the past year; and 4) if there were cases they suspected, how many could they recall?

In the article itself, the issue of recursivity is joined in two ways: first, the article is introduced by a historical overview of MBPS that reiterates the contents of a large number of articles in the field; and, second, the survey confirms the problematic status of MBPS by providing a statistically significant sample of health professionals who demonstrated familiarity with the disorder and who responded positively to the given definition of MBPS, to the extent of locating an additional "77 possible cases" that had gone previously undetected.

Regarding the historical introduction to their survey article, Kaufman et al. construct the first three paragraphs (some 14 sentences) out of data drawn from 33 previous articles. In effect, the entire introduction is but a "collage" of received ideas and opinions, uncritically and unreflectively stated as fact: "According to Meadow . . . ," "evidence also suggests . . . ," "Jones and colleagues reported . . . ," "Meadow found . . . ," and so on. What is culled and retranscribed, yet once again, is all the "alleged" content previously offered up as diagnostic and etiological fact: the same symptoms, the same deceptions, the "fact" that 95% of the perpetrators are mothers, the "fact" that mothers have their own histories of Munchausen's syndrome, the difficulty of diagnosis, nursing staff denials of diagnoses, perpetrators' denials, naive perceptions of mothers as "ideal parents," the legal system's skepticism, the psychiatric system's skepticism, doctor-shopping, unnecessary medical procedures and operations, infant mortality rates as high as 22%, repeated sibling deaths and on and on. Effectively, what these few paragraphs contribute to our understanding of MBPS is, at best, absolutely minimal. What they do, however, is to add seeming legitimacy to the ongoing discursive narrative about the disorder, reaffirming by reasserting, all the now classic observations, speculations, characteristics, types, and dangers.

To this muster role of allegations is added the responses of the concerned participants of the survey. Earlier, Meadow (1985) had vigilantly pursued MBPS perpetrators and victims throughout the whole of Great Britain ("and abroad," he tells us), examining information on some 90 cases during a two-year period (p. 385). But with Kaufman et al.'s (1989) four-question survey, 77 "possible" cases of MBPS are "identified" in central Ohio alone. The authors tell us that in their hospital, in Columbus, Ohio, 14 MBPS cases were formally diagnosed within the previous two years. All this polling data, it should be recalled, was drawn from a "captive" audience that was in the process of being "educated" as to the specifics and severity of the syndrome—an audience that may well have wished to demonstrate their newly found sophistication concerning MBPS identification. Nonetheless, the conclusion can hardly be suppressed: "findings suggest the possibility that the actual incidence of this syndrome has been grossly underestimated. . . . If our experience is at all representative of other metropolitan children's hospitals, MBPS is a more prevalent problem than the literature would suggest" (Kaufman et al., 1989, p. 145). Once again, the familiar call is sounded: "a study with larger samples of general practitioners, pediatricians, community mental health professionals, hospital-based mental health professionals, and community service professionals would better clarify these issues" (p. 145). Given this urgency, the only inference one can draw, even for the most skeptical observer, is that not only does MBPS exist as a dangerous disorder, but that—through the large number of surveyed Ohio health professionals, who retrospectively identified so many new cases—it seems to be spreading at an alarming rate. Hence, the ever more pressing need for a diagnosis!

An attempt to establish the breadth and significance of MBPS by another survey review of the literature (drawing heavily on Rosenberg and Meadow) and of a questionnaire sent to pediatric neurologists and pediatric gastroenterologists, was made by Schreier and Libow (1993b). The literature consisted of 178 papers on the MBPS syndrome, and the questionnaires. As with Rosenberg (1987) and Kaufman et al. (1989), little is offered, other than a vague reference to a "mothering as perversion" theory, that would definitively establish MBPS as a syndrome or as a disorder. In fact, the main intention of the article appears, once again, to repeat the received body of data about the disorder: there is a great risk of morbidity and mortality among children, the disorder is under-diagnosed, it is often mistaken for other disorders, siblings are at risk, and so on.

The methodology, like Rosenberg's, is highly questionable. Schreier and Libow (1993b) sent a questionnaire to a targeted group who, in the authors' words, "see the most common presentations of the syndrome" (p. 319). Although the readers of their article are not privy to the specific questions posed in the survey to the two subspecialty groups, one would expect the concern about MBPS to warrant a significant response from this highly qualified and most interested target audience. The authors determined that there was a total of 465 cases reported (273 "confirmed," and 192 "seriously suspected"). Rather than providing information as to how the cases were "confirmed" or "seriously suspected"— that is, to provide precise diagnostic information, clinical tests, frequency of patient visits, total number of cases seen, much less autopsy reports on mortality cases—Schreier and Libow make the completely recursive claim that the results were retrospectively confirmed by previous surveys and reviews, including that of Rosenberg (1987). Of 1358 possible respondents to the survey, 316 physicians replied. Not only do the authors lament the small number of these pointedly selected respondents, but there is no indication of the actual form of the questionnaire, for example, whether it had alternative forms of questions to counter controversial or negative aspects of the instrument. The results of the survey are really not used to make any substantive claims about the nature of the disorder itself, but only indicate, yet again, that "there may be a large number of Munchausen by Proxy Cases, and that many of them are not being diagnosed" (p. 319).

As with Rosenberg's case, this lamentable lack of specific data and actual confirmation seems oddly to lead to another "confirmation": this time, the appeal is to their own, earlier analysis of five MBPS patients they had already diagnosed at their Oakland, California hospital. In view of that analysis, they say, there probably are more MBPS victims than might have been thought, because untrained clinicians might have passed over or misdiagnosed them. Not so Schreier and Libow (1993b). Added to this massive sampling of the authors' five patients is a "reevaluation" of a review of cases at "a large children's teaching hospital in Boston." This review of a review is ostensibly meant to point out, once again, that MBPS prevalence is underreported. This time they take note of those people who compulsively seek physician care, that is, "doctor addicts."

In a six-month period, Hughes (1984) had evaluated 47 children with abdominal pain. Twenty-three of these were found to be 'without demonstrable organic etiology' (p. 146). Hughes concluded that these children, ranging in age from five to 16, were suffering from depressive illness. While many of the cases represented the more usual dynamics observed in children with chronic abdominal pain, there were indications that several of these mother-child dyads fit the 'doctor addiction' category of the report rather than depressive illness categories. In fact, Hughes observed that: "Mothers were neither significantly reassured nor encouraged by the absence of biological abnormalities but continued their efforts to help their children through an anxious, pessimistic pursuit of medical solutions" [p. 320].

Given that Hughes (1984) points out the mothers' anxiety over their own sick children, which would be fully understandable in the absence of quickly establishing an organic etiology, and that depression was probably behind the children's' symptoms, perhaps compounded by stress, Schreier and Libow (1993b) come to their own conclusion, one that now allegedly stands in confirmation of their previous five cases: "It is possible that at least some of these child patients were depressed because [like the group of patients at Oakland] they were colluding with 'Doctor Addict' mothers who needed their child to be sick as a means of enacting a particular relationship with the hospital system" (p. 320).

To say that "it is possible" that "at least some" (how many is unspecified) of these cases may have been depressed because they were "colluding" with "'Doctor Addict' mothers"—and hence, that they might possibly fit a vague profile of the MBPS victim—appeals, in turn, to yet another survey, this time of over 20,000 infant apnea cases, for confirmation: "In a survey of infant apnea monitoring programs (Light and Sheridan 1989), it was felt that 0.27% of the population of infants being monitored represented Munchausen by Proxy cases" (p. 320).

What can this statistical possibility concerning monitored apnea cases tell us about the underreporting of MBPS cases? What does it say about "Doctor Addict" mothers who "need" their children to be sick, not to speak of differentiating depressed and stress-suffering children from those with stomach cramps? What are we to infer from the claim that it "was felt" that two or three children out of a thousand who are actually being actively monitored may be MBPS cases, especially when apnea is held to be one of the most prevalent produced symptoms of MBPS? Given any normal statistical sampling margin of error, it could equally well be argued that MBPS no longer exists at all. Perhaps, as

Rosenberg (1987) suggested, the psychopathology was so occult that it barely registered. But, really, is this to be taken as a serious confirmation of Schreier and Libow's (1993b) five diagnosed MBPS cases? This invocation of unimpressive and uncompelling statistics makes sense only in the context of the recursivity of language, surveys, and statistical reviews themselves. Schreier and Libow, like Rosenberg and Kaufman et al., fail to make a case for anything having to do with the specifics of MBPS at all—its diagnosis, etiology, or treatment. But what they do is to perpetuate the disorder as a disorder by reinscribing the now-standard vocabulary and nomenclature within the extant literature (including, incidentally, eight references to their own work, four of which are listed as "in press," in the course of some seven columns) and by once again sounding the fateful call, in a concluding note: "we feel it important that the mental health community become more knowledgeable and involved in the understanding and detection of this severely harmful disorder" (p. 321).

To point again to the discrete origins of this sort of recursivity in the literature, we should recall that the emergence of Munchausen's syndrome as a syndrome was somewhat less tendentious. Asher (1951) described his first three cases in terms that were frankly humorous. In fact, Asher, who thought of himself as a satirist in the tradition of Lewis Carrol—he was a proud member of the Snark Society—creatively joined literary references, figurative usage, and humorous anecdotal images from a range of traditional and popular culture to his writings (Asher makes reference to the fact that he was a member of the Sherlock Holmes Society as well). In his initial Munchausen article, for example, he is clear to state the very nature of the disorder in terms of a simile: "Like the famous Baron von Munchausen . . . the persons affected have always traveled widely; and their stories, like those attributed to him, are both dramatic and untruthful" (p. 339). In the course of three pages, the ironic simile becomes a metaphor: The Munchausen patient. Practically every article or commentary to follow this begins by invoking the celebrated fabulist and thereby unwittingly reaffirms the entirely metaphorical basis for the "concept" of the disorder. Contrary to most conventional scientific or logically correct usage, it is the repetition of the figurative that literally constitutes the literal. In this sense, the very concept of this factitious disorder is itself affabulated.

Driving Asher's initial construction, as we have mentioned before, is the sense that these patients exert an unwarranted drain on the financial and personnel resources of the medical institution. But he is careful, at the outset, to specify that the "core" of the disorder, the "etiology and diagnosis," lie elsewhere: "these patients are often quite ill. . . . Perhaps most cases are hysterics, schizophrenics, masochists, or psychopaths of some kind" (p. 339). What is coded as Munchausen's syndrome from the start, then, are secondary qualities, incidental symptoms, personality "quirks" and behavioral abnormalities. And these secondary characteristics are what Asher (1951) finds humorous and interesting: "a passing doctor or sister, who, recognizing the patient and his performance, exclaims: 'I know that man. We had him in Dr. Quinidine's two years ago and thought he had a perforated ulcer. He's the man who always collapses on streets and always tells a story about being an ex-submarine commander and was tortured by the Gestapo'" (p. 339). Humorous banter among colleagues. By the very next sentence—and with the next humorous anecdote—the patient will have become a "trickster:"

> Equally often, the trickster is first revealed in the hospital dining-room, when, with a burst of laughter, one of the older residents exclaims: 'Good heavens, you haven't got Luella Priskins in again surely. Why she's been in here three times before. . . . She sometimes comes in with a different name, but always says she's coughed up pints of blood and tells a story about being an ex-opera singer and helping in the French resistance movement'" [p. 339].

Asher, in fact, ends his diagnostic section by likening the Munchausen trickster to the figure of Pooh Bah, from Gilbert and Sullivan's comic opera, *The Mikado*: "Often a real organic lesion from the past has left some genuine physical signs which the patient uses (to quote Pooh Bah) 'to give artistic verisimilitude to an otherwise bald and unconvincing narrative'" (p. 339).

Asher, who carried his sense of humor to the popular press (he wrote occasional essays for at least 13 different newspapers) and to the professional literature as well (composing such pieces as "Why Medical Articles are so Boring"), inspired a series of correspondence in *The Lancet* and elsewhere, which also was characterized by its lightheartedness, levity, and playful recounting of equally "unusual" patient anecdotes. Already mentioned, the two early letters by Stretton (1951) and Priest (1951) focused on the more bizarre aspects of two patients' behavior and their intriguing fabulations and carried on the music hall tradition by ending in a parody of "I Wonder Who's Kissing Her Now?" The humorous metaphor, however, quickly was transformed by subsequent writers into a real conflict between the medical establishment and these "trickster" patients—something also to be drawn from Asher's (1951) concerns. The developing conflict initially concerned the issue of resources to be allocated to the Munchausen's patients, but, more important, it grew into a struggle between the diagnosing physician and the patient who resists, eludes, and frustrates his diagnosis. More and more, the Munchausen's patient is understood according to the peripheral, unusual, boisterous, and deceptive behavior he exhibits, rather than to what Asher recognized as the primary concern of diagnosis, namely, that the patient was physically ill or psychiatrically disturbed in the first place. The culmination of this agonistic reading comes from Chapman (1957), who, as we have detailed, practically vituperates and criminalized this type of patient.

Once this conflictual orientation was taken toward Munchausen's patients the relation of the diagnosing physician became ever more central to understanding the dynamics of the patient's disorder. In fact, a great deal of the later literature tends to emphasize this theme and to repeat it. The basic presentation of the theme is twofold: 1) the doctor himself is portrayed as being a major figure within the etiology of the disorder, and 2) while the physician becomes central to the diagnosis, care, and treatment of the disorder, an exclusion occurs, whereby other health care professionals, nursing staff, and social workers become largely incidental to and totally dependent upon the centrality of the diagnosing physician.

With the appearance of Menninger's (1934) work on polysurgical addiction, the physician finally became the focal object of attention for the patient. This Freudian psychodynamic approach has it that the physician plays a role of transference for the oedipal father, and unwittingly becomes entangled in the entire set of psychosexual formations the patient has unsuccessfully engaged. Any resolution of the patient's problems necessitates recourse to the Freudian oedipal machinery, on one hand, and, on the other, must involve the very person of the physician, who has now become unconsciously embroiled in the patient's triangulation. A particularly striking example of such an approach is that taken by Cramer et al. (1971), which we have discussed at some length earlier. In a rather concise statement of this understanding, the dynamics are laid bare:

> The relationship with the physician is a reenactment of the relationships with the parents. This is made possible because physicians become objects with whom vicissitudes of object relationships at different stages of development—oedipal and preoedipal—are being acted out. At first, what the patient seeks is the re-establishment of a state of comfort and dependency where the hospital setting and the physician plays a caretaking, maternal role. The repetitive nature of hospitalizations indicates how powerfully they seek to reestablish a unity within the maternal atmosphere. On a higher level of development, our female patients experience physicians as ideal heterosexual objects whom they pursue and then resent for rejecting them; our male patients see the physician as a punitive father to whom they submit, seeking a regressive, more protective, and homosexual relationship [p. 577].

Such a Freudian psychodynamic model, as advanced by Menninger (1934) and Cramer et al. (1971), for the understanding of adult Munchausen's syndrome, rejoins one of the principal concerns advanced by Meadow (1977) in his early designation of MBPS. In his initial two case studies, he concluded that, for both mothers, "it was as if the parents were using the children to get themselves into the sheltered environment of a children's ward surrounded by friendly staff" (p. 345). Nonetheless, the claim that it was "as if" the mothers sought attention for themselves, became transmitted through the literature and through the medical environment, so as to be transfigured into the central core of the MBPS dynamics. Meadow (1985) later claimed that "a large number of British mothers have been seen by child psychiatrists who have not found any apparent disorder, and the psychiatrists themselves have written that they cannot believe the accusations that have been made against the mother" (p. 393). But, even while claiming that "the mothers do seem normal," except for the "small minority who have Munchausen's syndrome themselves" (p. 393), nonetheless, it was Meadow who called for early intervention and long-term care by the physician and psychiatrist. But Meadow's circumspect call for close observation and long-term treatment of the MBPS mother became reconfigured, according to his qualifying "as if" claim, into a contributing cause of the syndrome itself. Again, an effect (the call for treatment of the disorder) was transformed into a contributing cause of what needed to be diagnosed in the first place.

The mother–doctor dyad is thus twofold: the Freudian psychodynamic model integrates the physician into the very core of the disorder itself; and the long-term diagnosis called for by Meadow, and repeated time and again in the literature, reinforces this intimate, if unstable, connection, whereby in both cases, the physician is the determining element: causative and diagnostive. While there are many subsequent writers in the tradition who emphasize this double agency of the mother–doctor dyad, perhaps the most pointed and influential work has been that done by Schreier (1992). He fully exploits the Munchausen vocabulary in general while focusing directly on what he perceives to be the central role of the mother–doctor dyad in the etiology of MBPS.

Quoting himself in his own later review article, Schreier summarizes the position he took in the 1992 essay, namely, that he sees "the mother as involved in a perverse sadomasochistic relationship with the pediatrician, the infant serving as an 'object in the service of controlling the physician'" (Schreier and Libow, 1993b, p. 320). Indeed, he said "only when we examine the dynamics of the relationship between the doctor and the mother can we begin to understand this phenomenon [i.e., MBPS]" (Schreier, 1992, p. 422). The mother–doctor dyad of MBPS extends the patient–physician dyad, by which Schreier initially understands the etiology of adult Munchausen's syndrome. Repeatedly drawing on the work of Cramer et al. (1971), Schreier (1992) mines the language of psychodynamic analysis to find a connection between the adult form and the by proxy form of Munchausen. Munchausen patients, according to this model, see "the doctor as an idealized parent," they "project their own serious ego and superego deficits upon staff and doctors." By proxy mothers, likewise, and in an even more subtle way, continue the relationship with "the doctor, hospital, and ward staff," by dropping the "*Sturm und Drang* scene of the adult patient" (p. 424). According to Schreier, the angry confrontation is now, for the MBPS mother, replaced by the mediating role of her child, who serves as a fetishized object. This simple alteration of the continually repeated dyad and diagnostic model, leads Schreier to propose an extraordinarily complex and elaborate theory of "mothering" as a "masquerade," which incorporates a whole series of analyses of female perversions, fetishisms, object relations, and oedipal conflicts—a theory we attempt to analyze at length in the third part of this text.

The second aspect of the doctor's centrality, in the presentation of MBPS, directly results from the causative-diagnostic position the physician occupies. Since the physician is himself involved in the psychodynamic triangulation of the patient's disorder, and since he alone is uniquely qualified to diagnose and treat MBPS, there results a necessary exclusion of other participating parties within the broader health care community. While this exclusion in itself hardly seems unusual in ordinary medical or psychiatric diagnosis and treatment, the failure to diagnose correctly either adult Munchausen's or MBPS almost always falls exclusively on the doctor himself. It is the general range of doctors themselves who are initially most susceptible to failing to recognize the signs and symptoms of the disorder and hence fail to diagnose it correctly.

The rendering incidental of those health care professionals, other than the central agency of the diagnosing physician, is effectively expressed through a whole range of phrases, injunctions, and warnings—often directed to other physicians, who may be peripheral to the particular diagnosis of the MBPS case in question. Invariably, these injunctions warn that other, less qualified professionals are simply incapable of diagnosing MBPS in a particular case and that, by their skepticism—due to their own inadequate training and lack of theoretical sophistication—they risk misdiagnosing the patient, and hence, welcome her ruination.[2] The reasons for difficulty of prognosis are determined on the basis of the particular physician's claim that these MBPS mothers are unique and that their symptoms defy ordinary rational explanation. After all, mothers are supposed to care for children and nurture them, to offer them love and warmth, not the prospect of protracted illness and possibly death. It is only the esoteric knowledge gathered through the nomenclature and the by now sacrosanct "analyses" in the literature—and the familiarity with the case studies subsequently predicated on them—that fully warrants the physician to exercise his professional judgment. Ultimately, he alone is uniquely trained to diagnose this disorder. Other physicians must first be alerted to the danger and are warned not to be skeptical of this highly unusual, difficult to diagnose, yet widespread and underreported disorder.

The language of exclusion regarding the knowledge and treatment of MBPS is often far less subtle in practice. For example, Meadow (1985) warned of allowing this disorder to be treated by "outsiders": "Initially, I referred the child back to the medical and social services department of the home locality, sending them a written report. One or two tragedies have convinced me, however, that this is not the correct course" (p. 391). In this regard, the exclusions also extend to the testing

---

2. Meadow (1985, p. 386) stressed this. The theme is frequently reiterated in the literature, especially by Rosenberg (1987).

and surveying of various opinions about and knowledge of this disorder. In a more recent text about factitious disorders, there are several
references to various surveys regarding MBPS, all of which were administered to nursing staffs or various other community health professionals (Feldman and Ford, 1994). The decided focus of the authors' analysis
in one particular chapter—"The Deadliest Game of All: When
Factitious Disorders Become Child Abuse"—is almost exclusively centered on the concern that doctors alone can convey to others in the profession the precise knowledge of, and techniques for dealing with, the
disorder. In fact, there is a litany of cases in which nursing staffs or other
health care workers were repeatedly "duped" (these case reports pointedly exclude any mention of doctors who might have been similarly
"duped"). In one case, 20 nurses in a Midwestern hospital who were
questioned after dealing with a MBPS patient "were typically reluctant
to admit that they had been duped, and equally unwilling to accept that
the seemingly doting mother was a perpetrator" (p. 166). Similar claims
about nursing staff members being misled by MBPS patients, and being
repeatedly "tricked," "fooled," and "duped" furrow the literature from
Meadow's early work right through the most recent articles. Most often,
they express strong initial skepticism about the diagnosis (p. 389).[3] The
chapter concludes with a long personal narrative by the cofounder of
the "Munchausen by Proxy network"—not a physician—testifying to
the fact that she was continually fooled and duped by induced symptoms. She now "finds it hard to accept that there are still health care professionals, including pediatricians, who don't believe this behavior
occurs" (p. 167). Fortunately, her salvation was that she had "discovered
that there's a body of literature on MBP, and I read as much as I could,
and I found that so many of the cases had the same pattern" (p. 168).

Although we have touched on only a few of the patterns repeated
throughout the literature, the issue of recursivity remains a striking and
troublesome feature. Recursivity in the object field of an illness that has
been clearly illustrated and determined, such as, for example, tubercu-

---

3. Meadow (1985) goes so far as to characterize this behavior, when MBPS is diagnosed, and "surveillance" is called for by the physician: "Even when ward meetings
to discuss such plans have been arranged with care and tact, the senior nurse may
burst into tears, refuse to take part in the surveillance, or accuse the paediatrician
of uncaring outrageous behavior" (p. 389). As an antidote to these outbursts of
sympathetic emotion and skepticism on the part of the nursing staff, Meadow suggests that "It is necessary to enroll the help of a few key members of the staff
whom one can rely on to be obsessional" (p. 389).

losis, generally serves the purpose of expanding knowledge about the multiple aspects of the disorder. Granted there could well be mistakes, miscalculations, misdiagnoses, and deviations in the literature regarding a particular identifiable disorder, but at least these errors are situated within the context of that specified field. In the case of adult Munchausen's and MBPS, however, the repetitions and patterns are all based on a set of invented or secondary characteristics, which receive legitimation by virtue of their own reinscription within the literature.[4]

What we have tried to show is that this pattern of constant repetition contributes to the production of a disorder, which invariably becomes transformed and specified—sometimes narrowed, sometimes broadened—according to the weight of accrued instances, pointed focus, and professional and social concerns. What began with an ironically conceived "Luella Priskins" (an admittedly fabulated character), ex-opera singer, goaded on by Pooh Bah, now becomes, through an epistolary exchange, a noisome and troublesome commodity, only to be criminalized within a short period of time by the likes of Chapman. Within the course of some 150 subsequent articles, the FBI will have sounded a nationwide alert to local, state, and federal agencies:

> Unfortunately, more police agencies and medical professionals will be confronted with this form of abuse in the future. Hopefully, the information discussed here will alert law enforcement officers, especially those who deal with cases of abuse, to the warning signs of MBPS and will assist them in identifying the perpetrators and helping the victims [Boros and Brubaker, 1992, p. 105].

Cognizant of the widespread danger of typical and atypical Munchausen disorders, the *FBI Law Enforcement Bulletin* even goes so far as to sound the alert about one very peculiar variant—"Munchausen's Syndrome in Law Enforcement" (MSLE)—to be found within the law enforcement community itself:

> While Munchausen's syndrome is in no way limited to the law enforcement community, the unique demands of the law enforcement profession create an atmosphere in which this type of disorder may be more common than in the general population. For this reason, law enforcement managers should be aware of the specific causes and possible clues to this baffling and troubling disorder [DiVasto and Saxon, 1992, p. 12].

---

4. Two recent works, Levin and Sheridan (1995) and Parnell and Day (1998), strikingly confirm the persistence of this reinscription, even while contributing what appears to be new material.

PART THREE

THE CONSTRUCTION
COMPLETED: THE NEW
MBPS ORTHODOXY

CHAPTER SIX

THE PROMISE OF AN ETIOLOGY

> *The authors have admirably and intelligently stitched together the flotsam of available information.*
>
> —*Donna Rosenberg*

After a 42 year period of intensive study of adult Munchausen and MBPS—characterized by hundreds of articles, correspondence, reminiscences, and surveys—1993 saw the appearance of Schreier and Libow's (1993a) self-styled "encyclopedic" work on the subject, *Hurting for Love: Munchausen by Proxy Syndrome.* The book—even today the only full account of the disorder widely available to the medical, health care, legal, and social services professions—offered the promise of correcting many of the historical misunderstandings about the Munchausen by Proxy Syndrome and filling in important gaps in the information concerning this complex disorder. Through this volume the syndrome would finally be defined: the literature would be comprehensively surveyed, new clinical and psychometric material would be added, the legal implications of the disorder would be clearly stated, the socioeconomic and demographic aspects would be addressed, and, most significantly, a definitive etiology would finally be proposed. In view of these considerations, an effective treatment would be offered and a definitive prognosis would be forthcoming.

This newly defined account of MBPS would also affect its future control, management, and prosecution. *Hurting for Love* has become the central "expert" text in a variety and broad range of MBPS litigation. The unreflective psychoanalytic vocabulary it advances, such as "fetish," "sadomasochism," "sacrifice," and the like is commonly invoked in expert testimony in the prosecution of many of these cases and routinely applied to the mother—the "abuser," the "perpetrator"—in demonstration of her insensate criminality. After all, a mother who "fetishizes" her child, by that very token demonstrates her indifference to its humanity and welfare and, thereby, her incapacity to be a good mother. Not only have examples of this newly defined account of MBPS been found in practically all litigation against so-called MBPS mothers since the appearance of the book, but its claims of theoretical and diagnostic completeness have doubtless increased the number and persuasiveness of cases prosecuted. Effectively, with the publication of *Hurting for Love*, a *fully constructed disorder* has rapidly gained popular and professional credence as a diagnosable psychiatric disorder and as a criminally prosecutable offense.

Unfortunately, the foregoing promises remain largely unfulfilled. The reasons for this are basically twofold. On the metacritical level, it remains arguable that the disorder exists at all, thus rendering all the information yielded about it suspect at the very least. In fact, the very first sentence of the Preface in Schreier and Libow's book constitutes a decision not to problematize the existence of the syndrome: the authors begin by claiming to have "encountered several cases" of MBPS. Its existence *as* a disorder is thus secured *ab initio*—as the original disorder had been since Asher (1951) ("it is a common syndrome that most doctors have seen"). Second, and despite its largely unresolved and problematic character, the text proceeds to elaborate a whole set of unsubstantiated claims and empirically dubious "facts," all now collected in one place, under one cover. The earlier claims, the previous research, the uncritical methodologies, the questionable data, the incomplete case studies, the biases and prejudices exhibited in the more than 40-year history of Munchausen, *père et fils*, all are reinscribed, yet again, in this survey of all surveys, review of all reviews.

Although a multitude of inferential errors can be found throughout the text, we shall limit our critique, our reading of it, to but a few central and problematic concerns. Perhaps the most pressing of these concerns involves the newly proposed etiology of the disorder—as advanced by Schreier and Libow—and the various ways in which it is empirically verified and logically configured. Our reading of their etiological construct is thus directed to several specific areas, among which are the completely unreflective transformation of the doctor–patient dyad into the doctor–mother dyad; a number of questionable suppositions concerning the etiological centrality of the "loving, care-giving" physician; and the perhaps unintended use of the most obvious forms of socioeconomic and gender bias in their elaboration of the "mothering" subject. Indeed, the importance of the last is dramatically underscored by the claim that the MBPS mother offers up the child as a fetish at the altar of this most sacred of medical symbols. Other of our concerns focus on the abridged nature of many of the case histories, which effectively define and explain the disorder—case histories that, even at this late date, reflect the convenient selectivity of the earlier adult Munchausen case histories—that is, the unreliability and invalidity of much of the so-called clinical data, the lack of material evidence and attempted verification, as well as any detailed analysis of the extant materials. We also focus on the problematic nature of some of the legal and management aspects of the disorder. These continuing concerns also seem to be reflected in the way Meadow himself composed his Foreword to Schreier and Libow's volume. Oddly enough, he mentions the authors only once by name and devotes some three sentences to their work in the course of its four pages. He notes that they "have provided a wealth of carefully researched information, which they have analyzed thoughtfully and presented in a most stimulating way" (p. x). Nonetheless, as Meadow presciently remarks, "It will be some time before there is reliable information about prognosis" (p. x).[1]

---

1. At a meeting of the British Medico-Legal Society, at the Royal Society of Medicine, on March 9, 1995, Meadow was asked what he thought of Schreier and Libow's *Hurting for Love*. He replied, "I know them and their book and they actually invited me to write anything I wanted after I had read their manuscript, and I did so, and I was a bit critical of their hypothesis. They just abstracted the bits that praised their work and left out my critical bits from the book. I have never had that done to me before" (Meadow, 1995, p. 101).

THE CONSTRUCTION OF THE
MOTHER–DOCTOR DYAD

"Hurting for Love" is not merely a provocative title for the volume, but it serves as a concise epigram for the whole causal nexus of MBPS, that is, according to Schreier and Libow. Quite simply, the title raises the question, "Who hurts?" The mother. Why does she suffer? Because a) she was neglected herself as a child, or b) she has an unfulfilled, unsatisfying affective relation with her spouse. How does she obtain love? From an idealized parent/physician figure, whose construction entails a subtle combination of unconscious fantasy, compensatory mechanisms, and even, in certain cases, an all too believable attitude toward television portrayals of powerful and nurturing doctors. She likewise obtains love from an idealized spousal/physician figure, one constructed according to the erotic fantasy of a loving individual who will satisfy neglected sexual urges. In both cases and in both formations, the mother is deprived of affection, and in both cases, the mother believes she will be compensated with affection—familial admiration and respect, sexual and affective fulfillment: both aspects from the idealized and doubly transferred physician. Thus, the question, "From whom will the hurting mother find love?" From the physician. And, finally, how can she successfully obtain this double love—otherwise denied her—from the physician? Precisely by employing her own child as a fetish: as an affectively overinvested object, which will be used to draw and retain the concern and affection of the caring, loving, nurturing physician. In fact, she will go to great lengths of manipulating this child/fetish—even kill it—to maintain the desired relationship with the physician. MBPS! This brief trajectory of an etiology is succinctly stated as follows:

> An infant can be demanding, but cannot threaten to abandon or actually abandon his or her mother. Although a very intense relationship is possible, it can be heavily weighted with fantasy on the mother's part without arousing suspicion on the doctor's part. The relationship with the child lacks the threat to the mother's self-concept that a truly intimate adult relationship invariably brings. When the infant becomes demanding, the outlet is not to turn to the spouse for support (most MBPS mothers are married, albeit to distant, unavailable men), but to turn up on the doorstep of the newly found idealized parent, the doctor. The pediatrician's concern, perhaps fostered by a need to be up to the challenge of a difficult problem, the desire to be admired for successfully solving the case, and the need to be seen as

caring, keeps the game going. An intense relationship develops, albeit a narcissistic and sadomasochistic one, in which the mother needs to control the
distance and intensity of interaction between herself and the caring doctor.
The physician provides a safe theater and plays alongside her "reality" in a
very convincing manner . . . [Schreier and Libow, 1993a, pp. 87–88].

In an earlier article by Schreier (1992), a similar scenario is described.
Having "sought succor" initially from the obstetrician, which gained her
"an incredible entré to the theater of the 'patient,'" the woman reveals
her pathological desire for love from the pediatrician:

Soon after the baby is born, yet another physician appears at the bedside,
caring for mother and infant alike. The attention paid by the pediatrician to
the infant could easily cause rage in the mother, but the benefit of the physician's relatively nurturant, warm acceptance creates a totally new experience
for her, one that reflects—more than any other in medicine—the TV soap-
opera image of the kindly physician. Playing mother in the pleasant
atmosphere created in the modern obstetrics wing or in the warm room-
ing-in environment of the pediatric hospital comes easily to these women
[pp. 427–428].

Although some physicians might well fit this nurturing description,
it seems overly optimistic to claim that this would be an accurate profile of physicians in general. Most women would probably strongly dis-
agree with such a characterization. But Schreier and Libow find these
physicians precisely where the cultural stereotype (favored by physicians, especially) has encoded and deposited them: everywhere, regardless of space, time, insurance plan, or particular neighborhood. Like
virtually all the other major claims made by Schreier and Libow, this
one about the "caring physician" fails to trouble itself about the origin
or plausibility of the mythical stereotype that will be implanted at the
core of the claim; rather, it assumes this stereotype as empirical fact,
routinely retransmitted through the popular tradition. The sources for
this claim are far more problematic and complex than we are in any
respect led to believe in the authors' text.[2]
What is identified as a "caring" or "loving physician" has its discrete

---

2. Interestingly, Schreier and Libow do not even mention Freud, either in their text
or in their extensive bibliography. Doubtless there are practical reasons for this
omission. Rather, the Freudian-inspired dynamics are communicated by proxy,
through two particular figures, themselves heavily indebted to this tradition:
namely, Louise J. Kaplan (1991) and Karl Menninger (1934).

modern origins in the sacred mechanics of Freud's (1925) oedipal construction. For Freud, what will prove to be a long itinerary leading up to the physician as love object, begins with the preoedipal formation of the young girl.

> In little girls the Oedipus complex raises one problem more than in boys. In both cases the mother is the original object; and there is no cause for surprise that boys retain that object in the Oedipus complex. But how does it happen that girls abandon it and instead take their father as an object? In pursuing this question I have been able to reach some conclusions which may throw light upon the prehistory of the Oedipus relation in girls. Every analyst has come across certain women who cling with especial intensity and tenacity to the bond with their father and to the wish in which it culminates of having a child by him [p. 251].

This bond with the father has a considerable prehistory, of course, in the Freudian literature. Central to this prehistory is the discovery by the little girl of the little boy's visible sexual organ, her fantasized castration, and, ultimately, her subsequent penis envy. Effectively, this train of psychosexual "events" is the very core of Freudian theory relating to the development of femininity. The little girl is "assigned" a series of choices stemming from the situation of her inflicted "penis envy." Among these is the desire to be a man, which may persist and dominate her later life; she may even go so far as to deny that she "lacks" a penis or that she even suffers from penis envy at all. Alternatively, her penis envy may be transformed into a character trait of jealousy, which Freud saw as the most important female "deviation." The uncomfortable draw of the masculine on the feminine is ingeniously resolved by Freud by the introduction of the ubiquitous concept of masturbation. Women, castrated and without a penis, simply cannot compete with boys in this area. As a result, they withdraw from the masculine sphere, and, for many of these "defeated" women, hope is not lost. They can assert their femininity, and assume a distinctly feminine position, by wishing for a child instead of a penis. The father "naturally" becomes a love object, as the inseminating source of the wished-for child, and the mother thereby becomes the object of jealousy. For Freud, the once troubled little girl has grown to become the "ideal" woman.[3]

---

3. Freud's (1931) view of the father relation was modified somewhat with the appearance of "Female Sexuality," wherein he proposed that the intense bond with the father is really evidence of an earlier, preoedipal relation with the mother. In

With the power of the father figure in engendering femininity, and the addition of the transference relationship between the father and the physician, the conditions are readied to provide not only a "caring" and "supportive" physician, but also a "loving" one. As Wolman (1968) suggested, "Transference is a universal phenomenon, for everyone carries within his memory residues of past feelings and experiences" (p. 179). With transference, these intense emotional feelings are relived, often compulsively, but they are now attributed to someone other than the original source. Typically, these feelings "replace some earlier person by the person of the physician," in Freud's (1905) words, and

> a whole series of psychological experiences are revived, not as belonging to the past, but as applying to the person of the physician at the present moment . . . they may even become conscious, by cleverly taking advantage of some real peculiarity in the physician's person or circumstances and attaching themselves to that. These, then, will no longer be new impressions, but revised editions [p. 116].

Such feelings are relived—again, often they are compulsively repeated—precisely because they represent the earlier, unresolved conflicts that form the very core of the oedipal conflictual order. They can be resolved only by finding conscious expression; and, in the case of the mother who has not satisfactorily resolved her own development, the physician serves as the father substitute: the only figure—and here as substitute—who can effectively settle the initial, neurotic conflict of childhood. He is accessible by profession, he is present to the mother in her obvious feminine role as mother, as precisely the person who has literal and figurative authority over her.

Freud viewed transference not as a pathological condition in itself, but rather as a route to the discovery of certain earlier psychoneurotic conflicts, revealed through analysis. Since, for Freud, virtually everyone passes through various conflicts at the preoedipal and oedipal stages, retaining often powerful (if unconscious) memories of these earlier conflicts, regression to childhood is an absolutely necessary component

---

this sense, the relation with the father no longer consists in a reaction formation, so much as it is a less deviant repetition. The love of the father is not the culmination of femininity as such; rather, it is a symbolic representation of a much more powerful relationship with the mother. Menninger and his followers do not, however, appear to have been overly influenced by this revision of the father relation, which marked a significant reconciliation of Freud with his critics at the time.

of successful analysis. The causes of conflict must be brought to consciousness and dealt with. The physician/analyst becomes an important conduit for the expression, and hence resolution of these often disturbing conflicts from childhood. Problems do arise in transference when the patient is unable to break the transferential identification with the physician/analyst and continues to act as if he or she were still a child, beclouded by childhood memories. But even at this regressive stage, transference itself and the various object choices made, are seen not as being specifically pathological, but, rather, as forms of resistance. This might take the form of trying to undermine the "authority" of the analyst and render him a compliant lover, or it might take the form of making irrational demands or accusations directed to the analyst.

Even at these extreme points, the analyst is always directed by Freud (1915) and his followers to overcome such tactics with the goal of restituting self-control through the process of analysis. Hence, even in its most basic formulation, the transferential patient–doctor relation, with its various complexities and fantasy content, is not itself the basis of a pathological formation. Rather, it is the result of earlier conflictual relations, and its very presence testifies to the possibility of resolution. Freud did not employ this relation of transference in the etiological construction of any neurotic or psychotic position, however. Quite the contrary, he saw it as a great aid in effective therapy, in which the physician could establish a relation of intimacy and confidence with the patient and explore long-repressed areas of conflict, which would otherwise be practically impossible to expose and abreact.

Again, for Freud, there is little conscious agency at all on the part of the patient in the relation of transference to the analyst-physician. Rather, the conflicts stem from earlier developmental phases, which form an arrested emotional "cliché" or "stereotype" in the patient and thus lie quite outside the specifics and control of the present relation. If there are difficulties, they do not derive from the transferential relation itself. Rather, they testify to the resistance to and incompleteness of earlier attempts to stabilize one's own development and resolve the earlier conflicts of psychosexual maturation. In this sense, transference itself may create a heightened resistance to the attempted cure.

> Thus transference in the analytic treatment invariably appears to us in the first instance as the strongest weapon of the resistance, and we may conclude that the intensity and persistence of the transference are an effect and

an expression of the resistance. The *mechanism* of transference is, it is true, dealt with when we have traced it back to the state of readiness of the libido, which has remained in possession of infantile imagos; but the part transference plays in the treatment can only be explained if we enter into its relations with resistance [Freud, 1912, p. 104].

The dyad formed between the patient and the doctor is not the result of any specific agency on the part of the patient. Instead, it belongs to the analytic relation itself, which creates the structural possibilities for the very existence of such a relation. The patient does not actively seek out the doctor to create this relationship in the first place. On this very point, Freud (1915)himself insisted that "the doctor . . . must recognize that the patient's falling in love is induced by the analytic situation and is not to be attributed to the charms of his own person" (pp. 160–161). Instead, the patient can begin to explore his or her earlier conflictual difficulties only within the analytic relationship, which, in fact, permits the possibility of transference in turn. The time and space of this relationship is always limited to the locus of analysis, and the agency of the patient obtains, makes any sense, only within that locus.

How does all this reflect on Schreier and Libow's (1993a) account of the doctor–patient, doctor–mother dyads? They have borrowed— through intermediary analyses, particularly those of Menninger, Klein, and Kaplan—significant portions of the preoedipal and oedipal theory of Freud, which accounts, in part, for the "formation" of the "feminine." From this material, they have isolated the element of the "father-figure," as well as the theoretical apparatus of the child, the phallus, and penis envy, and conflated these otherwise conceptually interdependent notions with a naively construed sense of transference. The immediate effect of their conception is to take a theory of already perverse femininity and mother–child relations and offer it as an etiological source for a specific perversion of mothering: MBPS.

Many contemporary feminists have pointed to Freud's notion of femininity as posing a culturally preconditioned view that women are by "nature" perverse. A woman's whole development is simply directed toward overcoming this perversion and pathology, that is, being female in the first place. This development is accomplished, according to Freud, by women's fulfilling their procreative role through some real or idealized male figure (or both). Women are, in any case, excluded from real genital sexual satisfaction. Hence the claim that MBPS mothering is a perversion, given that Schreier and Libow's theory is ostensibly (if not explicitly acknowledged) Freudian in origin, is to say absolutely nothing new about mothering and even less about the understanding of MBPS mothering. In the end, the account simply invokes a universal characteristic of mothers and mothering out of the cultural soup, namely, that they have children as a requisite to their own development as women. And this is the core of their perversion. If MBPS mothering is indeed a perversion and a pathology, it hardly seems to be adequately distinguished from the "normal" Freudian notion of mothering and femininity in general.

A similar misappropriation takes place with Schreier and Libow's treatment of the transference relationship. They abstract from the whole theory of psychoneurosis, especially the role of analysis itself, but, most important, the specific nature of the transferential relationship as a means of understanding and dealing, therapeutically, with the initial neurotic symptom formations. As a result, they over determine the agency of the patient and establish this agency as a pathological element in MBPS. By the same token, they construct the physician into a surrogate or substitute parent or lover. Transference becomes itself transformed into some factually conceived serial substitution or replacement. The patient's familial and sexual agency remains fully in force but merely redirected to the "powerful physician"—almost in the sense that the woman patient goes "shopping" for the substitute, for the absent father or for the missing husband. Hurting for love becomes doctor shopping, window- or otherwise. The various specific parameters of the transferential relation with the analyst thus become extended and reconfigured, in a quite "literal" way, as a search for any doctor—gynecologist, obstetrician, pediatrician, surgeon—who would serve as a present place holder, an active and available substitute object of affection, of respect, admiration, and love.

THE MEDIA EFFECT: THE DOCTOR HERO

This serial replacement raises the question: Why a doctor, and why not someone else? With the theoretical failure to demonstrate the physician's central importance in the psychodynamic construction of the doctor–mother dyad, or "dialectic," the answer seems to lie either in the domain of popular culture (from TV soap operas) or in the generally inflated view of physicians taken from the discourse of physicians (which, after all, constitutes the literature about physicians). In the first instance, Schreier and Libow (1993a) propose that our image of "the good doctor," is generally derived from and reflected by "TV portrayals" of doctors: "Our idealized images of doctors are reflected in the media portrayal of a certain kind of fantasy based on traditional sexual politics. It seems we can't get enough: there were 7 medical dramas on TV in the 1950s, and 28 in the 1970s" (p. 59). Schreier and Libow go on to quote the work of J. Turow:

> Ben Casey (Vince Edwards) and Dr. Kildare (Richard Chamberlain) found themselves beseiged with letters and people asking for advice: According to *McCalls*, "Chamberlain received 3500 letters a week . . . women opened their hearts to him." The two actors found that everywhere they went they were subjected to mobs of screaming fans [p. 59].[4]

Although Schreier and Libow qualify their presentation of the "good doctor" by stating that they are not suggesting that "MBPS was created by expectations raised by TV soap operas or in popular culture" (p. 60), their presentation still turns on a number of assumptions about the transmission and reflection of ideas, fantasies, beliefs, and images from popular culture in general, and from TV in particular. They seem to be saying that our population (and particularly young women) develops an idealized image of doctors as a direct function of repeatedly watching the broader popular reflections of these characters on TV and then by internalizing the messages contained therein. Clearly, the process is far more complicated than the authors allow. To begin with, one of the most difficult problematics in critically understanding television as a social and cultural medium is the question of how TV reflects, generates, provokes, and circulates meaning in the first place. To say that the image of the "good doctor," specifically for the MBPS mother, replicates

---

4. The particular quote that Schreier and Libow use to support their etiological theory has at least one obvious flaw. The "screaming fans" that surrounded Richard Chamberlain and Vince Edwards (Kildare and Casey, respectively) might very well have been reacting to the actors themselves, who were attractive men in their own right, and not to their fictional TV role figures. It seems, in this regard, perfectly plausible that, for example, women swooned at the very sight of Rudolph Valentino himself, not because they were compulsively attracted to Arabian sheiks.

"social forces of unequal power between men and women" (p. 60) is to advance a thesis far more complex than a simple explanation of how a very small group of women might come to identify doctors as the source of their salvation. This thesis incorporates a whole dimension of the understanding and critical interpretation of media-related meaning itself.

The conveyance of a message fueled by "social forces of unequal power between men and women" could never be represented in some simple, isomorphic image of a specific, individual figure, which would, in turn, be understood uniformly by an entire audience—or even by a specifically isolable segment of that audience. Rather, each representation of power, according to such media theorists as John Fiske (1987) and Mimi White (1987) is mediated by a complex of various factors, including the relationship between the viewer-reader and the TV "text" and the social, cultural, psychological and economic forces that contribute to the formation of the viewer-reader. Images—here of "the good doctor"—are not simply picked up at random from the culture and transmitted without mediation to just any viewer; it is not as if the image were itself some univocal testament to broader "social forces."

Power tends to be focused in the various images and persons of those individuals who are portrayed as elite figures, the power legitimating their own dominant interests. These aggregate interests would be congruent with broader economic and social forces, but there need not be any specificity of character, personality, or concern to any of them, save as ancillary dramatic characterizations. Power could be invested in virtually any imaged characterization and, in fact, has been. Lawyers, detectives, police officers, accountants, corporate leaders, teachers, clergy, sheriffs, cowboys, sales personnel, franchise operators, football players, all can be represented as good, bad, indifferent, humane, fatherly, powerhouses, wily, unscrupulous, diffident, charming, sexy, family oriented, loving, and so on. The associations are with embodiments of power, not with particular individuals or individual professions.

The concept of the potential MBPS mother, bedazzled and overwhelmed by the fantasy image of the "good doctor," thus fails to establish even the most fundamental precondition of a disorder. On one hand, it makes questionable claims about how these susceptible young women would both view and be influenced by certain images about doctors, drawn from television and popular culture. Schreier and

Libow (1993a) fail to take into account the extraordinary complexity involved in the transmission, apprehension, and understanding of media-generated images. They take for granted that there is a single dominant attitude that historically determines, over an extended period of time, exactly how a viewer should view television and precisely how a viewer should respond to a particular set of images. This naive, isomorphic reading is countered by the overwhelming majority of contemporary television criticism, particularly that involved with forms of ideological and cultural analysis, of which Fiske, for example, is merely one representative.

Moreover, not only do Schreier and Libow conceive of television meaning in an extraordinarily monolithic way, but they also fail to take into account the various diachronic changes involved over the several decades-long history of television. In the case of doctors, for example, they argue that there were only seven shows featuring doctors in the 1950s, but 28 in the 1970s, indicating that doctors themselves had become more popular and focal in the culture. While this assumption may have been true in part, the massive increase in programming, the growing number of stations, advertising sources and revenue, the increase in TV budgeting, audience growth itself, the proliferation of homes with television sets, the advent of cable programming, all these led to an explosive growth in the absolute number of all TV programs, including those featuring doctors. Similarly, they fail to take into account the change in the portrayal of doctors that occurred from the 50s to the 70s and beyond. Perhaps Ben Casey and Dr. Kildare were heroic figures, struggling against all odds, while fascinating a large audience of fantasizing teenage girls and aspiring health care workers. But the same could certainly not be said of some of the more realistically portrayed "M*A*S*H" doctors in the 1970s, nor of the 80s portrayals of the bungling, malpracticing group of physicians at "St. Elsewhere," nor the 90s team at "E.R." To suggest that the portrayal of doctors on TV has been constant over the decades—maintaining the same appeal, the same values, and same specific audience—is like claiming that sitcom family figures have remained by and large the same, that Ozzie Nelson and Jim Anderson, for example, are basically the same kind of sitcom fathers as Archie Bunker, Al Bundy, or Homer Simpson. Not likely.

Untested Realities: Women
and the Medical Profession

*Feminist theory must be diligently critiqued as any other, and I worry
that its current status is perhaps too cozy and unchallenged.*

—*Donna Rosenberg (commenting on Schreier
and Libow's deference to feminism)*

Another cornerstone of Schreier and Libow's (1993a) etiological theory
is the claim that doctors *actually do* provide a comforting, care-giving
environment for women in general and for MBPS mothers in particular—and that MBPS mothers-to-be are deeply moved and fatefully
influenced by such conditions. The authors give numerous examples of
the generously supportive and nurturing disposition exhibited by physicians and hospital staff.

> "Well baby visits" are very much a part of standard practice. These allow the
> pediatrician to bask in the special excitement and warmth of the early rela-
> tionship between mother and child when it occurs. Physicians whose prac-
> tice includes time spent with developing, healthy children have a chance to
> enjoy their child patients and interact with their parents, activities that are
> a valuable and valued part of their professional lives. Some pediatricians
> now make a well baby home visit just after the mother and newborn arrive
> from the hospital. One often hears them talking, as we psychotherapists do
> in our clinic, of valuing a family's warmth, caring, courage, and togetherness
> and their own relationship to the family. . . . Presumably, many pediatricians
> are particularly vulnerable to a "good mother," a woman who seems to
> embody our society's ideals concerning motherhood [pp. 56–57].
>
> Giving birth to a baby provides some women with the rare chance to
> assume a role in which they can enjoy constant attention and care. A fair
> percentage of these women have enjoyed something of a rehearsal for this
> role, having received extended treatment from a physician previously.
> Pregnancy, which brings the mother into close contact with her obstetrician,
> often serves to whet the appetite for more of the kind of attention that
> derives from being a patient. . . . Soon after the baby is born yet another
> physician appears at the bedside, spending time caring for infant and
> mother alike. The attention the pediatrician pays to the infant could easily
> cause jealous feelings in the mother, but the benefits of the doctor's rela-
> tively nurturant, warm acceptance of her, and the attention he must also
> devote to her, is a wholly new experience. It is an experience that echoes,
> more than any other she has had in the medical world, a throwback to the

TV soap opera and medical show image of the powerful and/or kindly physician [p. 92].

Pregnancy and the neonatal period put the mother in a relationship with physicians that appears to her to be significantly different from all other relationships in her life. For the MBPS mother-to-be, a "powerful" figure, perhaps for the first time ever, is sharing *her* emotional space, listening to *her*, perhaps valuing her opinion and even admiring *her* [pp. 93–94].

[F]or many women the care giving of her individual physician may be the most nurturance she has experienced since childhood. Certainly, there are many kind, sensitive, and caring physicians. . . . The physician appears to be interested in her, and is well-educated, caring, and important. Unlike most of the mother's other relationships with professionals and even with other physicians, this physician [i.e., the pediatrician] treats her perhaps less as the passive patient and more as an active and interested collaborator in the care of her child . . . the physician is one person who notices her good care and appreciates her for it, particularly when her child is most ill. Furthermore, by virtue of the social prestige afforded to medical care giving, a mother can at least bask in the glow of reflected glory when her pediatrician, with her help, succeeds in healing her child. . . . She and her child are drawn into this interesting and highly respected world of new people, new procedures, new ideas, and considerable attention to her child and her care giving [pp. 118–119].

If this is in any way an empirically and historically accurate portrayal of the full spectrum of real relations between women and their physicians—particularly between women and their gynecologists, obstetricians, and pediatricians—one can only conclude that universal, single-payer health care has arrived, *virgo intacto*, at the Emerald City. Although it is true that medical practitioners have recently become far more sensitive to women and their problems—in reaction, undoubtedly, to intense pressure from women's groups — the treatment of women by doctors continues to be far more problematic, oppressive, and insensitive than Schreier and Libow's idealizations suggest.[5] It is

---

5. Schreier and Libow do make some attempt to describe the relations between women and the medical establishment. The only conditions they focus on, however, are those relating to the education, employment, and advance of women within the medical profession. This concern is covered in but a few pages of text and then culminates in a discussion that seems to reemphasize the original etiological construct, that is, the authors claim that even though doctors and women have not had particularly good relations in terms of professional opportunities, for those women who are MBPS-inclined, it is ironic that their relations with doctors may well be the only ones with kind, sensitive, and caring individuals (see pp. 116–120).

important to point this out, after all, since it is precisely on these ideal-izations that Schreier and Libow's broader etiological construct rests. If their etiology is indeed correct, then it would be logically consistent to expect that all MBPS sufferers would, to a large degree, enjoy these benign and supportive conditions.

Without discussing the historical provenance of the relations between women and their doctors at length—space hardly permitting[6] —it is important to note that it was doctors, at least within the American system of medical care, who essentially created all the gyne-cological myths and procedures directed against women in the first place. These procedures covered a variety of forms of sexual surgery, including clitoridectomy and female circumcision (relatively common surgical procedures performed until the late 1930s, which were intended to insure that women would not masturbate), hysterectomy, mastec-tomy, oophorectomy, ovariotomy, and so on. The reasons for surgery of these sorts were historically ascribed to the aim of returning women to conventionally expected forms of female behavior.

> An 1893 proponent of female castration claimed that "patients are improved, some of them cured; . . . the moral sense of the patient is elevated . . . she becomes tractable, orderly, industrious, and cleanly." . . . Doctors claimed success for castration when it returned woman to her normal role, subservient to her husband, her family, and household duties. Her disorder lay in her deviation from that role, a broad enough characterization to explain the bewildering and suspicious variety of indications. Opponents of wholesale castration applied the same yardstick—they criticized the opera-tion because it failed to restore woman to her standard role [Barker-Benfield, 1978, p. 27].

Such physician-initiated procedures as unnecessary hysterectomies were hardly restricted to patients in the 19th and early 20th centuries. They were common throughout the 20th century and continue to be so today. Carol Tavris (1992) suggests that, of the approximately 650,000 hysterectomies performed annually in the United States, as many as 90% could be considered unnecessary. She goes on to argue that much

---

6. A full bibliography of works detailing the history of the relationship between women and the medical profession is a separate project. The most comprehensive recent work on the subject appears in Leslie Lawrence and Beth Weinhouse (1994). Some important select works on reproductive rights and childbirth are listed in footnote 7, this volume.

of the deeper rationale for such operations results from physicians' insistence that women's internal sexual organs are essentially useless after child-bearing age (pp. 162–163). The usual pretext given for such operations is that it is a convenient way of excising "precancerous" tissue, a claim that does not stand up to comparison with similar prophylactic surgery on the male's prostate gland.

> The idea of undergoing a surgical procedure for "precancerous" conditions that are statistically rare ought to be ludicrous on the face of it. The appropriate comparison to the uterus is the male prostate, which in the large majority of older men, actually does contain precancerous cells. These cells are very slow-growing, however, and do not pose a threat to most men who have them. Nevertheless, although prostate cancer is far more common than uterine cancer, no one recommends preventative surgery on the prostate. The very idea would make most men premurderous [p. 163].

Historically, women have not fared much better with their obstetricians than with their gynecological surgeons. The relation between the medical profession and the whole procedure of childbirth has been extensively criticized by a number of medical historians, sociologists, psychologists and feminist writers.[7] Although there are many paths of criticism regarding obstetrics and women, much of the literature falls into two broad categories: reproductive rights and the medicalization of childbirth and childrearing (not to speak of the pathologizing and medicalization of menopause). Reproductive rights can be further broken down into two important subcategories: forced sterilization and abortion rights.

Although forced sterilization has historically involved a number of institutions and players, including penal, political, and judicial systems, with their various authorities and facilitators, the actual surgical procedure could not have been carried out without the full cooperation of physicians and, by extension, the medical profession itself. Doctors have often been willing and entirely necessary participants in this long-standing and particularly egregious violation of women's reproductive rights. Like many "involuntary" procedures, sterilization has been almost exclusively practiced on working and poor women and women of color, frequently in an entirely clandestine way. The following excerpt from a

---

7. See, especially, Suzanne Arms (1975), Adrienne Rich (1976), A. Oakley (1985), B. K. Rothman (1982), Marielouise Janssen-Jurreit (1982, esp. pp. 87–205), and Betsy Hartmann (1987).

lawyer–client interview provides a harrowing example of just such a procedure, performed quite surreptitiously on a Mexican-American woman:

> Mrs. Acosta attended weekly prenatal clinic sessions at County—where, not once, was she counseled about sterilization. . . . However, on August 20, 1973, eleven months and eleven days pregnant, Lupe Acosta entered L.A. County in the final stages of labor. "When I was being examined, they pushed very hard on the stomach," she recalls, "Very, very hard. With their hands. One doctor would have one leg open. The other doctor would have the other leg open. And then, there were two doctors just pushing down on my stomach and I couldn't . . . I couldn't stand it. I pushed one doctor because I couldn't stand the pain. When he came back, he hit me in the stomach and said, 'Now lady, let us do what we have to.' I felt very sick. I was sweat all over, *sweat.* I kept telling them to do something to bring the baby. . . . They just kept me in that condition from six o'clock in the evening till three o'clock in the morning. That was the last time I saw the clock—the last time I remember anything.
>
> A question to Mrs. Acosta from her lawyer: "Do you remember signing a consent form?"
>
> "No," she answers, "I don't remember signing anything. Only when I left the hospital—perhaps an exit paper?". . .
>
> "When I asked the woman doctor, she asked me if I knew what had happened to me. I said, 'No.' And then the doctor told me, 'Well you won't need the Pill because they tied your tubes.' I said that I didn't sign anything. She said, 'Your husband did.' And then I told them he wasn't my husband" [Dreifus, 1978, pp. 106–107].

Testimony by patients is not the only source of these distressing images. An interview with an intern who had just finished medical studies at Wayne State University, in Detroit, reveals equally remarkable and outrageous acts:

> "Most of our patient population was black, inner city," he explains. "We had a lot of young girls come in . . . thirteen and sixteen and they'd have two or three children. In those cases, we'd ask 'em, often when they were in labor, if they wanted tubule ligations. There were *so many* young girls and most of them had a real low mentality. We'd tell them about birth control and they wouldn't take it. It would get some residents really mad.
>
> "With sixteen year olds, you needed parents' permission. *That* usually wasn't hard to get. The parents weren't in labor. Some of the parents said, 'No.' They liked having the babies around. Sterilization was offered to women in labor no matter what their age. Those over eighteen you didn't need the parents' permission. . . ."
>
> "You mean you sterilized *sixteen year olds?*" asks an incredulous intern from Milwaukee, who has been sitting on the side, taking in the discussion.

"Well, yeah . . . if they had two kids. . . . There was beginning to be a whole lot of trouble. Detroit's blacks, they're really very anti-white. They were having all these meetings about genocide" [pp. 113–114].

In the case of abortion rights, historians of abortion in America tend to single out the established medical profession in general and, particularly, the American Medical Association as the principal, if not the only, early source of opposition to this once completely legal procedure (abortion was not punishable by statute law in a single state until 1820). James C. Mohr (1978) for example, argued that the campaign to outlaw abortion in America was almost exclusively led by "the graduates of the country's better medical schools" and the members of the then newly established (1847) American Medical Association. The medical campaign, like the rationale of the sexual surgeons, also contained an aggressive attack on women, particularly with regard to their abandonment of traditionally conceived roles of bearing children and thus of ensuring population growth, demographic continuity, the continuance of male authority, and, ultimately, what was to be conceived as social, if not national, stability:

> [M]ost medical writers between 1860 and 1880, when the medical crusade against abortion was at its height and making its greatest impact on American abortion policy, continued to direct their sharpest accusatory arrows at women directly. Many physicians were determined to prevent women from risking the future of society as they understood it by denying what these doctors believed to be a biologically determined social imperative [p. 170].

Another pointed example of the vilification of women during the mid-19th century comes from the polemics of the extreme antiabortionist, Dr. Montrose Pallen, who wrote "that [because of abortions] duties necessary to a woman's organization [i.e., childbearing] are shirked, neglected or criminally prevented" (cited in Mohr, 1978, p. 105). Surprisingly, this avid medical support for outlawing abortion came in the face of considerable public indifference to abortion during the mid-19th century, an indifference that, quite remarkably, was shared by American Protestantism as well.

Group and individual physician-supported opposition to women and their abortion rights was not, by any means, limited to the 19th century. Like unnecessary sexual surgery, it extends well into the 20th century and is the subject of an impressive body of contemporary writing. One such writer, Susan Faludi (1992) argues that even though medical attitudes toward abortion had changed considerably by the late 1970s, the attitude toward mothers had not altered appreciably. Many physicians, influenced by the antiabortion movement, still placed a powerful emphasis on the fetus, leaving the woman to play, at best, a minor role in the reproductive process. This role was so denigrated by doctors, Faludi argues, that the image of "mother" became relegated to a mere receptacle, a vessel for carrying the child. Dr. Bernard Nussbaum, the creator of the film, *The Silent Scream*, portrayed the fetus as being trapped in "intrauterine exile" and as being behind what seemed to be "an impenetrable wall of flesh, muscle and blood" (p. 421). Other antiabortion metaphors depict the woman as a bombed-out shell, her body likened to "a haunted house where the tragic death of a child took place" (p. 421).

Antiabortion and antiwoman electioneering by doctors was not limited to bad metaphors. In 1982, in California—the proclaimed "woman's emotional space" capital—a group of geneticists and obstetricians met and agreed that they had enough scientific proof to treat the fetus as an independent "patient"—a remarkable claim, as well as a creative way of doubling fees. This "scientific" claim was immediately echoed in the experimental field of infertility treatment, where many doctors treated "the fetus as if it were a baby with a separate existence from the mother" (p. 422). Waiting rooms in in-vitro fertilization centers had "baby pictures" of fetuses posted on walls: " 'Our Katy,' read the caption of one of the many murky sonograms plastered on the walls of the Pacific Fertility Center in San Francisco" (p. 421).

The second category of birth-related "complications" suffered by women at the hands of their doctors and established medicine is the medicalization of childbirth and childrearing. Like forced sterilization and abortion rights, this category covers an enormous territory and has been extensively documented. A particularly representative example of this kind of medical hegemony over women is what Diane E. Eyer (1992) calls the "scientific fiction" of mother–infant bonding. Briefly, mother–infant bonding became a significant biomedical subject in 1972, when two pediatricians, John Kennell and Marshall Klaus, published a study that purported to demonstrate that women who had 16 extra hours with their babies following birth showed better mothering skills. With scant confirming evidence, Kennell and Klaus began to draw remarkable conclusions from their experiment. They postulated that the initial results indicated that a sensitive, hormonal period in women just following childbirth attuned them to either accept or reject their infants. Good mothers—that is, hormonally well-disposed mothers—stayed close to their infants, and, as a result, infants benefited. In fact, many experimenters in the field of bonding were willing to go even so far as to claim that healthy child development was a direct result of early mother–baby bonding. All this appeared to be an inspiring moment in the history of childbirth: mothers could pay much closer and more intimate attention to their newborns; it gave women much more control over their birth experience; and family members could all share the joys of the early birth experience. But, as Eyer points out, it had a darker side, a much darker side:

> Unfortunately, most of those who sought to reform hospital birthing practices (doctors and nurses as well as parents) failed to see the trap: Because bonding was a construction of medicine, it would ultimately serve to protect the interests of that institution. The promised revolution in childbirth became a product of the politics of science. . . . Bonding is another example of scientific fictionalizing. . . . By selecting the behavior of few species of animals that coincided with popular notions about women's maternal "instinct," bonding research reduced women to automatons who behave the way they do, not because of their capacity to reason, their complex psychology, or their economic or social circumstances, but rather because of their inherent and inevitable inferiority [pp. 3, 5–6].

The practice of mother–infant bonding, then, invented by doctors and to a large extent perpetuated by them, had two hidden agendas: first, it was a means of controlling the behavior of women and, in so doing, realizing the most entrenched stereotypes about them. Second, it helped to reestablish the centrality of the obstetrician and the pediatrician in the whole process of childbirth and childrearing—a centrality that was slowly eroding in the face of natural forms of childbirth, home delivery, and a revived interest in midwifery. These "alternative" procedures were advanced to counter the indifference so often practiced by the traditional specialists themselves. Hence, what appeared to be a "caring and concerned attitude" on the part of doctors secreted a bias as old as that of the sexual surgeons and antiabortionists. Rather than reasoning out and validly experimenting with the problems of childbirth and childrearing, doctors and other medical personnel simply transposed their own conservative views of women to these procedures. They failed to take into account the vastly different, sometimes unique approaches to childbearing and childrearing that often result from historical, social, economic, and cultural differences. Every woman, like certain animal species, was seen as compelled to behave in a certain manner, as having some "instinctual" need for mothering. Even well-meaning doctors and researchers who were relatively careful in their bonding experiments could not overcome the deeply rooted biases of the profession itself.

The foregoing accounts represent only a minute sampling of the negative relations between women and doctors. Volumes upon volumes have been written on the subject. This small representative sampling, however, provides more than sufficient evidence to mitigate the largely idealized version of women–doctor relations given by Schreier and Libow (1993a) in support of their etiological account of MBPS. The very conception of a fairly large group of women fully believing that doctors are "good" and "caring," that they will help them and add spice to their otherwise dull lives, that the medical environment is somehow benign and charged with excitement, love, and sexual fulfillment, seems quite unlikely in view of the complex reality of the matter. Moreover, this idealized conception, like those of the antiabortionists, sexual surgeons, and bonding specialists, is hardly more than a shallow characterization of women drawn from the perspective of their historically assigned roles. They fail as mothers and wives, a failure that is precisely what constitutes their deviation, their "perversion." Thus they seek fulfillment elsewhere, most commonly, with the fantasized father/physician, the ideal procreative, powerful male image.

With this in mind, one must seriously question whether Schreier and Libow have thoroughly thought out this etiological theory. How, if they indeed wish to explain MBPS in terms of a professed "feminist" reading, could they be so unaware of women's suffering at the hands of the medical profession? And, most significant, how could they be so dismissive of women's abilities to understand and respond to these everyday situations to which they are routinely subjected? Lupe Acosta would doubtless not be moved to share her "emotional space" in the future, however great an "entré" she might enjoy with the "well-educated" and "interested collaborator in the care of her child."

SOCIOECONOMIC UNREALITIES

The question of real economic and social differences between women is another entirely overlooked dimension in Schreier and Libow's (1993a) etiological theory. In the section of their book ostensibly devoted to analyzing the socioeconomic backgrounds of MBPS mothers, they claim that, even though the literature on social class distribution in MBPS is sparse, "cases have been reported in all social classes from the wealthy to the very poor" (p. 28). They also go on to state that the statistics on MBPS mothers more or less match those of average young mothers, generally. From this report, we are led to assume that MBPS mothers are not distinguished by social, class, or economic level; that the disorder cuts across the extremes of wealth, poverty, education, privilege, and position in the United States. If this assumption is true, we can then assume that, by implication, regardless of socioeconomic status, all MBPS mothers, to some degree or other, also share the common etiology offered by Schreier and Libow. They are all exposed to roughly the same preconditional elements; they enjoy exciting scenes and nurturing medical treatment in the hospital and are profoundly affected by this sort of environment; they are treated by "loving, caring" physicians; they witness the calming presence of a pediatrician: "Soon after the baby is born yet another physician appears at the bedside, spending time caring for infant and mother alike" (p. 92); doctors, perhaps for the first time, share the "emotional space" of these young mothers, really listen to them, and so on.

The brief—two-paragraph—section on the "Socioeconomic Backgrounds" of MBPS mothers serves once again as nothing more than a rhetorical strategy to defend the authors' etiological claims. Since the physician serves as the central agency of the woman's discomfiture, there is little need to examine what might be thought to be incidental or marginal causal factors of the disorder. Hence, Schreier and Libow commence the section by remarking that there have been "no population-based studies" on MBPS. Their bibliography of some 445 references confirms this assertion dramatically. Their commitment of some two paragraphs to analyzing the socioeconomic backgrounds of these patients only confirms the suspicion that such work would be but of marginal interest. The implied claim itself, namely, that all MBPS mothers, regardless of socioeconomic status, receive the same medical treatment and enjoy the same caring attitude shown them by physicians —since these mothers are alleged to be representative of the larger population of women—appears to be patently counterfactual.

To begin with, the broader claim that MBPS mothers are representative of the general population is simply not established. How could it be in the absence of any demographic studies? Two paragraphs hardly clarify matters, either. Remarkably, Schreier and Libow do mention that "the majority of suspected parents were receiving some form of welfare payments from the state" (p. 28). Would they maintain that the majority of women of child-bearing age enjoy such a common "socioeconomic background" as welfare? Invoking an earlier study by Meadow, who dealt with a total of 17 cases, they also maintain that MBPS parents "as a group" have a greater than usual discrepancy in the "social or intellectual grade of the parents" (p. 29). Yet what were Meadow's grounds for making this claim? Meadow himself (1985) seemed to equate employment status—at least of the father—with intellectual ability and emotional stability. Since, in the majority of cases where he explicitly discussed these issues, the husband was apparently of working-class origins (a "line-worker") and the mother herself was not characterized in working terms at all, he might understandably come to this conclusion.[8] But to generalize from 17 such cases in Britain to the broad spectrum of alleged MBPS mothers in Schreier and Libow's United States—in the absence of any focused studies whatsoever—appears to be significantly lacking in scientific rigor. To be fair, the authors do comment on this situation. They end their section on "socioeconomic backgrounds" with the remark that "a single case report (Sugar, Belfer, Israel, & Herzog,

---

8. In a later discussion, Meadow (1995) characterizes two sorts of Munchausen parents. In one, the woman is characterized as "a very inadequate person," whose partner is "an extremely unsympathetic and macho man, with no communication at all." The second sort of "inapt and absolutely wrong partnership," has the wife being "much more socially superior in terms of social skills, articulateness, and certainly intelligence," and the husband "frankly, is a sort of wimp. He takes no interest in things, he never asks to see the doctors, he is a real nobody. He is usually a sort of caretaker in a warehouse who does a 6-hour job and does nothing." While the latter is said to be "the commoner sort of partnership," Meadow describes a visit he once made to one of the former sorts of couples: "I went to a family in South London [a working class neighborhood] a year or two ago at night and I remember going up to their Council property [i.e., public housing] in the dark, and I knocked on the door and there was a terrible sort of scratching on the door and howling of a dog, and the door opened and the husband didn't even get up to call this Alsation off me. He was sitting by the gas fire reading 'Gun Weekly'. Meanwhile, his wife, a sort of small, sad lady, was cooking offal for the Alsation in the kitchen and that was their domestic life" (p. 97). It appears that, even at this later date, Meadow based his conception of spousal relations, comparative intelligence, and compatability on what are highly subjective, simple, unscientific, and arguably biased observations.

1991) from Massachusetts General Hospital noted a similar discrepancy between the spouses" (Schreier and Libow, 1993a, p. 29). The only discernible trait that MBPS mothers do have in common with the larger population—at least according to Schreier and Libow's brief account—is that "the age of most mothers of infants ranged between 22 and 35" (p. 29). In other words, they were of normal child-bearing age.

If it appeared to be relatively inconsequential to physicians that the majority of MBPS mothers were welfare recipients, it is arguable whether such circumstances would be inconsequential to the mothers themselves. Even if it were established that MBPS mothers came from the spectrum of different classes, representative of the population at large, it still would not be true that they all receive the same kind and level of treatment, as Schreier and Libow imply precisely to establish a common etiology. There is no reliable evidence at all to establish that poor or inner-city or minority women receive the same degree of medical care as upper and middle class white women do. In fact, all the studies examining public health care for broad population samples indicate just the opposite, namely, that poor, inner-city, and minority patients routinely receive substantially inferior medical care—and, in many cases, no medical care at all. For such women, the very notion of "well baby home visits" is itself inconceivable, not to mention basic pre- or neonatal care. Exciting and fascinating visits to gynecologists, obstetricians, and pediatricians, as well as intriguing hospital experiences, could also be largely ruled out.

Against the lack of documentary and literary evidence of "good doctor–woman patient relations," there is a massive body of evidence testifying to inequitable medical treatment for poor and minority women. Some few examples would be instructive. Nationwide, a third of Latino women have no health insurance whatsoever—private or public-assisted. Fully 22% of black women have neither. A quarter of all separated women have no health insurance at all, the same figure holding for single women of all races. Over 20% of divorced women suffer the same lack of any form of health insurance (Taueber, 1991, p. 242). The prospect of receiving loving care from nurturing physicians for these women is unlikely indeed. Of course, they hardly fit Schreier and Libow's etiological model of women who find social, psychological, and emotional fulfillment from doctors and hospitals. Unless, that is, such hospitals and physicians were willing to forego compensation.

Conditions of inequality among poor and minority women are reflected in a number of other ways. Minority and welfare patients are sometimes segregated into separate and inferior hospital wards. Two such instances have been reported in two of New York City's most prestigious hospitals, Mount Sinai Medical Center and Columbia-Presbyterian Hospital (Sullivan, 1994). According to another *New York Times* report, one entire floor of Mt. Sinai consisted mainly of poor Medicaid maternity patients, who were predominantly black and Hispanic; the other floor included mostly privately insured maternity patients, most of them white. Not only were the patients separated according to their "socioeconomic backgrounds" and race, but the number and types of services available to the patients differed considerably. The "white" floor enjoyed a series of exciting and nurturing events, including classes in childrearing, information on breast feeding, personal instruction and individually oriented services, and opportunities for entertainment; the "minority" floor enjoyed none of these nurturing activities. The separation seemed to be so racially grounded that three minority women accused Mt. Sinai of segregating them by race, along with the Medicaid patients, even though they were fully covered by medical insurance. One of these patients, Deborah Ford, told the *Times*, "I saw some white patients in the elevator, but never on our floor—not even one" (Sullivan, 1994).

In another case (Hilts, 1994a) a complaint was filed with the National Institutes of Health against the Medical University of South Carolina in Charleston for conducting illegal human experimentation on maternity patients. In the course of their hospital treatment, the maternity patients, "virtually all African-American," were tested for possible cocaine use, but without their knowledge or consent. A spokesman for the hospital, Scott Regan, said that "consent was not required to turn information from medical records over to the police." According to the *Times*, "once a woman tested positive on a drug test, she was told to sign an agreement that she would complete a drug-treatment program. If she refused to sign, the woman was to be arrested. If she did sign, but later tested positive again or failed to appear for treatment, she was arrested." The administration of these experiments resulted in the arrests of more than 40 patients: "Some were arrested hours after they gave birth. Some of the women were handcuffed and put in leg shackles or handcuffed to hospital beds during the arrest." Asked to respond to this experimentation program, Regan replied, "This was never intended to be an experiment; it was strictly a treatment program. . . . These cases are a burden to their families and the state." Interestingly, the *Times* continues, "the women chosen for testing were those who had no prenatal care or inadequate prenatal care [or] went into labor early or had previously known drug problems." Those patients who tested positive were told by the Charleston county prosecutor, "If you fail to complete substance abuse counseling, fail to cooperate with the Department of Social Services in the placement of your child and services to protect that child, or if you fail to maintain clean urine specimens during substance abuse rehabilitation, you will be arrested by the police and prosecuted." Unfortunately for those people who were arrested and given appointments for drug treatment, "there were no drug programs in South Carolina for pregnant women. No provision was made for the women to be transported to their appointments, and no provision was made for taking care of their children if they did get to their appointments" (pp. A7, A12).[9]

Given the disparity between medical treatment for poor and minority women and middle and upper class women, the broad claim that all MBPS mothers share a common etiology can only be a painfully gross distortion of reality. The etiology advanced by Schreier and Libow (1993a) is predicated on the effective fulfillment of an idealized paternal/spousal figure by an actual physician, and it supposes the reality of a warm, supportive, friendly hospital environment. These considerations, in turn, suppose equal access to physicians and to medical institutions; equal treatment to all individuals, regardless of their social, racial, economic, class background; not to speak of the nature and comparative quality of the medical institutions themselves, their neighborhood or regional locations, the financial health of these institutions, and the availability of adequate insurance coverage. Perhaps the only positive thing to be said about the fourth floor at Mt. Sinai, and about the Medical University of South Carolina Hospital "maternity program," is that they are unlikely to generate very many cases of MBPS in the near future.

---

9. In a follow-up article in the *New York Times* (Hilts, 1994b), we are informed that, as a result of the investigation of this program by the Federal Government, the Medical University of South Carolina was placed on probation for violating ethical standards in human testing. If the ethical violations are not corrected in a year, the University could lose its federal funding.

The Confusions of Explanation

Not only does the etiological model of MBPS advanced by Schreier and Libow (1993a) fail to address adequately the socioeconomic conditions of the patients or to deal extensively and objectively with the historically strained relations between women, their physicians, and the medical establishment generally, but it introduces a number of explanatory concepts that appear to be ill considered, if not fully unwarranted. Perhaps foremost among these are the notions that MBPS is a special kind of "perversion," that the MBPS subject uses the child as a "fetish" to "regulate her disastrously ambivalent relationship with the physician" (p. 97), and the entirely unreflective and retrograde use of "sadomasochism" to explain this particular female "perversion."

Schreier and Libow, claiming that MBPS mothers "challenge and push to new limits psychodynamic theories of developmental psychopathology and personality disorders," appropriately do likewise when they stipulate the nature of MBPS as a "perversion":

> From the perspective of the individual mother, we have come to see the dynamics as a perversion, a form of mothering imposture. The term "perversion" is used here neither in its common pejorative sense, nor in its traditional psychoanalytic sense, relating it to particular sexual practices. It is rather used to describe a particular form of "unreal" [sic] relating and the mental processes that permit its continuance. The object of this unreal relationship is to connect to a powerful and unattainable person, the doctor, who in fantasy can repair early experienced trauma. The sick child is not the object of this process but rather provides the means for the connection and allows these patients to live out their fantasies, much the way the fetishistic object allows for "sexual activity" for the person with a sexual perversion [pp. 80–81].

Given the generality of such a use of the term perversion, it would be difficult to exclude any statistically aberrant behavior from its stipulative web. With such a definition, one could well describe chronic schizophrenia or practically any other unusual mental state as a perversion; any sustained attempt at "unreal relating" conjoined with its underlying "mental processes" would, by definition, satisfy the description of a perversion. Such a definition, precisely by pushing psychopathology to new limits, could well include any number of creative acts—from the inner visions of poets to the rhetorical impostures of great orators. Or one could easily apply the term pervert to a child who compensates for loneliness by making up his or her own games, played with imaginary friends (unreal relating), by imagining the games and friends (the mental processes that permit its continuance), and so on.

To makes things even more complicated, despite the disclaimer that the term perversion is not to be taken either commonsensically, or in its psychoanalytic sense, this is precisely what Schreier and Libow, in fact, do. The core behavior of the alleged MBPS mothers and the motivations underlying it are consistently portrayed throughout the text as being specifically sexual in nature. Schreier and Libow continually explain to us how the mother seeks sexual satisfaction and personal respect from the idealized—and idolized—figure of the loving physician, precisely because of her own sexual frustrations and loss of psychosexual valorization from a spousal or parental figure. This behavior, in turn, is simply a reiteration of the conventional Freudian apparatus of "female perversion," which is, after all, exclusively sexual in nature— the entire feminine oedipal drama. Effectively, Schreier and Libow draw so extensively on such intermediary Freudian readings as those offered by Menninger (1934) and Kaplan (1991) that their account of perversion differs from Freud's only in name.

The question raised by the etiological argument, then, is to what extent MBPS—if it exists in the first place—is a perversion in any traditional *or* contemporary sense of the word at all. It is defined so broadly as to be all-inclusive (of fantasy, psychosis, imposture) or, alternatively, as an effective reiteration of Freud's notion of perversion generally, that it is difficult to ascertain the specificity of MBPS as a unique form of perversion (as characterized by Schreier and Libow). On one hand, it seems to be inseparable from any number of conditions, psychopathological or otherwise, on the other, it is claimed to be a nonpsychoanalytical form of perversion, but one that is characterized strictly in Freudian terms all the same. It is alleged not to be sexual in nature, yet the female "sufferers" are afflicted precisely because of sexual deprivation or childhood trauma and are motivated to continue their "mother's masquerade" in hopes (fantasized or otherwise) of affective fulfillment. If MBPS is just a form of "unreal relating," how are we to distinguish it from any number of other conditions, and why is it perverse? If the answer is that it is perverse because the MBPS sufferer has a need for sexual fulfillment, originating either in early childhood development or in later adult spousal relations, then one can hardly characterize the perversion as being nonpsychoanalytic in nature, especially when the dynamics used to describe it are explicitly attributed to Kaplan, who borrowed quite directly from Menninger and Freud. Once again, as they have with other aspects of the MBPS etiology they have advanced, Schreier and Libow have failed to examine sufficiently the basic logical coherency of their claims and have failed to give an adequate etiological account of their own claimed etiology.

If the answer to the question as to why MBPS should be considered a perversion is that the mother employs the child as a "fetish," then this recourse likewise seems to hold little promise of resolution. The concept of fetishism employed here seems vague and self-serving, and as they have with so many central notions, the authors seem disinclined to examine the provenance or the traditional usages and contexts of fetishism. While they maintain that the child serves the MBPS mother as a fetishistic object that "permits her to regulate her disastrously ambivalent relationship with the physician" (p. 97), their explanation of this concept—which is central to their account of MBPS—is simply nonexistent. In a brief description, the crucial agency of the child as fetish is itself imbued with the "magical causality" of the passive voice: "in the case of MBPS, the infant is first dehumanized and then anthropomorphosized, that is, turned into a fetish like object to sustain the relationship the mother compulsively seeks with the child's doctor" (pp. 97–98). This assertion constitutes the authors' complete explanation of fetishism stated in the section devoted to this very subject matter, "The Infant as Fetish"—which section consists of a *single paragraph*.

An adequate explanation of exactly how such a "perverse" relationship forms, both theoretically and in practice, between a mother and a child is not the only element missing in the authors' treatment of fetishism. They also fail to explain how such a notion can explain an exclusively "female" form of perversion, namely, MBPS mothering. In fact, Freud (1927) himself—from whom the very concept derives—and most of the tradition following him view fetishism as an exclusively male deviation in sexual development.[10] Theorists following Freud have gone so far with this distinction as to propose a completely different but parallel form of deviation or perversion in females, namely, kleptomania (see, e.g., Kaplan, 1991, pp. 284–320). But the only mention of this

---

10. Most sociologically oriented investigations of fetishism also confirm that, by and large, fetishism is a male perversion (see, e.g., Gosselin and Wilson, 1980, pp. 158–163).

issue by the Schreier and Libow (1993a) is used simply to qualify and dismiss it: "The fetish, like those so often found in male sexual perversions .... enhances feelings of powerfulness and wards off fear" (p. 97). Thus, also dismissed by this remark is Freud's (1927) conception of the entire psychosexual formation of sexual difference, at least with regard to its "perversion." If males are prone to forming perverse fetishes and this tendency is a specific deviation in their psychosexual development, then how is it possible that this large group of MBPS mothers are suddenly afflicted by this peculiarly male deviation?

What becomes even more bizarre in Schreier and Libow's (1993a) account of MBPS as a form of perversion, where the mother uses the child as a fetish to obtain close relations to the "loving doctor," is their insistence that the perversion is not sexual in nature. Their complete silence concerning the nature of fetishism only adds to this increasingly perplexing claim. Given both Freud's and Kaplan's readings of fetishism, the very act of forming the fetish cannot even be conceived without some sexual motive—without taking psychosexual development as its very context—or without a strong libidinal investment. Typically, the traditional account places the fetish as a substitute for the missing "maternal phallus." The young boy is initially confused by, and in denial of (Verleugnung, or disavowal), the enigma of sexual difference with respect to his mother. He is also fearful that he might suffer the loss of his own phallus. Freud's (1927) celebrated remark is cogent and to the point on this issue: "Probably no male human being is spared the fright of castration at the sight of a female genital" (p. 154). With all this at stake, the male child is compelled, in certain cases, to deny that the female does not have a penis and also to invent one for her. This will ultimately serve the male as a substitute for the female sexual organs and can take a variety of well-known fetishistic forms. By the same token, such a fetish will also serve to protect the boy's own sexual identity in the face of the feared "castrated" and "castrating" woman. Hardly an account that fails to recognize the agency of sexuality at work in perversion or fetishism.

Given such mechanics of fetishism, traditionally conceived, it is hardly remarkable that neither Freud nor Kaplan, whom the authors quote at length, sees any relation at all between fetishism and, of all things, a female perversion of mothering. Indeed, in discussing the female equivalent of male fetishism, Kaplan (1991) remarks that the illusion of being fixed and transformed by a magical phallus is, to my mind the most common manifestation of perversion in women, and it gives reason to all the other perversions of female desire. That central illusion, that particular method of defying and short-circuiting reality, is a psychological equivalent of the fetishistic perversions of men [p. 527].

In other words, female perversion is governed by the desire to be transformed by the male phallus. Thus, for Kaplan, at least, female perversion is explicitly sexual and in no way directly involves the mechanics of male fetishism. But, of course, in Schreier and Libow's (1993a) explanation of MBPS behavior, there is a third element in the mother's relation to the physician: the child. Hence, the authors hope to explain the mother's relation to the physician as being mediated by this third factor, understood by them as a "fetish."[11] If it is convenient to ignore the male provenance of the mechanics of fetishism in their rush to construe the child as a fetish—particularly convenient in the absence of any explanation of how the fetish is constituted by the mother—it is equally understandable that they wish to ignore the entire sexual provenance of both fetishism and perversion. What they apparently wish to derive by borrowing the now desexualized notion of fetishism is the one power that fetishism and sexual perversion had in the first place, namely, the character of blurring the distinction between reality and fantasy. This magical property, in turn, sustains the contradictory and ambivalent relations the MBPS mother is alleged to entertain between herself and the physician.

One might just as well term what Schreier and Libow call "fetishism" —especially in their curiously desexualized notion—"sacrifice." The mother "sacrifices" the child as an offering on the alter of the godlike

---

11. The notion of using the child as a fetish is particularly confusing in view of a work that Schreier and Libow liberally refer to, namely, Renik's (1992) "Use of the Analyst as a Fetish." Renik gives the clear impression that the patient in analysis uses the fetish—that is, the analyst—as a means of either fulfilling or breaching the transferential relation in analysis. Indeed, according to Renik, the introduction of an intermediary fetish, such as a child, would be counterproductive, since it would fall outside the direct transferential relation between analyst and patient. From this view, it seems that, if the mother wanted to establish a relation with a caring and nurturing figure, at least in the form of a psychiatrist, psychoanalyst, or psychotherapist, she would do so directly, rather than employ the child as a proxy. In this sense, instead of Renik's theory substantiating that of Schreier and Libow, it seems to counter it; it offers a more feasible way for the MBPS mother to present a relation with the doctor—enter into therapy.

physician, thereby propitiating him and gaining his love and attention. The authors continually speak of the physician as "symbolically powerful." Indeed, in Schreier's (1992) article on MBPS, he claims that *society's two most powerful symbols*—fatefully bound—are the "mother" and the "doctor/healer" (p. 435). In view of such a virtual deification of the doctor, perhaps "sacrifice," rather than "fetish," would be the more appropriate, and less sexualized or "psychoanalytical" term. With such a dynamic, it is interesting to see how Schreier and Libow (1993a) "desexualize" the allegedly core "perverse" relation in the first place. Quoting from Kaplan's major study on female perversion, and stressing, rather than predominantly sexual concerns, the authority of the doctor (as priest, as authority figure) as being at the center of the MBPS relation, the authors lay the foundation for the use of the child as a "sacrifice" rather than as a sexualized "fetish." This shift of emphasis, once again, is meant to reinforce the centrality of the physician as the dominant, if not deified, authority figure. But this contention is not supported by the tradition, which Schreier and Libow often fail to acknowledge—and it certainly is not supported by Kaplan. Their careful editing and convenient use of ellipses in dealing with Kaplan's aforementioned study is instructive. Here is their key quotation from Kaplan:

> A woman dissatisfied and disillusioned with everything the real world has offered to her, is possessed by the idea that a certain kind of person does have the power to fix her—a father, a priest, a husband . . . a movie star, a surgeon . . . a son or a daughter ... and to bring her illusions to life and satisfy all her frustrated desires. He or she will compensate for the humiliations of her childhood and rectify the mortifications of her feminine condition. When that certain kind of person . . . is found, . . . created . . . invented . . . the . . . pursuit of this fictive phallic power assumes a force and intensity that eventually subsume and consume all a woman's strivings and ambitions [Schreier and Libow, 1993a, p. 94].

The following is Kaplan's (1991) original text from which Schreier and Libow quote. We have added italics where Schreier and Libow inserted ellipses:

> A woman, dissatisfied and disillusioned with everything the real world has offered to her, is possessed by the idea that a certain kind of person does have the power to fix her—a father, a priest, a husband, *a teacher, a lover, a hairdresser, a toreador, a dry goods merchant, a fashion designer,* a movie star, a surgeon, *an analyst,* a son or a daughter *or female lover whom she invests with phallic power*—and to bring her illusions to life and satisfy all

her frustrated desires. He or she will compensate for the humiliations of her childhood and rectify the mortifications of her feminine condition. When that certain kind of person—*the ultimate phallic being*—is found, *that is*, created *and* invented *by the woman*, the *erotomanic* pursuit of this fictive phallic power assumes a force and intensity that eventually subsume and consume all a woman's striving and ambitions [p. 527].

Kaplan sums up her account in the sentence following this citation, also omitted by Schreier and Libow: "Yes, an erotomanic pursuit of phallic perfection does succeed in circumventing and undermining reality" (p. 527). Perhaps it is a perverse reading of perversion, traditionally conceived, to lend such stature to it: neither commonsensical nor psychoanalytic.

If Schreier and Libow (1993a) cast the MBPS child more in the image of a sacrifice than a fetish, a problem still remains as to why this perverse behavior is consistently described as sadomasochistic, by the authors themselves as well as by the more psychoanalytically expressed tradition. In the context of Schreier and Libow's study, the term is invoked only in very cursory detail. But if we take the term with the full impact of its force, with regard to contemporary feminist thinking concerning women's assigned gender roles, it seems to require much greater attention and specificity. Given the much discussed inadequacy of such a term to describe women's behavior, to say that the relationship between the MBPS mother and the doctor is a sadomasochistic one, and that "the mother's masochism appears in a message to the pediatrician: do anything to my infant, but don't *leave* me" (p. 96), leaves such a characterization open to a number of criticisms.

To what extent is the term sadomasochism adequate to describe the behavior of the MBPS mother, when the term is generally, if abusively, used to describe the normal behavior of women as mothers, homemakers, and spouses? (See Caplan, 1994.) This invocation of sadomasochism is particularly troubling in view of the fact that Schreier and Libow give us no specific definition or explanation of sadomasochism, and only the slightest sense of where it fits and how it operates in their etiological model. For example, they claim that the MBPS mother sadistically contests the authority of the doctor by controlling, devaluing, and confusing the pediatrician, ultimately by lying to him. The reason for this sadomasochistic behavior, it is alleged, is to prevent the mother from getting too close to the physician, whom she attempted to ensnare in her elaborate plot in the first place. Thus, the MBPS mother employs a form of sadomasochistic behavior as a defense against her successful seduction or "entrapment" of the physician: if she becomes too close to the physician, too successful in her willful guiles, she becomes vulnerable to and dependent on his authority, his affection. He may, in turn, withdraw his affection, leaving her fully abandoned, abjected, as she was in her youth, in her marriage, in her thankless tasks as a mother.

But isn't this entire dynamic based on the power and dominance of the *male* physician and the submissiveness and inferiority of the woman? And isn't this precisely what feminists point to as the stereotypical, self-denigrating and self-defeating sorts of behaviors that have been historically attributed to women and that have been institutionalized as "disorders" by psychoanalysis and psychiatry? The infamous Masochistic Personality Disorder, which first appeared in the *DSM III* (American Psychiatric Association, 1978) (later renamed in the *DSM III-Revised* (American Psychiatric Association, 1985) edition as Self-Defeating Personality Disorder), presented a veiled description of "masochistic" women in terms of the most commonplace male prejudices, preconceptions, and projections. In fact, any of the several variations of Self-Defeating Personality Disorder could easily characterize the typical MBPS mother: Histrionic (formerly Hysterical) Personality Disorder, for example, describes this person—always a woman—as attractive and seductive: "this individual [read: woman] tries to control the opposite sex, tries to enter into a dependent relationship. Flights into romantic fantasy are common" (Tavris, 1992, p. 184).

In the context of biases against women, we should also note that Schreier and Libow (1993a) identify mothering—casually absolving both parenting and fathering—as the sole source of the MBPS perversion. Fully employing Rosenberg's (1987) literature review of the syndrome, they simply restate, in slightly modified form, her statistics on mothers: 95% of the perpetrators are mothers, either biological or adoptive; sometimes mother surrogates are involved. The other 5%, which includes MBPS fathers, adult male MBPS perpetrators, and adult females who induce symptoms in other, unrelated adult females are simply thrown out of the sample. We are never really given an adequate explanation for this significant omission. Such nettling questions as how fathers could engage in a strictly "female" perversion and why adults would perform such perverse operations on each other, if indeed infants are the sole "fetishistic objects" of the disorder's etiology, are never addressed. The only explanation advanced by the authors appears in a single sentence, in a footnote: "Because 95% of the parents *directly* involved are mothers, we will generally use the female pronoun" (p. 7n).

At any rate, this exclusive stress on mothers and mothering not only fails to take into account inconsistent data, it also completely overlooks a question central to virtually all contemporary feminist thought regarding women's roles, namely, to what extent is "mothering" a socio-cultural myth? And, if it is a myth, how can one speak of it outside the sociomythic forces that created it? (See Rich, 1976, Caplan, 1989.) This failure on the part of Schreier and Libow to address the broader question of mothering affects their entire etiological model. For, if mothering is a myth of woman's place, a largely sociocultural gender construct, then the very model for good mothering on which the "perversion" is based is itself perversely constructed. In other words, "good mothering" (as opposed to bad mothering: MBPS mothering) is, at least in large part, determined by the gender-based, patriarchal construct of women's behavior: they must nurture their children, demonstrate powerful maternal instincts, stay at home to care for their children, feel fully compensated by childbearing (i.e., receive the longed-for penis), place foremost emphasis on marriage and conjugal relations, and so on.[12]

The importance of the mothering-as-myth concept regarding female roles is evident in Oakley's (1976) widely received sociological study of women's societally assigned gender roles. She attacks psycho-analytic theory, among other things, for fostering a myth of motherhood. As we have seen, Freud made motherhood the practical resolution of penis envy. By bearing a child, preferably a male one, the woman finally receives the longed-for penis, which, remarkably, is the fulfillment of her femininity. It then follows, Oakley argues, that a woman who chooses not to have a child also rejects womanhood: femininity and childbearing are, in the psychoanalytic perspective, inseparably bound. As is so often the case, this theoretical imperative gets inscribed in the practical. As a result, many of the popular books devoted to mothering and childbirth tend naturally to equate maternity and femininity. Oakley offers a popular British work on proper gender roles as a condemning example:

---

12. A particularly powerful condemnation of society's distorted vision of mothers appears in Chodorow (1989, pp. 79–96 and passim). An interesting and diverse collection of contemporary feminist views on mothering appears in Trebilcot (1984).

Lundberg's and Farnham's *Modern Woman: The Lost Sex*, an early example
of the popularization of the Freudian perspective, shows clearly the identification of maternity with femininity and the question of any other 'career'
beyond the maternal one as "masculine." Published in 1947, this treatise
blamed most contemporary ills on women's deviation from their proper
gender role—maternity looming large in the list of feminine activities thus
neglected in the course of women's progressive (pathological) masculiniza-
tion. Childbearing and childrearing represent for women, assert Lundberg
and Farnham, "almost their whole inner feeling of personal well-being"
[pp. 188–189].

The intense maternal pressures on women are manifest in numerous
other forms of socialization. For example, little girls have universally
been pressured by parents, early education teachers, and friends to play
with dolls, in an attempt "to make this identification with the doll as
symbolizing maternity" (p. 191). Other outside pressures on young girls
include the immense stress toward marriage and homemaking, which
also take a coercive form, in both home and school settings. As for
women's relation to their children, the standard assigned role model
leaves little room for ambivalence about offspring. Mothers must be
committed to liking their children and to all the little chores associated
with childrearing. Another book on mothering, also cited by Oakley,
describes this ideal mother's behavior as follows: "A child is for her, in
one of its major aspects, a passive object to be hugged close, or to deck
out in appealing clothes. . . . As an expression of her protectiveness . . .
[she] devotes many hours a day to the physical care of her children"
(p. 195). Despite these idealizations, Oakley argues, many women do
not in fact like their children, and even more despise the everyday
chores associated with their "physical care."

Oakley's descriptions of the socialization of mothering go on at
length. What is important to note here is that what we have come to
believe is "good mothering" is really no more than an extraordinarily
complex sociomythic construction, one that entails a wide variety of
opinions, ideas and images, all derived from a preconceived cultural
notion of woman's place. We believe that mothers must nurture their
children because maternity is a biologically determined instinct. But this
belief is based on the thinnest of behavioral comparisons, usually
between women and observations of various animal species. We believe
that it is impossible for mothers not to want their children, but many
studies of voluntary abortion indicate overwhelmingly that these mothers-to-be do not suffer any psychological damage (p. 200). We assume

that mothers must love their children, but many do not. And so on. In the end, Schreier and Libow (1993a) fail to factor all of this into their vision of mothering and therefore present only those aspects of mothering that are congruent with their theory. The "perverse" mother abuses her child because of a pressing need to form a fascinating relationship with a powerful, caring physician. But what ultimately supports this "perversion of mothering" is the assumption that there is some universally accepted, objectively determined activity called mothering from which certain mothers deviate. As we have seen, recent feminist writing casts considerable doubt on this sort of assumption.

CONFUSING CASES AND INCONSISTENT DATA: READING "THE CASE OF CHRISTOPHER"

Chapter 5 of *Hurting for Love* (Schreier and Libow, 1993a) is devoted to the analysis of the core perversion: "The Perversion of Mothering."[13] The case study that introduces the sections entitled "Mothering as a Masquerade" and "MBPS as a Perversion" concerns a young boy, Christopher, who, we are told in the very first sentence, "died at the age of 4, after 25 hospital admissions and over 300 pediatric office visits." Surely, this is a dramatic opening—the death of an MBPS child in the wake of such extensive medical attention—to what promises to be the central case study of the crucial MBPS dynamics. Earlier, in the Preface, Schreier and Libow were careful to articulate their concern for the social and historical contexts of such studies, as well as the need for precision and detail in recounting the dynamics involved:

> We are now much more aware of the dangers of taking such formulations out of their social and historical context. . . . We hope, in our attention to the details of these dynamics as well as their social context, to provide the element often missing from clinical texts: that of leading the way toward an understanding that will then provide the means for prevention [pp. xiv–xv].

---

13. The whole section is virtually a reprint of Schreier's (1992) article, "The Perversion of Mothering: Munchausen Syndrome by Proxy." One obvious difference consists in the authorship of the two versions. In the earlier article, Schreier begins his case study of "Christopher" by stating, "In one fairly typical case *I* consulted on . . ."(p. 424). In Chapter 5, the analogous passage states: "In one not particularly unusual case on which *we* consulted . . ." (p. 88).

Such concerns are indispensable to the analysis of MBPS dynamics, especially in view of the authors' stated intention of making the volume "as encyclopedic as possible." Indeed, they go on to say, "We hope we have offered enough descriptive material to be practically useful and at the same time enable readers to arrive at their own hypotheses" (p. xiv).

It is hard to imagine that the readers of *Hurting for Love* could arrive at anything but "their own hypotheses" if they take Schreier and Libow at their word, namely, that "The Case of Christopher" is "not particularly unusual" at all in this literature—at least in its lack of detailing dynamics, its failure to provide an adequate social and historical context, and its scarcity of descriptive detail. Perhaps this explains why the authors inserted a brief caveat the end of their Preface: "Clearly, our dynamic formulations are open to different interpretations" (pp. xiv–xv).

The case of Christopher starts when he is one month old and ends when he is four, the mother having been indicted for his murder, but ultimately convicted of manslaughter. The mother (Edith) first brought Christopher to the pediatrician's office suffering from what she reported as projectile vomiting, runny stools, and crying during bowel movements. Apparently convinced by these "reports" of the child's illness, his physicians fitted him with a nasogastric feeding tube, which they later replaced with a percutaneous gastrostomy tube (surgically implanted). The early diagnosis was "failure-to-thrive." The authors tell us that this initial set of events occurred somewhere "in the southeastern United States."

Young Christopher soon "was receiving as many as 14 medications for chronic infections, asthma, allergies, and feeding disorders." Presumably physicians diagnosed these various illnesses and disorders, but Schreier and Libow seem to qualify this diagnosis by going on to say "a purported 'immunoglobulin deficiency' turned out to be a delayed maturation of immunoglobulin synthesis" (p. 89). But what is the difference between a "purported" immunoglobulin deficiency and the fact that Christopher was not sufficiently mature enough to synthesize it in the first place? It is fully understandable that a child lacking immunoglobulin would be particularly susceptible to the illnesses mentioned, which is doubtless why medication was prescribed. The authors then relate how Edith claimed that the child had a high temperature at home but often had a normal temperature in the doctor's office: "Frequently Christopher would show up with a history of 105–107°F temperature the night before, but his temperature was found to be normal in the doctor's office" (p. 89). Of course, it is altogether possible that a fever might be misread or that it might go down in the course of a day. It is equally possible that the pediatrician was disinclined to make a "well-baby visit" at night to a single-parent mother who lived in a one-bedroom apartment and who slept on a couch. Single parents usually have to wait until office hours begin the following day. Aren't they frequently instructed to give the child two aspirins and bring him to the office the next day? And is it unusual that a child who is diagnosed as having frequent infections and immunological disorders might, in any case, have frequent high fevers?

What is unfortunately typical in "one fairly typical case" is the typical lack of detail given about any of these health concerns. It is assumed in the case history—which is supposed to establish a diagnosis and etiology—that the mother is already caught up in her MBPS behavior, that from the start she is practicing her deception on everyone: surgeons, doctors, pediatricians, consultants, and therapists. What Schreier's role was as a consultant (Libow was added as a consultant only when Schreier's earlier article was subsequently republished as a book chapter under both of their names) is not stated either in the article or in the book. Was Schreier brought in as "expert witness" only at the mother's trial? He has served in this capacity on several occasions, after all, in the Ellen Storck case, the Yvonne Eldridge (Serra, Gilg, and Wohaldo, 1997) case, and the ongoing Kathy Bush case. Indeed, both authors have enjoyed considerable professional celebrity, having been—in their own words—"interviewed for three news magazine television programs" and having been "approached repeatedly by network talk shows to see if we would agree to appear alongside a Munchausen by Proxy mother" (Schreier and Libow, 1993a, p. 221).[14] But the nature of their consultation on the case of Christopher remains unstated. What is voiced is the typical suspicion directed toward the mother: as mentioned, the section's first sentence announces Christopher's death. His mother "reported" a series of symptoms, which led to the surgical implant of Christopher's gastrostomy tube. The implication is that the symptoms were induced by the mother. The nasogastric feeding tube and the gastrostomy tube were resorted to "despite normal workups at a major

---

14. They continue, "As a friend put it, 'You're hot,' meaning, of course, that the syndrome has suddenly caught the eye of the media and the fascination of the public" (p. 221).

medical center that specialized in the treatment of children" as the authors relate it (p. 88). Why should this be "despite normal workups"? The mother was not authorized to perform a diagnosis or surgery. We are given no information that she even so much as requested the procedures. Was the surgery performed in this "major medical center that specialized in the treatment of children"? (p. 88). After all, the physician's own diagnosis was "failure-to-thrive." This initial suspicion is maintained by the invocation of "as many as 14 medications," which were prescribed by physicians after all. Even though a "purported" immunoglobulin deficiency did not register, the fact that Christopher could not himself synthesize immunoglobulin did. Why the use of the word purported if not to maintain suspicion about the whole case? The issue of disappearing fevers is likewise brought forth as if to suggest that they were simulated outside the pediatrician's office. The authors hardly blame the pediatrician for not responding "frequently" to Christopher's late-night fevers by making a house call or for failing to instruct the mother to take a cab to the hospital ER room should the child once again have one of his 107°F fevers.

Schreier and Libow (or Schreier) go on to relate a series of disturbing and painful symptoms suffered by Christopher in the course of his brief four years: bruises ("secondary to a fall or running 'into a concrete wall'."), vomiting, low sugar levels (the mother, "though medically knowledgeable, was 'using the wrong scoop for his glucose'"), weight loss, diarrhea, dehydration (p. 89). Numerous steps were taken to correct his continuing problems, but, "despite all these efforts, Christopher continued to fail. But it came as 'a surprise and a shock' to Edith when he died, for he appeared to her to be doing so much better physically" (p. 89).

In the end, an autopsy revealed that Christopher had died of chronic ipecac poisoning, and that "the poisoning had to have gone on for 2 to 3 years to have caused the deterioration in the heart muscle that was found at autopsy" (p. 89). What 25 hospitalizations—at least some of them at a major medical center somewhere in the southeastern United States—and over 300 pediatric office visits failed to disclose, an autopsy did. Assuming that the ipecac poisoning was the cause of the deteriorated heart muscle (discounting a marathon four-year period of intensive medical treatment, medication, and the attendant stress all this would impose on an already sick infant), Edith was charged with murder. This sentence was reduced to manslaughter "once the dynamics of

MBPS were explained to the district attorney" (p. 91). Presumably, the diagnosis of MBPS was arrived at after Christopher's death, after all the hospitalizations, pediatric visits, and autopsy reports. Schreier and Libow do mention a conference held at "the medical center" to discuss Christopher's case at which a child psychiatrist suggested the possibility that the child's disorder might be based on a "learned behavior pattern"; but Edith declined to have the child submit to an inpatient psychological examination. Her reasons are left unstated by the authors/consultants. It would be consistent to surmise, certainly by this point in this typical case history, that, if she were aware of her own alleged MBPS disorder, she would hardly wish her imposture to be discovered.

Edith, we are told, was shocked by the child's death. She admitted to giving Christopher ipecac "only a few times in the last months of his life" (p. 89). Her reasons for administering ipecac to her child are, in this case, at least stated: "Edith later admitted that because Christopher begged for food and because he was denied so many other activities of a normal childhood, she felt that she should give him something enjoyable to eat, followed by ipecac to cause him to vomit" (p. 89).

About Edith herself, her own history, the circumstances of her life, her employment, her friends, the social context she occupied, we are given precious few details. Information must be inferred from what little data we are given. How old Edith was when she had the child we are not told. Nor are we told if she was married at the time of Christopher's birth. About her first marriage, which is, after all, a significant detail in the life of a mother, we are told absolutely nothing nor about her first husband. This omission is itself peculiar in a chapter entitled "The Perversion of Mothering," especially when Schreier and Libow end the chapter by stating their hopes of "attempting to understand the prerequisites of normal female development" (p. 102). Here is the summation of Edith's formal education, her employment skills, the first husband, and the marriage: "Following a junior college education, Edith went to work in a hospital, where she met her first husband. After about 2 years the husband left her" (p. 90).

Edith's employment history is then related to us in likewise cursory detail: "she subsequently held a number of low-paying jobs. . . ." Two years after the breakup of the marriage, she had herself admitted to a psychiatric hospital. Some time after this—how long is not specified—she married again, to "a young man" (p. 90). By the time of Christopher's protracted medical visits, however, Edith's godmother (familiar with the family dynamics) recounted that they "lived in a one-bedroom apartment" and "the mother slept on the couch so that Christopher could have his own bedroom." With no mention of the husband's sleeping anywhere, nor any detail about him at all, not even a name, one suspects that the second marriage also suffered what Schreier and Libow dismissingly term a breakup.

Interestingly, a third "breakup" figures prominently in Edith's history, but Schreier and Libow fail to pursue this — as if two divorces were already more than sufficient to account for the traditionally expected "absent father" component of the MBPS syndrome. This third breakup was that of Edith's own parents. The account is given in striking brevity. Edith, we are told, "came from an upper-middle-class family that lived in a suburb where her father held a responsible executive position. The marriage broke up when Edith was in elementary school" (p. 190). The version given in Schreier's (1992) *Menninger Bulletin* article differs, in that Edith's age is given at the time of the divorce, the status of the father's occupation is somewhat differently related, and, most important, an extremely significant mention is made concerning the father's philandering—something that is simply omitted from the later version. "Her father worked as an executive in a large corporation. He had reportedly had affairs before the marriage broke up when Edith was 7 or 8 years old" (p. 426).

Recall that young Christopher underwent 25 hospital admissions and 300 pediatric visits, that a conference was held on the case, that extensive court proceedings were held, and that consultants and evaluators were brought in on the case. The documentation alone must be archival in proportions! That Schreier and Libow, who claim to advance a sociodynamic model of understanding the MBPS syndrome, fail even to mention the possibly disastrous role of the father in this case is inconceivable. In the absence of communicating this information, much less raising it as an issue, the remark about Edith's own mother, just seven lines further on in the text, seems relatively innocuous: "Edith's claim that her mother was upset when she found out she was pregnant with Edith was confirmed by her mother" (Schreier and Libow, 1993a, p. 90). If this remark is taken in conjunction with a subsequent recollection, given on the very next page, one begins to see the possibility of an enormously precarious situation for the young Edith: "She said that she always felt that her mother had not loved her, and indicated that there were no physical expressions of affection in the family" (p. 91).

It is clear that Schreier and Libow have not troubled themselves too deeply about the family dynamics of the case—this central, defining case of "the perversion of mothering." In fact, one is tempted to think that family history and social context are merely afterthoughts. The extent to which the authors have looked into the family at all, much less into its dynamics, can be illustrated by comparing two brief passages. Schreier (1992) begins the paragraph on "Edith's history" with the following sentence: "Edith was the fourth of five children in an upper-middle-class family" (p. 426). Schreier and Libow (1993a) have it otherwise: "Edith's history provides many clues to why she developed MBPS. Christopher's mother was the second of 4 children" (p. 90). So many of their "clues" drop any mention of the father's reported affairs, alter her relative position as a sibling in the family, and even change its size.

Edith's own medical history appears to be an afterthought as well. It occupies only three and one-half lines of the text: "Edith's medical history included many visits to emergency rooms, claims of numerous miscarriages, a history of peptic ulcer disease, some dysfunctional uterine bleeding, hypothyroidism, and chronic laxative abuse" (p. 91). Schreier (1992) added mention of the former "psychiatric hospitalization," and specified that "she claimed to have had 8-10 miscarriages" (p. 426).

We do not know Edith's age at the time of her ordeal with Christopher, or anything at all about her two husbands or two marriages (and even granting the need for patient confidentiality). We know nothing about her background, other than that she came from an ostensibly middle-class family (probably retaining this status until "her father's leaving") located somewhere in a nameless suburb of the Southeast. She is void of any markers to the family's general education, culture, race, ethnicity, income, religion, or community standing. One can only speculate as about to "who" Edith might have been, and how she might have found herself in the situation she did.

Edith certainly seems to have been a single parent at the time of Christopher's illness. She also seems to have fallen considerably from any middle-class status, having passed through a series of low-paying jobs and sleeping on the couch so her son could occupy the only bed. If her father's reported philandering preceded Edith's birth, or was concurrent with her mother's pregnancy, it is understandable that her mother might have felt rage toward the father, and, in all probability, would have at least mixed feelings toward the child who was his offspring. She probably would have felt betrayed and misused, at the very least. That the mother displayed "no physical expressions of affection" toward Edith, indeed that Edith felt the mother did not love her, would certainly be consistent with such a dynamic. Having left the family years earlier, the father remarried and, in Edith's words, was "obviously not interested in her."

Given such circumstances, it is understandable that Edith would seek affection outside the family. Two marriages and 8 to 10 miscarriages would certainly be sufficient proof of her repeated attempts to achieve some form of emotional fulfillment, however tragic the results. The court evaluators, we are told, noted that Edith had "a fairly normal affective range in interviews" (p. 91). The number of miscarriages might also have damaged her health, resulting in "some dysfunctional uterine bleeding" and "many visits to emergency rooms." Nonetheless, Schreier and Libow are completely silent as to how these medical disorders might have played into her history and may have altered the diagnosis. But, once again, the authors qualify her every move with initial suspicion: all these disorders are merely "claims," and no one seems to have thought of discussing these "claims" with her or with the attending physicians at the emergency rooms she ostensibly visited.

Perhaps even more telling is their failure to explain to us the role of her "claimed" hypothyroidism. Was she hypothyroid or not? If she was, this would lend some explanation for why she may have had some degree of mental impairment, a decreased tolerance for medication, anemia, menstrual disorders, and numerous miscarriages. This might also have a strong bearing on why she was a chronic laxative abuser since one of the most common symptoms of hypothyroidism is constipation. Typical of many hypothyroid patients is that they have serious problems with weight gain and loss. Overweight is common in this population, as is extreme thinness. Such people tend to have serious eating disorders, with attendant feelings of guilt, inadequacy, perceived loss of self-control, poor self-image, and depression (see Tierney, McPhee, and Papadakis, 1998, pp. 1049–1051). The psychological burdens suffered by such people often result in compensatory eating binges, followed by induced vomiting and laxative use—to assuage their own sense of guilt for having binged in the first place. (In fact, Edith's explanation of why she gave young Christopher ipecac closely follows this rationale.) As often, they seek to compensate for feelings of personal inadequacy and emotional frustration by an increase in sexual activity.

Feelings of inadequacy may also result in a dramatically decreased sex drive, or, indeed, and commonly so, in the need for a range of ordinary human affective relations, such as friendship, and, even, maternity. It would not take a clinical pathologist to note that all these indications could be suggested, and discussed, simply by following up on Edith's "claims." Also, that hypothyroidism is often related to autoimmune disorder (p. 1050) might well account for her own repeated visits to the hospital. Add the frustration of a childhood abandonment by the philandering father, a mother who is emotionally dead to the world, the accumulated stress of two divorces, poverty, and being a single parent with a chronically sick child, and a peptic ulcer would hardly be out of line, either.

But the medical indications are simply sidestepped in Schreier and Libow's account, as the mother's early "reports" about the child's illness were greeted with outright suspicion and as are the social and historical contexts of the case. Why? Because the whole of Edith's behavior and alleged history is held to be an imposture. From beginning to end, we are repeatedly told that she is a liar, a simulator, a living imposture of motherhood itself. Her illness, her disorder, consists in a "perversion of motherhood." Even her "appearance" of being a good mother is part of the MBPS imposture, an imposture, we are repeatedly told, that is difficult for nonspecialists and for the judiciary to understand. Despite Edith's own mother's claim that "she was the happiest person alive with that child. She kept him spotless. Everyone loved him" (Schreier and Libow, 1993a, p. 90). Despite her godmother's assurance that "she was a wonderful mother," despite the psychiatric hospital admissions note testifying to her kindness and generosity, despite the court evaluators' claim that there was no sign of psychosis and that she seemed to have a normal affective range—despite all these claims, Edith's whole life is said to be but a masquerade of mothering: "As the case of Edith suggests, the mothers involved in MBPS appear on the surface to be constant, caring and concerned attendants to the needs of their infants" (p. 92). But this is, after all, only apparent. The key to the MBPS mother's "grossly disturbed behavior" of "masquerading" as a mother is reasserted, once again, to be the child's physician: "We believe the key is to be found in the mother's intensely ambivalent *fantasy* relationship with her child's physician which in astounding ways defines the use of her own infant" (p. 93).

Edith's imposture is purportedly exposed through her frequent lying.

After noting that Edith was a relatively "mediocre" student in comparison with her siblings, Schreier and Libow quote one of her sisters as saying that after the parents' marriage broke up, "she 'got away with a lot more' than the rest of the kids, and was always a 'poor-me' person once she learned that she could get what she wanted that way" (p. 90). This claim is doubtless meant to suggest that Edith was destined from youth to be deceitful. But if we recall that Edith's mother was upset when she realized she was pregnant with Edith—in the context of the poor relations with the husband—and that Edith, perhaps quite justifiably, felt unloved by the mother, this quote from one of the sisters might be read somewhat differently. In fact, Schreier (1992) himself read it differently, just one year earlier, when he quoted the same sister as saying that "Edith 'got by with a lot more' than her brothers and sisters. . . (p. 426).[15] In the latter quote, the suggestion seems less that Edith is deceitful but that she was able to profit from the mother's guilt over the earlier rejection of this unwanted child, a form of *schuldgelt* perhaps. But this is a minor affair compared with the two "lies" that Schreier and Libow next bring forth.

Following the "breakup" of the first marriage, and the succession of low-paying jobs, Edith had, "as she admitted, a problem with 'lying.' She checked herself into a psychiatric hospital 2 years after the breakup of her marriage; the immediate cause was her failure to fulfill a promise to some friends that she could get them a producer for a show" (Schreier and Libow, 1993a, p. 91). The extent to which this so-called lie is a plausible "cause" for psychiatric admission is testified to only by the failure of Schreier and Libow to discuss it. After a broken family, a ruined marriage, and the dreary prospects of a lifetime of poverty ahead—not to speak of her physical aliments—is this really a case of "lying"? She may well have felt upset that she let some friends down. After all, how many producers are there in the southeastern United States who are willing to employ someone like Edith as an agent? Alternatively, she may have met a producer, or even a "faux" producer, who let her down with his promises to advance her career as an agent. Who can tell? The authors don't even bother to try. In fact, as Schreier (1992) phrased this damning episode, "she checked herself into a psychiatric hospital after she was

---

15. Here, the brothers and sisters are spoken of in the plural, since Schreier claims that the family has five children. Schreier and Libow (1993a) say that the family has four children.

unable to follow through on a promise to some friends that she could get them a producer for a television show" (p. 426). Being "unable to follow through on a promise to some friends" becomes transformed, in the course of one year, to a "cause" for psychiatric admission! And this serves as evidence to indicate that compulsive "lying" is part of the etiology of "mothering as a masquerade," the duplicitous "perversion" of MBPS.

The second "major lie" committed by Edith followed her release from the "psychiatric institution." How long after is unclear. Whether she was already a mother by then is typically unspecified.

> She told a major lie to a young man whom she subsequently married. She told him that she had cancer ["leukemia," in the earlier version] and required chemotherapy, an admission that apparently hastened their marriage. She would occasionally leave the house, telling her husband that she was going out for kidney dialysis but actually spending 4 or 5 hours driving around aimlessly before returning home (Schreier and Libow, 1993a, p. 90).[16]

One is tempted to think that the authors, both of whom have extensive professional experience in the field, have on occasion met someone in desperate enough circumstances to have employed an element of "deception" to achieve a bit of stability in his or her life. Primary gain and secondary gain are not, after all, terribly remote from ordinary human experience. We have seen several examples drawn from the history of factitious "disorders": the French soldier who feigned myopia so as not to get slaughtered with Napoleon's armies on the Russian front; the British soldier who preferred to feign a stiff joint at the base infirmary rather than taste the fare offered up at the malaria and yellow fever wards of India or the Caribbean; the Munchausen patient feigning various disorders so as to obtain morphine, Demerol, food, and shelter. If one were confronted with hypothyroidism, chronic substance abuse, a series of miscarriages and uterine bleeding, poverty, no family, perhaps a child, a stint in a psychiatric hospital, and a broken marriage behind her, would it not seem to be perfectly normal behavior to employ a bit of deception in hope of finding a sympathetic husband? Perhaps one equally needy? Perhaps a lonely someone who is also "hurting for love"? After the marriage, one could always "claim" to have been

---

16. The incident is referred to in Schreier (1992) as "one of Edith's lies" and as a "deception."

misdiagnosed earlier. And what cost is there, really, to anyone, for taking a nice summer's drive for a couple of hours?

Earlier, in the context of discussing her psychiatric admission, Schreier and Libow (1993a) claimed that Edith admitted to having a problem with "lying." But it was not clear, at that point in their account, exactly when Edith said this or to whom she said it. In the penultimate paragraph of their "Case of Christopher," they specify this charge:

> With one of her psychological examiners, Edith talked about her lying problem and noted that she had "fabricated a life for herself to such a degree that she began to believe her fabrications." Personality testing suggested dynamics of angry feelings, overt and covert, related to a sense of being hurt or unfairly treated [p. 91].

Well, if this confession of her persistent lying is meant to be conclusive, it at least concludes the case study. The final brief paragraph, which we have already quoted, relates how once the dynamics of MBPS were carefully explained to the court and, especially, to the district attorney, the state felt compelled to reduce the charge from murder to manslaughter. Subsequently, the court have become better informed as to the perplexing character of MBPS, and the mothers who suffer from MBPS would doubtless be better understood and more compassionately treated.

There is yet one more striking difference, however small, between the text composed by Schreier in 1992, and the text jointly composed by Schreier and Libow in 1993. The year-earlier passage corresponds to the penultimate paragraph of the Christopher case study in *Hurting for Love*. In Schreier and Libow (1993a) the account of Edith's "lying problem" is brought full circle: to her own confession of having "fabricated a life for herself to such a degree that she began to believe her fabrications" (p. 91). The only problem is that Edith doesn't say this at all in the earlier version. Such confessional testimony would be an elegant segue into the following section of "Mothering as a Masquerade," and would lend some degree of credence to their already implausible account. The year-earlier version reads as follows (emphasis added): "Edith talked about her lying problem to one of her psychological examiners, *who* noted that she had 'fabricated a life for herself to such a degree that she began to believe her fabrications'" (p. 427). Hence, the confession to the "lying problem," the veritable descent into a world of fabrication, is one fully advanced by the "psychological examiner," not by Edith. This—if the earlier claim is to be believed—is subsequently, and in turn, fabricated into a confession precisely by the very medical authorities who claimed deception to be the core of the MBPS disorder. Given the series of tenuous assertions in their analysis, the lack of any published confirmation, the absence of detailed medical or psychological data in their analysis of this typical case, it is hardly surprising that Meadow, in his Foreword to *Hurting for Love*, once again raises the real question: "What is the correct diagnosis: Munchausen by Proxy syndrome abuse or medical negligence?" Indeed, he continues, "It will be some time before there is reliable information about prognosis" (Schreier and Libow, 1993a, p. x). It is likewise hardly surprising that, in the end, Edith "suggested dynamics of angry feelings . . . related to a sense of being hurt or unfairly treated" (p. 91).

Psychometrics: Quantifying the MBPS Profile

Given the egregious oversights in the "Case of Christopher" and those we have touched on in many of the earlier case histories, there is probably much more that needs to be said about the method, validity, and accuracy of these accounts of adult Muchausen's and MBPS—both in *Hurting for Love* and in the literature in general. Space hardly permitting, however, we would like at this point to examine some of the basic errors, unfounded assumptions, and biases underlying the testing of MBPS patients (read: mostly mothers). Schreier and Libow (1993a) devote an entire chapter, "Psychological Testing of MBPS Patients," to develop a "standard profile" of the average MBPS sufferer. They claim that, even though there is a wide variability to the manifestations of MBPS, parental dynamics "reveal a remarkable consistency when viewed from a clinical standpoint" (p. 165). How they arrive at this conclusion—particularly in face of the (admitted) lack of sufficient data from previous testing, a number of special conditions that affected those who were tested, and a "comprehensive" theoretical model that is being proposed for the first time in the very same book that is seeking to establish retroactively clinically objective facts about MBPS patients—makes for an interesting bit of invention by the authors.

Given those considerations, one might hesitate even to list the test results of MBPS patients, especially when the authors themselves indi-

cate that many of these results may be unreliable owing to special testing conditions and a lack of sufficient long-term test data. But this lack
does not seem to deter Schreier and Libow. Their proclaimed goal is to
use testing data, not as a means of collecting information about a wide
range of MBPS behaviors, but, rather, to draw up what amounts to a
characterologic profile that would help support the "diagnosis of these
mothers in the courtrooms" (p. 165). In their attempt to do so, the
authors begin their account by invoking professional articles that
"allude to the use of psychological testing for specific cases" of adult
Munchausen's Syndrome. They justify this recourse by claiming that the
"available data . . . contained in the adult Munchausen's Syndrome . . .
may provide clues to the pathology in the by-proxy disorder, given the
overlap in the two syndromes" (p. 165). This recourse is perhaps not
unusual in itself, but Schreier and Libow, at the very outset of their
work, make a very specific point of distinguishing and separating these
two forms of Munchausen:

> The name "Munchausen by Proxy Syndrome" was coined from the adult
> "Munchausen's syndrome" because it seemed to mimic the adult disorder of
> illness fabrication but involved the use of a child as a type of proxy, or sub-
> stitute, for the adult's own body. Unfortunately, the similarity in names of
> the two disorders has engendered considerable confusion about the rela-
> tionship between the adult factitious disorder and the "by-proxy" syn-
> drome. The name "Munchausen's syndrome by Proxy," still widely in use,
> makes the unwarranted assumption that the proxy syndrome is simply a
> variant of the adult disorder. *We have chosen to use the term "Munchausen
> by Proxy syndrome" throughout the book to clearly distinguish it as a separate
> entity from Munchausen's syndrome. While some patients share symptoms of
> both disorders, in fact there seem to be distinct differences in behavior for the
> two syndromes. What they share most clearly is the "Munchausen" name* [p. 6,
> italic added].

If it is true, then, that the two syndromes are connected only nomi-
nally and that there are "distinct differences in behavior for the two syndromes," why would the authors choose to present data from adult
Munchausen testing as "providing clues" for the by-proxy pathology?
After all, the distinct differences between the behaviors manifest in the
two syndromes would largely negate the association of such statistics or,
at least, render them unreliable. Given the authors' stress on distinguishing the two conditions—they even go so far as to call one a "disorder" and the other a "syndrome"—theirs certainly appears to be a
classic, but somehow unrealized, case of an invidious comparison.

A possible answer to our question, we suggest, lies in the self-serving character of Schreier and Libow's use of test information in general. Their expressed concern in the section on psychological testing, as we have mentioned, is to piece together a characterologic profile of the average MBPS mother. But this ostensive claim, it appears, is driven by a much more ambitious agenda. What the authors really want to accomplish—the unavowed objective of *Hurting for Love*—is to establish firmly their own etiology and diagnosis of MBPS, in this case, based on "objective" test data. This objective will, in turn, lead to an extraordinarily creative attempt on their part to combine disparate, sometimes inadequate, and often contradictory bits of data about MBPS mothers and eliminate or pass over whatever data seem inconsistent or inconvenient.

Several examples of this stratagem occur in the section on adult Munchausen test data. The presentation of Wechsler Adult Intelligence Scale (WAIS) scores, for instance, seems to have absolutely no bearing on any aspect of the disorder, nor do the results show any statistical pattern, inherent or otherwise. If we are to assume that the WAIS data that do not give the number of adult Munchausen patients tested refer to only one patient, the total of patients tested amounts to four. (There are several more patients who were administered a Wechsler-Bellevue test, but this test is not included expressly in the authors' summation: one explanation for this particular exclusion may be that the group so tested by Lidz et al. (1949), and listed as a source of data for adult Munchausen's syndrome, predates Asher's (1951) discovery of the syndrome by two years.) The findings regarding these four patients seem patently routine and descriptive of virtually any individual or group that might be subjected to the same test: "Reported scores range from below-average to above-average on the Full Scale IQ., with 'minimal' to 'considerable' scatter. Where data are available, it appears that verbal IQ generally exceeds Performance IQ" (p. 169). Clearly, such generalized test results could just as well profile the intelligence functions of a group of opera lovers, physics teachers, or even physicians (but probably not surgeons).

The MMPI (Minnesota Multiphasic Personality Inventory) tests administered were, by the authors' own admission, even less conclusive. Two of the four MMPIs presented were possibly invalidated by what the authors call "faking bad." According to them, this phrase means that the Munchausen patients were trying to appear as if they had a psychopathological condition. Such a pretense seems odd since much of the literature on these patients expressly states that they were indeed suffering from some form of psychopathology (indeed, adult Munchausen's is itself seen as a psychopathology, precisely one involving "faking" behavior). There are other curious claims along these same lines: "The response to duress and/or a 'cry for help' might also explain these elevated MMPI profiles. Alternatively, such profile elevation may reflect rather florid histrionic elaboration of emotional and physical complaints" (p. 169). It is difficult to comprehend why the authors expected to see results any different from these in the first place. After all, "histrionic elaboration" and "emotional and physical complaints" are the very behavior adult Munchausen patients are supposed to demonstrate. Why even bother listing the test results? The only conclusion that one can draw from this scant sample of MMPI tests is that adult Munchausen patients will act like adult Munchausen patients are alleged to act under clinical testing conditions as well as under nonclinical conditions—not exactly the kind of statistical data that will "provide clues to the pathology of the by-proxy disorder" (p. 165).

Projective tests, such as the Rorschach inkblot test and the TAT (Thematic Apperception Test) are equally inconclusive, although the authors attempt to salvage some case-to-case consistency in their summation of these test scores. Like other adult Munchausen tests, these are represented by an extremely small sample. According to our count, only five of the authors listed in Table 10.1: Summary of Test Data of Adult Munchausen Syndrome (Schreier and Libow, 1993a, pp. 166–168) actually administered any projectives tests at all, and two of them reported nothing of consequence in their interpretations. The authors' claim that "perhaps the most consistent data come from the reports of projective test results" is thus based on three papers—those of Stone (1977), Victor (1972), and Cramer et al. (1971)—which are risible in the lack of specificity and, we should add, the irrelevance of their interpretations. Schreier and Libow (1993a) summarize these interpretations as follows: "In general they reported themes of preoccupation with decay, death, and loss. Identity confusion as well as sexual and aggressive impulse control issues came up several times. Defense mechanisms of acting out, projection, somatization, and denial were all described" (p. 169). These interpretations, once again, are standard psychodynamic ones and could be applied to a broad range of individuals suffering from any number of psychological dysfunctions. Drug abusers are often described in similar terms. "Preoccupation with decay, death and loss" are exactly the terms repeatedly used in describing the famous mental patient, Daniel Paul Schreber, who has been alternately and retroactively diagnosed as schizophrenic, paranoid, paranoid- schizophrenic, manic–depressive, hypochondriacal, suffering from a bipolar disorder, depressive, and, recently, even as reasonably sane (see Lothane, 1992). The only consistency in these kinds of data, then, seems to be that almost any sufficiently disturbed person can fit the profile of an adult Munchausen's sufferer. And, we should add, all these machinations on the part of Schreier and Libow (1993a) were grounded in their earlier insistence that the Munchausen and by-proxy forms of the disorder are not in any real sense connected at all.

Although the test scores of MBPS parents seem much more substantial and extensive than the thin data on adult Munchausen's patients, they also have their shortcomings. The authors, to be fair, allude to some of these weaknesses at the beginning of their summary of MBPS parent data. The greatest problem with the data, they suggest, seems to center on the orientation of the test administrators, which differed significantly: two took an individual approach, whereas the other focused on family systems. But, even given these different orientations, Schreier and Libow are able to elicit some continuities and connections in the test data. Interestingly, they do this not only in the face of inconsistent testing methodologies, but also with full knowledge that one of the three test sample groups was interpreted by "a British clinical team [that] had access to extensive and detailed social, historical, and psychiatric data on their patients and were likely more aware of the presence of serious, if subtle, parent psychopathology in MBPS mothers . . ." (p. 170). This bit of information should, at the very least, raise some concern about the comparative consistency, if not the objectivity and validity, of this particular test result. After all, if the testers were already fully knowledgeable of "parent psychopathology"—which, it would seem, the tests are intended to reveal—then their interpretations might be significantly biased by such foreknowledge. This situation, however, does not really faze Schreier and Libow, and, as always, they go on to draw connections between these MBPS parent tests and conclusions about the subjects' respective behavior patterns. Their less than intrepid conclusion reads:

> This (*sic*) very scant data currently in the literature suggests that Munchausen by Proxy syndrome mothers may utilize more denial and dissociation

than adult Munchausen's syndrome patients while making a more conscious effort to appear psychologically healthy and functional. However, more subtle and indirect measures of assessment seem to yield the clearest evidence of psychopathology [pp. 172–173].

Despite the fact that the various test results say practically nothing useful or new about adult Munchausen's syndrome, its connection to MBPS, or MBPS parental behavior, the authors persevere in their desperate attempt to make this test material relevant. Their final effort at unraveling "the complexities of the dynamics and personalities underlying MBPS" (p. 173) consists of collating and interpreting detailed psychological data obtained from testing 12 MBPS mothers. The caveat on this material is that the clinicians and the mothers alike were under some restrictions when the tests were administered. The clinicians were "generally operating without an existing theoretical model or test profile" (p. 173), which, according to the authors, resulted in their basing their selection of test instruments on personal preference and familiarity. How much familiarity and personal preference they may have had regarding MBPS patients, without either a theoretical model or a test profile, remains an open, and potentially problematic, question. At any rate, the MBPS mothers tested were more aware of their own predicament. Indeed, Schreier and Libow warn the reader that the "Wechsler Test subscale scores" that show a generally low intellectual functioning might not be generalizable to the larger population of MBPS mothers because all of the mothers tested either "willingly" submitted to the testing or were ordered to do so by a court. The reason that this sample may be exceptional is: "It is quite possible that mothers of higher intellectual functioning and/or social class may not be caught as readily, may be less cooperative, or have access to legal representation that helps them to avoid court-ordered psychological assessment" (p. 173).

Without our going into excessive detail, it is important to note a serious oversight in the foregoing quote. The authors warn that the WAIS-R tests may not be generalizable because "higher intellectual functioning" MBPS mothers may avoid them or alter the final results in some way. But then they simply go on to generalize and find consistencies in the existing seven test scores that will, ultimately, be used to formulate a "psychological profile" of MBPS mothers. What is overlooked here, however, is that the seven mothers of "lower intellectual function" were tried and, presumably, convicted of various forms of child abuse, including poisoning and suffocation. If the absence of "higher intellectual functioning" MBPS mothers can, de jure, seriously affect the generalizability of the test data, why don't the real conditions affecting "lower intellectual functioning" mothers—mothers who have most likely been arrested, subjected to long, draining hearings or trials, convicted of abusing or killing their children, and, in some cases, incarcerated—also affect the results and generalizability of these tests?

We, of course, never find in Schreier and Libow's book anything that even remotely resembles a response to that question. Rather, the authors immerse us, inundate us, with an impressive flow of statistics, of seemingly objective numerical scores. None of these convicted MBPS mothers was able to attain a WAIS-R full-scale IQ score of higher than 92. One even fell into the dangerously "feeble-minded" range of 71. That all the women tested demonstrated low full-scale IQ scores was not, however, of much concern to the authors, who apparently failed to see a trend in this otherwise interesting phenomenon.

They were, however, able to find several trends in the various subtest scores. The subtests—a battery of performance and comprehension tests, ranging from picture arrangement to arithmetic—appeared, from the authors' standpoint, to yield certain data consistent with their own theoretical model. For instance, they point to the fact that Picture Arrangement (a task of sequencing cards depicting stories) was the highest subtest score for "several subjects" (actually, for three out of six). Using these data, the authors propose that "this finding suggests that these women can successfully focus on sequencing information about social relationships and interactions" (p. 174). And, further, if this is combined with their difficulty in using spatial and visual skills (five out of six subjects had higher scores in Picture Arrangement than in Object Assembly and their inability to express or even to comprehend the more abstract principles underlying social rules and expectations (lamentably, half the subjects [3] had higher Picture Arrangement than Comprehension scores), one can safely draw the conclusion that they are "likely to appear more socially adept than they are in terms of mature, abstract understanding of the social world" (p. 176).

Of course, this is precisely how MBPS mothers are *supposed* to appear. They are insidious and clever in their manipulation of the often overly caring physician, but yet are blithely unaware of the real social and psychological repercussions of such behavior. In fact, they are so cleverly manipulative that they can maintain their "masquerade" for years and often, through a virtually endless number of pediatrician and hospital visits, as Edith did (see Part III, chapter 6, this volume). What Schreier and Libow fail to point out, however, is that the subtest scores they have singled out neither are extraordinary within the full sample itself nor do they carry any unusual comparative weight if we view them in relation to a broad range of other subtest scores rather than limiting them to a single focus of comparison, as the authors do.

Regarding the former, we should point out that five of the seven subjects tested scored quite high in both the Digit Span and the Digit Symbol subtests. In fact, there appears to be a more substantial overall trend in the tests of these two performance categories than in that of Picture Arrangement. Yet we are never informed of what the high subtest scores in these performance categories might indicate. Regarding the latter, the only subtest comparison made by the authors is that between Picture Arrangement and Object Assembly and Comprehension skills, which of course yields the "self-fulfilling prophecy" of the authors' earlier stated diagnosis and etiology of MBPS. But what about other subtest comparisons? "Patient 11," for example, scored quite high on the Arithmetic subtest but rather low on the Picture Arrangement subtest (p. 176). Is this just an isolated anomaly, or does it indicate an example counter to the authors' comparisons, that is, good abstract reasoning skills but a poor ability to sequence information about social relationships and interactions. After all, this single inconsistent case represents 33% of the full positive sample referred to by the authors (three cases). Or do the consistently low Vocabulary scores in the sample have any bearing on the low Similarities scores of subjects? Might these relatively low Vocabulary scores have any effect on the subjects' ability, say, to "sequence information about social relationships"? Unanswered questions. We should also add that a perennial problem among psychometricians is that not only are WAIS subscale scores unstable, but difference scores based on between-subscale score comparisons are even markedly more unstable.

The MMPI data on these MBPS mothers are treated in a manner somewhat different from the data on the WAIS subtests. What distinguishes this section on psychological testing from others is the dexterity shown by the authors, who proceed to sustain their fully preconceived profile of MBPS mothers by neatly generalizing and tying together a host of what appear to be ungeneralizable trends and "themes" in the data. Given that there is a considerable amount of material in this section, a salient example will have to suffice.

The authors begin this section with a warning: "it is difficult to summarize and compress even this small number of MMPI profiles into a single meaningful description." But, even so, they feel that they can extrapolate themes from the data and confidently state that "the following themes from the profile configurations emerge" (p. 177). One of these "themes" emerges from the MMPI high negative scores in F–K Index, which, the authors stress, is "the most striking consistent finding in these nine MMPI protocols" (p. 177). The consistency here is that virtually all the subjects demonstrated (by their high negatives on F–K Index) that they were lacking in personal insight, highly defensive, or, even worse, were deliberately attempting to "fake good" and deny pathology as much as possible. The authors then admit that this "faking good" element could very well invalidate the protocol "by suppressing the overall profile toward the non-pathological range of scores" (p. 177). They also, for the first time in the chapter at least, take into consideration the fact that since *all* these evaluations were court ordered (a statement that appears to contradict an earlier one claiming that the evaluations were both willingly submitted to *and* court ordered), it might well affect the overall test results. But, in the end, they do not see this as a major problem, at least with regard to preserving their favored themes:

> While the fact that these evaluations were court-ordered could to some degree explain the motivation of the examinees to try to appear psychologically healthy in order to regain custody of their children or escape prosecution, these F–K Index scores are probably still diagnostically significant given that the clinical scale configurations give other supporting evidence of high denial and antisocial tendencies [pp. 177–178].

But what the authors seem to forget here is that, if a conscious motivation—the MBPS mothers' desire to regain custody of their children—can suppress the "overall profile toward the nonpathological range," why wouldn't the deeper and far more compelling force of the mothers' punitive circumstances move the profile toward the pathological range? In other words, what effect would the mothers' immediate circumstances have on the overall test results? Many of the described themes— "boastful," "reactive in the face of frustration," "flight of ideas," "overactivity"—might well be at least partially motivated by these MBPS mothers' continuing life situation. The inclusion of this variable might prove especially helpful on a test like this one, given the fact that the MMPI results are best interpreted when they are "correlated with other behaviors" (McCullough, 1992, p. 262).[17] What is also interesting in this regard is that the "faking bad" behavior indicated by the F–K Index of the adult Munchausen MMPIs is seen by the authors as sufficient reason to eliminate two sets (Sussman et al., 1987; O'Shea et al., 1982) of these test scores, while the "faking good" indicators in the F–K index of the MBPS mothers are routinely dismissed because of other "clinical scale configurations." In other words, you can't really be determined to be crazy if you are trying to be crazy; but you can, if you are trying not to be crazy—provided you are an MBPS mother in the first place.

Projective test data (TAT and Rorschach) provide an even better medium for creative statistical manipulation. The tests themselves are far more open to a broader range of interpretation and elaboration than either the intelligence or performative tests are, since both consist of creative operations on the part of the subjects themselves (i.e., story construction and projective figure identification). The authors, to be sure, take full advantage of this range of interpretation. They begin by stating that, even though the subjects were of "limited intellectual ability" and might show concern for the "legal implications of their evaluations," there was a broad spectrum of "pathology," from mothers with very loose association with "bizarre" and sometimes violent material, to "Polyannish" stories with "magical problem resolutions" (Schreier and Libow, 1993a, p. 180). The MBPS mothers also demonstrated overall undertones of dysphoric feeling, which was described mainly as "frustration," "dissatisfaction," or "sadness" about loss. Consequently, "several of the other protocols describe characters who passively try to resist doing what is expected of them but ultimately are presented as helpless in terms of having an impact on events in their stories" (p. 180).

Now, if we consider that all the women tested were subjected to punitive conditions (if they were all ordered by the court to take the tests, then they must at least have been indicted on some criminal charge or remanded to family court), and the fact that in at least two of these

---

17. James Neal Butcher (1990) makes a similar point with regard to MMPI profiles: "The interpretation of any psychological test proceeds best in the context of a personal history. Important aspects of the case—for example, ethnic group membership, education level, marital status, and the presence of precipitating stressor or trauma—are important variables to consider when MMPI-2 profiles are interpreted. Errors of interpretation can occur if MMPI-2, or other test protocols, are considered apart from nontest parameters" (p. 21).

cases the mothers seemed to be facing murder or manslaughter charges, the imagery in these stories may very well recount or be motivated by their current situations rather than any deeply rooted pathology. After all, mothers who have abused their children, been arrested, tried, subjected to court-ordered tests, who may face having their children removed from their custody, and possible long-term incarceration would tend actually to be "dysphoric." They might also invent "Pollyannish" stories with fairy tale endings or feel helpless about having an impact on events in their stories.

There is another curious oversight in the section on TAT scores. The authors describe several other protocols as distinctly featuring "characters whose murderous or suicidal impulses got out of control and resulted in unintentional murder." The various examples chosen by the authors read as follows:

> For example, one patient described a woman who chokes a man to death but "the thoughts running through her head is she wished she didn't have done it." Another patient told a story about another loss of control involving both sexual and aggressive impulses: "He killed her. He didn't mean to but he did . . . killed her by accident. He did whoopee too much . . . he goes to jail, and get a long sentence." Another example is the patient who described murderous feelings that got out of control when a small disagreement between husband and wife escalated into the husband bludgeoning the wife to death. "After he realized that she was dead he couldn't believe what he'd done" [p. 181].

The authors interpret these stories as indicating that the patients themselves "vacillate between states of passive helpless resentment and the fear of explosive anger with unintended murderous consequences" (p. 181), which neatly fits the preconceived notion of how an MBPS mother should feel and act. But there are certainly a number of other possible interpretations of these protocols. One that immediately comes to mind is that the women were not revealing their own murderous feelings but, rather, were conveying feelings of horror about the real abuse and battering to which they themselves might well have been subjected.[18] Most of the aggression cited here is male initiated. With the exception of the first example, one of the women in the stories had been "killed by

---

18. The authors do make reference to physical and sexual abuse near the end of this chapter (see pp. 184–185). Their response recognizes the outside interpretations of experts on TAT and Rorschach tests, which indicate that the protocols are

accident" by a man and the other was "bludgeoned to death" by her husband. The first instance, in which the woman kills the man, could very well indicate feelings of retribution or frustration directed at an abusive male figure. Given the significant number of incidents of abuse in the family backgrounds and case histories of many MBPS mothers, this possibility should have at least been taken into consideration as an alternate reading. Perhaps even more remarkable about this oversight is that the authors actually claim that "some of the stories seemed to suggest a perception of men as more nurturing and supportive figures than women" (p. 181). "Some of the stories" turn out to be an unspecified number of those of "patient 6." Including these data does fit nicely with the supposedly compulsive need that MBPS mothers have for nurturing males, particularly physicians. All this male "nurturing," it should be added, is despite the fact that three out of the eight mothers tested either were killed by or killed the male antagonists in their stories.

---

often weighted toward abuse. The authors acknowledge that this may be a factor in the interpretations, but they further state that only two subjects in the testing sample openly reported abuse. Since fear of reporting abuse and other forms of domestic violence is common, particularly among women who themselves are accused of abusing their children, the issue of possible abuse would require further consideration and study.

It should also be noted that the authors are at considerable odds with a large portion of studies of child abuse (Burgess and Draper, 1989: Leehan and Wilson, 1985). Schreier and Libow attribute little causative value to abuse in the family background of the MBPS mother/perpetrator. In fact, there are only two brief index listings of background family abuse involving MBPS mothers. Such a paucity of information is extraordinarily unusual; most studies of child abuse in general find the abusive background of the parent to be a major contributing factor in the abuse of the child. In fact, in a particular instance, the authors seem to go out of their way to argue that reports of childhood sexual and physical abuse initially suffered by the parent herself may very well be part of the MBPS mother's "exaggerated medical history" (p. 93n).

Eliminating a commonly accepted causal factor underlying child abuse seems to have been advanced, at least in part, to support the authors' novel etiology for MBPS in the first place. To weaken consideration of such a factor as the MBPS mother's own possible abuse, the primacy of the mother–doctor dyad appears to remain relatively more immune to the complications of competing—and historically and empirically better established—etiological claims. The only support advanced for this unusual elimination of the mother's own possible abuse is, once again, Rosenberg's study (1987) (which we have addressed at length) and a handful of other professional articles that, the authors claim, only "inconsistently" uncover early parental abuse.

A further attempt to legitimate these data, and, most important, the authors' reading of the data, is made by submitting selected results to experts in TAT and Rorschach interpretation. In the matter of the TAT, there may be a particularly subtle subterfuge at work. The authors inform us that they sent five of the TAT protocols to Drew Westen, director of psychology at The Cambridge Hospital in Massachussets. Westen returned an assessment that was notable in its partial confirmation of some of the authors' initial interpretations. For example, he confirmed their reading of a "minimal sense of causality in the social realm," while also stressing "defensiveness," "loss" and "sexualized aggression." What we are not told, however, is why only five of the eight protocols were sent to Westen, or even which ones were sent. If the authors suppressed protocols that presented data inconsistent with their own readings, such an omission would no doubt significantly alter the results. If, for instance, they eliminated all three of the protocols that contained stories referring to killing or being killed, would the interpretation still be weighted toward "defensiveness" and "sexual aggression?" At any rate, Westen's interpretation also contains some interesting insights:

> Defensively, most of the responses are "shut down," as the subjects appear to be clamping down on associations to painful experiences, perhaps of abuse, and their internal lives more generally. Denial is prominent, and many of the protocols have a childish quality, although it is difficult to know how much of this may reflect age or intellectual factors as much as psychopathology or emotional issues [cited in Schreier and Libow, 1993a, p. 182].

Perhaps the best way to conclude our critique of this chapter on psychological testing is to turn to the authors' own concluding remarks. On the surface, the remarks are sympathetic to MBPS mothers; they focus mainly on the fact that many women are treated by society in a biased way. Women are undervalued and neglected emotionally. They experience lack of recognition, which in turn may contribute to a disorder that is marked by defensiveness and denial. While the authors are correct in their initial conclusions, the entire chapter—indeed, the entire book—does not really deal with these problems in any substantial way. Rather, what seems really to be at stake is establishing a profile of the "classic" MBPS mother that corresponds perfectly to the diagnosis and etiology advanced in *Hurting for Love*. In this particular chapter, the profile is accomplished by stipulating that there is an "impressive consistency in the patterns of these mothers" regarding all the earlier mentioned diagnostic and etiological characteristics of MBPS: defensive styles, denial, self-centeredness, intense passive conformity, dependency on males, and so on.

We say "stipulated" because, as we have demonstrated, the relatively small number of test samples, the authors' skewed interpretations, the prevailing testing conditions—not to mention the questionable validity and reliability of psychological testing itself—fail to meet even the most basic standards for objectively and validly establishing the authors' proposed conclusions. If we take a straight count of those test subjects represented in the entire chapter, we find that they total approximately 39 (exact numbers are not given for some of the adult Munchausen tests). About 23 of these subjects fall under the category of adult Munchausen patients. Given that the authors themselves, seeking to sever the two "syndromes," argue at some length that the connection is only nominal, and given that very little, if any, conclusive data are drawn from these tests, it seems reasonable to eliminate this group from the overall total. That leaves us with 16 subjects (12 from "colleagues' tests" and four from professional papers). In the case of the 12 patients, varying tests were administered. Three subjects took a relatively complete battery of tests. Others took only two or three tests. Eight out of the 12 subjects took projective tests, but we are not, for example, told how many pictures were used in the TAT to elicit stories from each subject. The conclusions drawn by the authors, then, are based on only three relatively complete batteries of tests and nine relatively incomplete sets of testing data. Without corresponding test scores for all the subjects, it is difficult to draw such distinct conclusions from the available data, not to mention that sufferers from this "pervasive and underreported" disorder are being profiled on the basis of two small sets of incomplete test scores (16 subjects), which, in both cases, were not administered by the authors themselves.[19]

There is also little detailed mention of the conditions under which the 16 subjects were tested. Testing conditions often are a significant

---

19. Butcher (1990) also makes a point of the need for "direct contact" between the therapist and the MMPI-2 test subject: "Blind interpretations of test profiles can provide general information about a client's symptoms and behavior. These impressions, however, need to be verified by direct patient contact" (p. 21).

variable in test results. The skill of the examiner on WAIS-R tests, for example, is usually considered of singular importance, as the examiner will often be called on to eliminate one or more subtests, depending on the prevailing test conditions (e.g., time constraints). Overall reliability of the WAIS-R test may also be seriously compromised "when the client is anxious or tense, heavily medicated, or otherwise impaired" (McCullough, 1992, p. 280). TATs require highly skilled, expert examiners, as their interpretations tend to be more subjective than those of most other tests.

The importance of test conditions is likewise plainly demonstrated, for example, in Gould (1981). He argues that army intelligence tests administered in the earlier part of the century were so skewed against minority and poor, uneducated recruits, that the exam became virtually useless (pp. 194–214). Gould also argues that the widely varying conditions under which the protocols were administered clearly affected the end results. Many recruits were required to take the exam in extraordinarily hot and uncomfortable conditions; many were badgered by the examiners, both for disciplinary reasons and time restraints. Similar conditions might have affected the test scores of the MBPS mothers, although we cannot know this for certain. Their tests, we are told, were collected from different professional papers, on one hand, and, on the other, from tests of MBPS mothers "seen by a number of our colleagues." There appears to have been no uniform standard for or control applied to the varying testing conditions. Indeed, from time to time, the authors themselves warn us of special conditions that prevailed. Combine these warnings with the fact that all the mothers were tested under court order, that some, at least, had been arrested, had undergone a preliminary hearing, and may have been subjected to a long trial, and the possibility that the test conditions were a significant variable in the overall scores becomes increasingly real.

In the end, the chapter on psychological testing does not really differ substantially from any other chapter of *Hurting for Love*. Ostensibly, the authors set out to develop a relatively objective profile of MBPS mothers for strictly legal purposes. They give the appearance of being completely detached and circumspect in all their interpretations and claims. But, beyond this appearance, there is an underlying and powerful motivation—an apperception, perhaps—both to fulfill and to legitimate their own medical and social agenda, one that is driven by the etiological, diagnostic, and theoretical trappings of the relationship between

MBPS mothers and their physicians. What under other conditions might represent significant methodological difficulties—that is, insufficient data, unknown testing conditions, external stressors—is here largely overlooked or evaded. All this, it seems, is to elaborate a profile that would remain consistent in the way it might be viewed by professionals in related fields and within the context of the argumentative structure of *Hurting for Love* itself. To paraphrase F. Allen Hanson (1993, p. 7), the psychological test data used by Schreier and Libow do not so much corroborate and record the behaviors associated with MBPS as they help *invent* them.

MEDICAL–LEGAL "DILEMMAS": MANAGING MBPS

Do not become enamored of power

—*Michel Foucault*

The two final chapters of *Hurting for Love* deal with the legal and management issues of MBPS, respectively. The chapters are related to the extent that both seek to provide a sort of working hypothesis regarding the treatment of MBPS "perpetrator" mothers and their children within the framework of the medical and legal establishments. This working hypothesis (what Schreier and Libow term "an effective response" to MBPS), however, is weighted toward the pervasive, though unstated, goal of the entire text: to legitimate the nearly absolute power of the physician so as 1) to determine the "correct" diagnosis and etiology of a "disorder," 2) to determine the disposition of all the parties involved (notably, the MBPS mother and the child), and 3) to be in a position to control the full range of MBPS's social, institutional, and legal ramifications. This desire to legitimate the physician's authority involves a number of interesting strategies, many of which, remarkably, aim to undermine or evade the conventionally established legal rights and precedents that would otherwise devolve to the MBPS mother. Rather, these will be largely suppressed in the authors' drive to intervene on behalf of the child, who is alleged to be the victim of the mother's abusive behavior. In short, these two chapters represent an activist (or, perhaps better, reactivist) attempt selectively to circumvent common legal safeguards and due process in the treatment of MBPS mothers. The goal stresses instead a set of punitive and surveillant operations originating with the physician's presumed authority and implemented by the professional hospital staff.

Because the battery of psychological tests administered to what are claimed to be MBPS mothers are incapable of establishing a reliable profile for the MBPS "disorder," it is not surprising that Schreier and Libow present their psychological test data *after* having discussed the viability of therapeutic practice.[20] In the absence of objectively specifying exactly who is an actual or potential MBPS mother, any discussion of therapy becomes somewhat otiose. The authors, in their rush to avert any potential damage to the child caused by parental abuse, largely pass over their earlier claim of wanting to "treat" such MBPS women. Their attempts to devise a plausible therapy for the MBPS mother are thus effectively dropped, and this for two reasons. On one hand, the literature shows no practical or effective means of treatment; on the other, their principal concern, and a very real concern it is, is to prevent the possibility of child abuse in general, and its dreadful companion, SIDS.[21] These two factors—namely that psychological testing indicates little or nothing about the MBPS mother, as well as their concession that psychological or psychiatric therapy is effectively nonexistent—permit their deeper concerns to emerge: the child, above all, must be spared the potential of abuse. The authors maintain that the only reliable means of demonstrably establishing child abuse, at least in a hospital setting, is through covert videotaping, that is, to "catch" a mother in the act of

---

20. Although an entire chapter is devoted to "Psychotherapeutic Work with MBPS Patients," the authors acknowledge that to date there remains little "information about psychotherapy and the healing process." Indeed, they remark, "To a large degree this vacuum is due to the unwillingness of identified Munchausen patients to seek therapeutic help, to use words rather than physical symptoms to express their pain, and to achieve the insight and skills necessary to discard Munchausen behaviors" (pp. 149–150). Remarkably, then, the failure of therapy—even in the absence of established therapeutic practices—lies once again with the patient. The only positive suggestion made by Schreier and Libow in the entire chapter is to warn the therapist about the dangers of countertransference, whereby the physician may be tempted to fall into the deceptive snares of the dissimulating patient.
21. The authors devote an appendix to SIDS and cite several authors, notably Meadow, who relate breathing disorders, especially induced infant apnea, as possible clinical indications of both MBPS and SIDS. Reported cases of child abuse rose dramatically in the 1980s, as did reported cases of SIDS.

abusing her child. The elaborate discussion of the MBPS mother–child dyad—bound by the mother's fetishizing of the child in the attempt to gain the respect, trust, love, and affection from the physician—becomes a concern at best secondary to obtaining irrefutable photographic evidence to document child abuse.

The objective of establishing convincing evidence of actual child abuse becomes the single dominating concern of the latter part of their work. In practical terms, any concerns for the MBPS mother—her diagnosis, her treatment, therapy, and ongoing care—come to a halt. The entire syndrome now becomes transformed into a series of "management" and "legal" interventions, initiated solely on behalf of the child and performed by the directing physician and the hospital staff. MBPS therapy is replaced with a series of well-planned means to remove the child from the mother's care, to obtain court intervention and social services placement for the child, and to "recommend" court-mandated, long-term psychiatric therapy (however unsuccessful that is, as the authors themselves admit) for the mother. Of course, long-term, court-mandated psychiatric therapy would confirm the assertion that the MBPS mother is unstable, if not dangerous, and thus incapable of properly looking after her child in the first place—all the more reason for social services to intervene and supervise the outplacement of her child. Effectively, then, the entire discussion of MBPS—its etiology, diagnosis, treatment, and therapy—devolves to a single issue: the presence or absence of videotaped surveillance demonstrating an act of child abuse. The entire diagnostic apparatus, which sought to establish MBPS as a distinctive disorder, as a unique and "much underdiagnosed syndrome," now becomes secondary to preventive and punitive concerns. The only positive determination of this allegedly complex syndrome is precisely the common denominator for all child abuse, namely, demonstrated child abuse.[22]

Although this sounds like a practical, legal, and humane way of controlling MBPS child abuse, there are numerous legal and ethical implications involved in the whole process of gathering evidence, particularly by covert surveillance. In this regard, the authors provide extensive and

---

22. After extensively reviewing the MBPS literature, Judge Miller would summarize the determinations of the offending MBPS mother's behavior, in the case of "Jessica Z": "The child's illness is the only reliable symptom of the mother's disorder" (Miller, 1987, p. 13).

detailed guidance on what evidence is considered to be admissible in the court of law, in the prosecution of MBPS mothers. They indicate three important elements that the pediatrician/social worker/psychology consultant ought to beware of: 1) the importance of the admissibility of indirect evidence; 2) the acceptability of the use of professional opinion as evidence; and 3) the surveillance of MBPS mothers using covert videotape monitoring. To satisfy the first two factors, the authors call on the personal and professional initiative of doctors to make an unusual and prolonged sacrifice of their time to establish the presence of MBPS abuse. Indeed, by calling attention to the MBPS mother within the legal system, the doctor may well be burdened by a long "process of evidence gathering, testimony, acrimonious relations with the press and defense attorneys" (Schreier and Libow, 1993a, p. 190). In other words, the physician's centrality in determining the legal implications of the case is highly significant. The inordinate burden falling on the physician regarding these legal matters may not, of itself, appear to be particularly unusual, but the amount of latitude given the physician regarding the covert surveillance of suspected MBPS behavior is extraordinary.

As we discussed earlier, surreptitious videotaping in a hospital setting is not a simple matter. Indeed, in their thoughtful article on the ethical use of covert videotaping, D. M. Foreman and C. Farsides (1993) make a very strong argument for implementing a procedure that would guarantee the legal rights of the mother, the child, and the physicians involved and that would assure the active participation of the proper legal authorities. Such a procedure would follow the strict guidelines stated in the British Children Act. This act assigns the primary responsibility of investigating child abuse to the local authorities, but it is broad enough to include an insistence on establishing a partnership with the parents, even in those cases where active abuse by those same parents is suspected. In certain important respects, the Children Act is designed to require permission from the concerned parties to conduct an investigation of child abuse allegations. Foreman and Farsides argue that the logic of this stipulation within the Children Act serves precisely to remove the management of child abuse cases, especially MBPS cases, from the exclusive domain of physicians (p. 611). One of the problems they see with physicians' personal demand for surveillance is that such a recourse actively involves them, as physicians, in inducing the MBPS behavior they found so reprehensible in the first place.

Our objection to covert videoing is that "information to act on" is not the same as certainty. If a doctor is sufficiently confident that someone has Munchausen's syndrome by proxy, then allowing an additional event to prove this does harm without any useful gain in knowledge, which is unethical. Proof can be obtained by less contentious investigations, such as careful interviewing of multiple informants or a trial of physical separation between carer and child. As these methods present less risk to the child, covert videoing can be ethical only if they fail to provide sufficient evidence. It cannot be substituted for them [p. 611].

Apparently unmoved by such ethical considerations, Schreier and Libow (1993a) counsel a much different course of action for medical practitioners regarding covert videotaping. In brief, they strongly advocate that, once "convinced" that a child's life is at stake, physicians and other associated health care workers should take matters into their own hands. Largely following the advice offered by Meadow (1985), the authors defend violations of privacy rights and due process by painting a grim picture of the effort to detect abuse by MBPS mothers—a futile process described as "exponentially more difficult" than the detection of standard forms of child abuse (Schreier and Libow, 1993a, p. 193). They further make a case for immediate medical intervention by stating that "nonconcealed close human observation of a child in a hospital is difficult and far from infallible" and that reports of severe abuse are, in the authors' experience at least, "usually futile in the absence of hard evidence" (p. 193). Besides, other measures, like confronting the mother or her husband (if she has one), often do not lead to a cessation of the endangering behavior. In fact, these sorts of confrontations "may even cause the parents to intensify their efforts to demonstrate that the child is really ill" (p. 193), or, in certain cases, may drive them to relocate.

The only choice, then, is between protecting the child's life—who, the authors stress, cannot speak for himself—or violating the parents' constitutionally guaranteed rights to privacy and due process. Schreier and Libow argue that such a dilemma is only apparent, however. The decision to violate the MBPS parents' rights may be perfectly legitimate, they maintain, given an obscure Supreme Court ruling, *Burdeau vs. McDowell* (1921). It seems that as a rule, the Fourth, Fifth, and Sixth Amendment rights of protection from unreasonable searches and seizures and against self-incrimination, and the Fourteenth Amendment's due process clause are sufficient to exclude evidence that is surreptitiously obtained. But these protections apply only to officials

working under the direction of some specific law enforcement or government agency. They do not apply to private parties that might collect
evidence covertly. The authors argue that physicians and other hospital
personnel may be considered private parties for purposes of this exclusion. In other words, as "private parties," physicians may choose to
videotape suspected MBPS mothers covertly *without* violating their
constitutional rights.[23]

The authors also repeatedly stress that the various covert interventions should be kept strictly within the closed confines of the medical
institution itself. This is done in a subtle way. After stating several cursory warnings about the rights violations involved in covertly searching
the personal belongings of suspected MBPS parents, the authors cite
articles describing instances in which in-hospital closed-circuit video
monitoring would be justified as a means of protecting the baby. This
restricted surveillance would, of course, allow hospital personnel—who
would have the final say on the gravity of an abuse situation—to circumvent obtaining appropriate search or show cause warrants. This
suggestion is accompanied by several quotes from an article by Southall
and colleagues (1987) which demonstrably supports the use of police-
managed video surveillance and the breach of confidentiality. They also
quote Meadow (1987) at length, who, quite emphatically, defends
Southall and his colleagues (Schreier and Libow, 1993a, p. 194). To add
to this growing litany of medical self-governance, the authors cite
Williams and Bevan (1988), who strongly recommend that a small
group of hospital insiders, led by a consulting pediatrician, and staffed
by other medical consultants, a social worker and a senior nurse, should
be the final authority in determining whether covert surveillance should
proceed (pp. 780–781). This article is particularly distinctive in its stress
on restricting decision making on surveillance to members of the hospital staff and to hold dissenters within the hospital to "strict confidentiality." The secretive and limited nature of this sort of decision is even

---

23. The decision in *Burdeau vs. McDowell* (1921) was not unanimous. The two dissenters, Justices Brandeis and Holmes, argued that even though the private seizure
of evidence may have been constitutional, the same results might have been
obtained by other, proper, means. They concluded their dissent with the rather
striking observation that "in the development of our liberty insistence upon procedural regularity has been a large factor. Respect for law will not be advanced by
resort, in its enforcement, to means which shock the common man's sense of
decency and fair play" (p. 477).

extended to the family's general practitioner. On this, Schreier and Libow (1993a) write: "Consultation with the family's general practitioner is *not* felt to be useful and may be inappropriate because of the conflict of loyalty that he or she would then feel" (p. 195). This general claim, it should be noted, is based on one incident experienced by the authors involving an uncooperative family practitioner (p. 195).

The question of whether or not to inform the police and other authorities provides yet another pretext for establishing medical hegemony over MBPS and its supposed sufferers. Typically, the authors initiate the discussion by feigning a "balanced" view of the rights and obligations of all parties involved in notifying law enforcement authorities. They set up the now familiar bifurcation: "It is unclear whether an appropriate search warrant for hospital surveillance is the better route or whether the 'private party approach' is more appropriate" (p. 195). This assertion is directly followed by quotes from two professional articles that seem to present opposing views of surveillance and police involvement. On closer inspection, however, both appear to favor unrestrained medical intervention. The first article gives the impression of full enthusiasism about the prospect of video evidence's being admissible in court. That article cites a number of incidents in which such evidence led to convictions; the other article seems more circumspect about such interventions but nonetheless only warns that the physician must not be overzealous and must take the parents' legal rights into consideration (p. 195). Schreier and Libow tend to dismiss even these vestiges of medical restraint by stressing the enormous difficulties that members of the judicial and social services systems might have in understanding the whole MBPS phenomenon: "Underlying our concern is the lack of knowledge and inability to appreciate the potential for parental causation of the child's serious recurrent illness on the part of the protective or judicial system" (p. 195). The solution to this extremely complex issue is simple: go ahead and videotape.

> Given the potential for severe risk in this disorder, the helplessness of the infant, and the great skill of the parent at hiding the abuse, we think that surreptitious surveillance is sometimes necessary. After all, physicians often screen for toxins in blood drawn from other tests, without parental consent. Telemetry, involving video monitoring of children, is becoming a common part of medical practice, particularly in hospitals. It has been argued that this type of surveillance does not involve entrapment by enticing the parent or in any way changing the environment in a fashion that might induce

behaviors. . . . We feel that as MBPS becomes firmly recognized as a disorder, surveillance will be seen as part of the standard treatment for documenting abuse [p. 196].

Before we discuss Schreier and Libow's account of the management
and control of the MBPS scourge, we must point out two extremely
important, though, totally unaddressed, implications in the foregoing
statements regarding MBPS "private party" surveillance. First, the argument that a "preverbal infant's life" or "severe risk" may be at stake in
the MBPS relation and that some form of covert surveillance is therefore needed and justified is so general as to be virtually useless.[24] MBPS,
as it is described by the authors and others, *always* poses a potentially
life-threatening danger to the infant or child involved. Forms of abuse
associated with MBPS, by the authors' own admission, are so varied and
complex that one can hardly predict either the precise nature of the
purported behavior or even what sort of medically deceptive stratagem
or device the abusing parent might be using. Inducing apnea, for
instance, could eventually lead to suffocation. The use of prescription
and over-the-counter medications sometimes leads to death or serious
injury in the child-victim. Tampering with the urinary tract can often
lead to dangerous or deadly sepsis. Even a physician's care could eventually wind up killing the child. (Indeed, the generality of MBPS causes
closely corresponds to Asher's configurations for adult Munchausen's.)

The threat of death or serious injury to a child, and particularly to an
infant, is present, then, in virtually every alleged case of MBPS. If this
suspicion is honored, then the physician has virtually total freedom to
choose to intervene. He may designate a case of apnea inducement or
ipecac poisoning as life threatening and, as a private, concerned party,
may at any time violate the personal and privacy rights of the suspected
MBPS parent. This possibility is particularly troublesome when one
considers that there is really no fool-proof way of determining MBPS
other than actually catching the perpetrators "red-handed" by videotaping them in the act of abuse. In effect, the decision to videotape is

---

24. Surveillance could be justified in the course of a particular case of suspected
child abuse when a definite pattern of suspected abuse emerged. The case might
involve a parent who consistently removed feeding tubes from the child when the
nurse or physician left the hospital room or an adult who allegedly repeatedly
struck a child on a particular street corner every day on his return home from
school.

initially made on the basis of uncertain and inadequate evidence, so as, ultimately, to "produce" direct evidence, which would have been the principal justification for videotaping in the first place. Due process is ignored, if not largely inverted, by precisely such a move, since everyone who has a child with a diagnostically troublesome illness would thereby be suspect.

The second point to be made regards the degree of legal power ceded to doctors. One shudders to think of doctors—who, arguably, know as little about the subtleties of legal matters and constitutional rights as judicial and social service authorities know about MBPS behavior— being placed in a position of virtually absolute authority regarding the disposition and determination of certain cases within the medical ambit. Although there are calls in Schreier and Libow's chapter on legal issues for "consultation" and careful deliberation of these matters, nonetheless, the "doctrine" of self-initiated covert action provides a con- venient means of evading many, if not most, of these expressed obliga- tions and responsibilities. The problem also arises in this regard as to what limitations can be placed or enforced on medical personnel in their zeal to "protect life." Could, for instance, a doctor who is being sued for malpractice by a terminal cancer patient surreptitiously record evidence favorable to his case on the grounds that a long, agonizing court trial could hasten the patient's death? Might an aspiring physi- cian/detective—someone seeking the "preconditions" for criminal behavior in the hospital—invoke the "private party" precedent in order to realize his "a priori" suspicions? And, in the end, who would be answerable for this sort of behavior by physicians or other medical per- sonnel? The institution? The particular individual involved? What agency would redress the grievances of "violated" and "abused" victims of wrongful or unwarranted surveillance? Unfortunately, the authors provide us with no answers to these vexing questions.

It is not unusual that we receive no answers to these troubling ethical and legal questions regarding physician initiative and jurisdiction. The underlying purpose, as we have often stated, of the whole argumenta- tive and theoretical structure of this chapter, and of *Hurting for Love* in general, is to establish complete hegemony for those physicians who are able to diagnose MBPS. With the removal of the mother–doctor dyad and the mother–child dyad, as the central motif of medical power and determination, the seemingly far less problematic route to the central- ity of the physician—the complete, unrestricted power to determine the

CHAPTER 6

existence of MBPS through covert surveillance—suddenly becomes enormously attractive. Hence, each consecutive stage of the legal issues chapter addresses precisely this hegemonic possibility, although often in liberalized terms. The initial "dilemma" is cleverly erected: the "preverbal infant" is at dire risk; should the physician take the baby's possible death as justification for possibly violating the parents' constitutional rights? After some obligatory soul searching, the answer is an unqualified yes.

This determination, in turn, places the doctor directly and exclusively at the center of the entire decision-making process. He alone is able to determine definitively the existence of the very disorder that has continually frustrated him and that most certainly will escape his less knowledgeable colleagues, not to mention other hospital personnel. He will maintain his authority in the face of other concerned agencies, since he is capable of providing the irrefutable evidence that is necessary to their very function. The authors insist that outside agencies are reluctant to deal with MBPS perpetrators without hard evidence. In short, the MBPS specialist will institute a medical "fiefdom," where he permits himself to act in violation of commonly guaranteed rights; where it is not necessary to inform local authorities of possible criminal behavior (by the purported MBPS mother, much less by the surveillant physician); where he can make clear that anyone opting out of surveillance "must be held to strict confidence" (i.e., to the physician himself); where he may determine, on subjectively arrived at evidential grounds and without extensive consultation, that a life is at stake; where he may form small consultation groups, but, according to Williams and Bevan (1988) only groups consisting of underlings; where he does not even have to consult with the family practitioners of his patients (pp. 780–781). All this authority devolves to the physician despite the fact that he is not yet able to establish his centrality in managing MBPS—or, we should add, despite the fact that he is not yet able to establish the very existence of the disorder itself.

With little indication of a typical MBPS profile, with no sure psychological testing data to confirm or disconfirm such a profile, with complete disarray, disagreement, and perplexity as to what constitutes therapy for the MBPS mother, much less, what the prognosis is for the MBPS child, Schreier and Libow (1993a) nonetheless conclude their extensive treatment of the MBPS phenomenon with a set of prescriptive strategies for its "management." Schreier and Libow commence their account with a summary of purported "signs," which would serve as "guidelines for suspecting and identifying MBPS" (p. 202). The series of "signs" they advance is taken, once again, from the previous literature in the field, extending from Meadow (1977) through Kaufman et al. (1989). Thirteen of these "most commonly noted signs" (p. 202) are given in series, with no analysis of them whatsoever, nor is there any indication of which of these signs may be relatively more or less important in raising "suspicions about MBPS."[25] Nor is there any explanation of how many of the 13 signs may constitute a base for the suspicion, nor of which configuration of signs may be telling. One could, for example, take one or two of the signs they advance and come up with what appears to be a highly suspect parent. Alternatively, one could select several of the signs and find absolutely no suggestion of MBPS. A parent with "an emotionally distant relationship with her spouse," who "reports dramatically negative events, such as house fires, burglaries, car accidents," and works "in the health care field" would hardly exhibit a combination of characteristics that strongly point to MBPS. Would an X-ray technician with a difficult marriage and whose house was recently broken into qualify for court-mandated child placement and long-term psychiatric care, simply because a physician's suspicions were raised by these three "signs"? On the other hand, a single sign, for example, "a child who presents with one or more medical problems that do not respond to treatment or that follow an unusual course that is persistent, puzzling, and unexplainable" might well serve as a strong indication to suspect possible abuse.

Moreover, the language involved here is extremely provocative. This listing of signs by which one might suspect a parent in certain instances contains phrases like the "suspected parent" (p. 203). These signs, which are meant to raise suspicions, state the "suspicion" in the very description of the parent herself. To indicate suspicion, it seems enough to predetermine that the parent is a "suspect" in the first place. All this variant of the "liar's paradox" does is to tell us that the suspect is suspicious. In other cases, the purported warning signs are simply contradictory: a parent who is calm in regarding her child's treatment and is at the same time "highly supportive and encouraging of the

---

25. For an interesting analysis of these signs and an alternative view to the prevailing model, see "Guidelines for Suspecting and Identifying Munchausen Syndrome by Proxy," on the M.A.M.A. website (www.msbp.com).

physician" is held to be suspect of MBPS. But, at the same time—and according to the same announced indication—the mother who is not calm, who is "angry," and who, far from encouraging the physician, devalues the medical staff and demands further medical intervention is equally suspect of MBPS.

One particularly troubling "sign" of the MBPS "Guidelines for Suspecting and Identifying MBPS" (pp. 202–203) is the observation that the child's health improves when he or she is removed from the parent. Indeed, when all else fails, this guideline intuitively seems to be a reliable marker for MBPS abuse. Simply stated, when in the parent's care the child is ill; when removed, the child improves. Missing from this forumla, however, is the vast number of reasons for the improvement in the child's health improving, as well as the occluded fact that, in some cases, the child's health worsens. Often in cases of suspected MBPS abuse, the child is removed by Child Protective Services (or a similar public agency) and placed into hospital care or into a situation where there is readily available and effective medical care.

Such was clearly the case in the instance of an appellate court decision (Kawamoto, 1996). In affirming the judgment of the circuit court, which found J.N.'s parents innocent of any child abuse, the presiding judge decided that "J.N.'s improvement was not the result of his parents' inability to care for him but rather the result of more effective treatment for his illness" (p. 19). Besides hospitalization and better medical care for removed children, there are many psychological and emotional factors that can also contribute to the improvement. Moreover, certain childhood illness that are often associated with MBPS abuse, such as apnea, frequently improve, if not disappear entirely, with the passing of time. Such would also be the case with allergic or other environmentally related disorders. A child presenting respiratory problems associated with environmental factors would most likely show marked improvement if removed to a more salubrious climate.

Nonetheless, this "sign" of suspected MBPS abuse—that the child's health improves upon removal from the family—is often held to be the single most important marker, in the absence of any verifiable parental abuse, for imposing the MBPS diagnosis. Serving as an expert witness for the prosecution in the Ellen Storck case, for example, Schreier himself—never having interviewed Ms. Storck—felt completely assured that the diagnosis was MBPS, precisely because her son's apnea disappeared when he was removed from her care. Judge D. Freundlich (1993) remarked:

> Dr. Schreier testified that based on the profile of Ms. S provided him and an examination of [the child's] medical records, coupled with the complete absence of any apnea once [the child] was removed from his mother, that this was a case of MSP [i.e., MBPS]. Dr. Schreier also went on to explain why he felt it unimportant that he had not interviewed Ms. S. MSP [MBPS] is a very complex syndrome and the most perplexing facet is the ability of the parent to present an extremely caring and credible adult, one who would never be suspected of inducing or fabricating illness, yet an adult capable of lying consistently. He himself cannot discern from parent interviews who is telling the truth and who is not. Again, the final piece to complete the picture is the abatement of the illness in the absence of the parent; regardless of the parent factors, if the child remains ill when removed completely from the parent then there is no MSP [pp. 17–18].

To enhance the set of signs for suspecting and identifying MBPS, Schreier and Libow (1993a) append a set of "guidelines for verifying MBPS"—again, without so much as mentioning what constitutes a defining set of suspect signs. Nonetheless, they claim that the MBPS diagnosis "can be verified or rejected in a speedy fashion" (p. 203). Again invoking the common sources in the literature, the authors advance some 18 guidelines for verification. Principally, these guidelines enjoin the physician to seek verification of the disorder through surveillance, review of medical histories, case histories, interviews with concerned parties, medical testing and screening, and so on. Given all these operations, one is fairly well certain—eventually—to come up with a disorder that plausibly appears to be MBPS, especially if that is what the examining physician is being advised to pursue. Indeed, the authors, who seem to be concerned about the reliability of the medical testing procedures—that these procedures may not demonstrate the intended results—counsel that "the range of possible falsification [by MBPS parents] is beyond most screening tests." This concern to assure physicians that MBPS is really present, even if it appears not to be, is continually underscored, and perhaps reaches its apex in the final guideline for verifying MBPS, in which the authors stress that "the fact that these children often have a previously *explained* disorder, should not deter suspicions. Previously explained disorders in MBPS make it harder to suspect falsifications, *but* they do not negate the presence of past and current *un*explained disorders" (p. 207).

They conclude the section on "guidelines" with two rather remarkable statements, remarkable only, however, if one has followed their earlier accounts. On one hand, they state that the problem of previously unexplained disorders is extremely common. They base their claim on their own earlier survey of neurologists and gastroenterologists. It would seem difficult to make such a strong claim on the basis of a study that they themselves characterized as having a very low rate of response, one that—unfortunately, and by their own admission—"cannot in any way be used as a valid estimate of incidence or prevalence" (Schreier and Libow, 1993b, p. 319). The other rather remarkable statement is that the careful development of profiles would help to "avoid the draconian methods entailed in surreptitious surveillance," which surveillance, of course, they proposed several pages earlier would routinely become "part of the standard treatment for documenting the abuse" (Schreier and Libow, 1993a, p. 196).

What is to be done to prevent further cases of MBPS? This is the final question posed by the authors of *Hurting for Love*. One fears that the answer to this question also strikes a certain finality. Much like the physicians who earlier dealt with the perplexing adult Munchausen's disorder, Schreier and Libow call for a series of measures undertaken nationwide that would reveal the identity of MBPS patients and their whereabouts, as well as catalogue their respective symptoms, case histories, relations, medical experiences, and the like. All this would be in the service of future detection and management of MBPS. Schreier and Libow lament the present liberality of the "free-enterprise health care system," since it positively "encourages open access to caregivers," limited only by "the patient's ability to pay for services." Likewise, they even argue that "Medicaid encourages such behavior" (p. 210). If such profligate abuse of the health care system might result in "doctor-shopping," in the repeated visitations of the MBPS mother and her child to physicians and, thereby, to the uncontrolled spread of MBPS itself, then, the authors argue, two things must be done: access must be limited, and information must be collated to designate the identity of the suspected MBPS abusers. These objectives would be most easily met in the case of "families with limited income and mobility," since, without "prepayment" as an option, poorer families could not easily engage in the peregrinations of doctor shopping, and their medical records would thus be locally contained and more easily accessible to "private party" physicians. Ultimately, a clear medical profile of the offending MBPS mother would more quickly present itself to the responsible physician. This example of access-restricted medical care is generalized into a prescriptive model. It would first emerge on the local level, but, given the serious imperatives of MBPS abuse, the model would ultimately be extended to a national computerized data bank for all "suspected" MBPS candidates:

> Local areas could potentially develop flagging systems for alerting hospital personnel, via medical charts or computer screens, about "overutilizers" or children with multiple suspicious emergency room or clinic visits. A "red flag" might alert a physician to do a more thorough examination, pursue psychiatric/psychological consultation, and be less-liberal in prescribing medication or yielding to parent-requested tests and procedures. Such a system requires clearly defined sets of rules delineating adequate grounds for suspicion and requires trained medical staff to make judgments of when to flag cases for possible MBPS behavior [p. 211].

One of the many limitations of this "local" model is the assumption that people visiting emergency rooms or hospital clinics with some frequency might do so out of some perverse need to subject their children to excessive and dangerous medical treatment. For most poor and uninsured individuals or families—and this is certainly the case with inner-city families—emergency rooms and clinics are the only source of medical attention and care. If this concern is taken into account—along with the fact that poor medical care (especially, the lack of adequate preventive medicine), the potential for injuries resulting from neighborhood violence, and inadequate nutrition are central factors that would also contribute to the creation of "overutilizers"—the potential for error and abuse, of the patients themselves, here seems dramatically increased. Remarkably, then, it may well be the very lack of care given to patients by "the free-enterprise health care system" that propels Schreier and Libow to condemn those patients "with limited income and mobility" for "abuse" of the system. At the same time, the repeated appearance of those patients in the emergency rooms provides a convenient model for monitoring all patients, even if this restricts subsequent access to medical care and, especially, when treatment is said to be "parent requested."

This same lack of sensitivity to the real needs and lives of patients is perhaps at the root of another of the authors' suggestions: the extended model, which they term "the national electronic medical network." This sort of national model was initially proposed by the U.S. Secretary of Health and Human Services from the Bush administration, Louis W. Sullivan. Schreier and Libow (1993a) are quite enthusiastic that such a nationwide system of computer monitoring "holds out the possibility of a dramatically more powerful means of centralizing information and tracking and flagging potential health care abusers such as MBPS mothers" (p. 211). There is no mention, of course, of the considerable controversy that the proposed measure, had caused when it was first introduced by Dr. Sullivan. To begin with, such a system would clearly violate a whole set of patient–physician rights and privileges, as well as dramatically affect personal privacy rights, claimed by all citizens despite their incomes and mobility. There were also strong accusations leveled at the Bush administration, and particularly at Sullivan, for trying to introduce surreptitiously a system for closely monitoring public assistance and Medicaid recipients, as well as undocumented aliens, under the guise of an "electronic medical network." The import of such a system would be to impose full government surveillance on every poor person in the country and potentially on everyone else.

Even more pointedly, Schreier and Libow propose that, on the community level, "multidisciplinary teams or task forces on MBPS" be established. The teams would be composed of "social service providers, pediatricians, public school staff, child protection workers, court representatives, and attorneys" (p. 212) They would "collect data, establish general policies" and lend formal support to those "professionals likely at some point to become involved in cases involving factitious illness" (p. 212). Not only would they maintain "a high level of awareness about the [MBPS] syndrome," but they would "enable faster, more confident diagnosis" (p. 213) of the syndrome.

With such a task force empowered to heighten our awareness of this hitherto underdiagnosed disorder, Schreier and Libow advance a plan, suggested by A. Markantonakis (1989) recommending that, once MBPS mothers have been diagnosed, a nationwide registry "of convicted MBPS parents" be maintained so as to prevent them from continuing their "deceptions by moving to another part of the country, once court supervision" is terminated (pp. 130–131). Schreier and Libow liken such a "registry" to "the registry of convicted sex offenders used in California," used to notify law enforcement agents when such previous offenders move into a new community. They qualify this model somewhat by noting that not all MBPS mothers are convicted criminals and that the records of many of them remain sealed in juvenile courts. Nonetheless, to decriminalize matters—after all, the initial comparison was with convicted sex offenders—they suggest that such a central registry be a medical one and that it would be appropriate that the registry be maintained by the National Center for Disease Control, precisely the agency Louis Sullivan would have drawn on for his national monitoring network.

But, in the end, why advance these measures to control the movement of such patients, to survey their residences, to maintain extensive histories and profiles of these MBPS mothers, to the extent of having national electronic networks and trained task forces on the alert? Schreier and Libow's concern is that some MBPS patients, once properly diagnosed and identified, may not be "successfully rehabilitated." Ultimately, they argue,

> even if they lose permanent custody of their "proxy" child, they may eventually establish residence in new areas of the country and have more children or assume a responsible role with children, meanwhile escaping any surveillance regarding the status of their new children's health [p. 213].

In truth, how serious a threat is this? Realistically speaking, the statistically minute possibility of a repeat "offense" could be of significance only within a broader agenda that seeks to establish this disorder, using virtually any form of social and medical urgency to do so. If psychological profiles are virtually nonexistent, if the symptomatology borders on the fanciful, if the etiology is no less magical, if therapy proves elusive and unproductive, if the medical establishment itself often meets the MBPS diagnosis with skepticism, if the case studies are notoriously vacuous—how dangerous can the disorder be in the first place, much less, to warrant a nationally orchestrated surveillance of possible repeat offenders? What studies or statistical analyses confirm this as a compelling national concern? There are not even reliable statistics to confirm the initial incidence of MBPS.[26] Even given these obvious drawbacks, the authors go on to state that it really may not appear to be a problem, but—like many another occluded danger—it *must* exist!

---

26. It should be noted that McClure et al. (1996) have conducted a differential epidemiolgoical survey of MBPS in Great Britain and Ireland.

Once again, we encounter a central fabulation that permeates virtually all of the Munchausen literature, both the adult and the by proxy variety: "We have no statistics and no idea how prevalent this problem may be, but it certainly must exist" (p. 213).[27]

---

27. Yet another curious manifestation of this "central fabulation" regarding MBPS can be found in an article by another expert in the field, Marc D. Feldman (1994). He writes: "the lack of an adequate explanation of the denial in most cases is mirrored by the absence of effective strategies for reversing it . . . MSPB is also not considered to be a psychiatric diagnosis by the Munchausen by Proxy Network of the National Association of Apnea Professionals, and the American Psychiatric Association's *Treatments of Psychiatric Disorders* contains no entries on MSBP. Similarly, no authors describe consistently effective or specific treatment programs for the MSBP perpetrator herself, particularly if an acknowledgement is not forthcoming. Psychological and psychiatric evaluations have been reported to be unrevealing and nonspecific. The results of psychiatric intervention have seldom been published but are believed to be poor" (p. 125). Remarkably, rather than questioning the specificity of the scientific foundation of the disorder itself, Feldman concludes his remarks by stating: "Nonetheless, psychotherapy (individual and/or family) would seem to offer the best, and perhaps the only hope for treatment of the MSBP perpetrator." It seems that denial is prevalent not only among MSBP perpetrators.

CHAPTER SEVEN

MUNCHAUSEN NOW!

SUMMARY

As the dynamics of social urgency gave rise to the construction of MBPS—as a distinct and threatening form of child abuse, coupled to familial dysfunction and rooted in what was alleged to have been a uniquely female axis of behavior, so will that same sense of urgency oversee its conversion from a narrowly construed psychiatric disorder into one more amenable to intervention by the broad range of public agencies that deal with the continually evolving forms of social change. The name Munchausen has just recently passed out of favor in the official language of psychopathology: *DSM-IV* (American Psychiatric Association, 1994) simply deleted the Munchausen label for both the adult and the by proxy disorder. The term had begun its trajectory in the standard diagnostic manual as a specific and exemplary "form" of Factitious Disorder with Physical Symptoms (301.51), but its adult formation has now reverted back to the more general "Factitious Disorder." Likewise, the by proxy instance has now simply become "Factitious Disorder by Proxy." For the "victim" of what was formerly held to be MBPS behavior, the appropriate designation is once again the standard

"Physical Abuse of Child" (995.5). Indeed, Factitious Disorder by Proxy remains relegated to the Appendix of the *DSM-IV*, as an entry deserving of "further study." In the official usage, then, after nearly 50 years of intensive research, beginning with Asher's (1951) pioneering work, passing on to the work of Chapman (1957) and Meadow (1977), traversing some 300 professional studies, and culminating in the definitive account of Schreier and Libow, "Munchausen's" has lost its nominal distinctiveness as a psychiatric designation—but only to be preserved as a more practically applicable and less obviously contentious form of disorder.

Although both adult Munchausen's and MBPS have lost their official status within the psychiatric nomenclature, in the popular and medical mind they remain very much alive. Like witchcraft and hysteria before them, adult and by proxy Munchausen have outlived their demise as officially sanctioned and designated disorders. The reason for their remarkable survival is that they were not effectively self-standing disorders at all but, rather, were particular pretexts by which social power, authority, and control could be established and propagated. In each case, a complex set of dynamics gave rise to a widely perceived threat of social, familial, and institutional disorder. In each case, a specific institution or political agency sustained and directed the construction of the threatening formation, and in each case, there was a targeted group that would be its host: women.

With witchcraft, the institution of the church would aggressively seek to remove the threat perceived to be incarnated in the person of the demonized witch. Even when the church relented in its pursuit of witches, the danger and threat of witchcraft nonetheless remained in the popular mind, and the pursuit of witches assumed a more specifically political and cultural cast. The mutations of witchcraft were several, but in each instance specific interests assumed the authority of persecution and prosecution—from the political state, to religious sects, to avaricious landowners, to individuals and families who felt threatened or challenged by what eventually mutated into socially unconventional and unacceptable behavior.

When hysteria declined as a definable physiological pathology, it was "rescued" as a psychopathology and given new life in the form of the unconscious and its determination of psychic and somatic dysfunction—typical of predisposed and overly sensitive, sexually traumatized young women. Hysteria moved from the neurologist's office and the hospital ward to society at large during a period of social and economic transition, when women's overall role behavior was being likewise dramatically transformed and reconceived. During the late 19th and early 20th centuries, when Western industrial society was being progressively secularized, it was the institution of medicine, enhanced by its increased professional status, that assumed a position of authority to determine personal and cultural "normalcy." Medicine (and particularly psychoanalysis and psychiatry) advocated a set of behavioral norms, of physical and mental health standards. While intended to prescribe what was felt to be a model of individual health and family stability, these prescriptions also tended to preserve a most traditional model of the social status quo. Much of the authority for this social project was derived from the treatment and control of socially disruptive disorders, like hysteria and other aberrant or deviant forms of observable behavior.

In much the same fashion, adult Munchausen's arose as a medical response to a peculiarly aberrant form of behavior, one construed by physicians and hospital staff to be an unwarranted and opportunistic assault on the system of health care generally. Adult Munchausen's first emerged in the difficult period following World War II, when Britain nationalized its health care system. Many physicians remarked that a small number of individuals was appearing to exploit the medical care and treatment offered by that system, for no apparent reason. These individuals so repeatedly presented themselves for care that they were viewed by the profession as manipulative and, indeed, deceptive in their insistent appeals for attention. It was the residue of this negative feeling experienced by physicians that was to intensify what began with a rather humorous designation, that is, "hospital hoboes," into an urgent search for causes, cures, diagnoses, and means of controlling such patients. In effect, virtually every behavior that was viewed as a negative assault against the medical system could be reduced to this "disorder." Adult Munchausen's became a "lightning rod" for doctors who were beset by "hateful patients," "undiagnosable disorders," "derelicts in the emergency room," "multiple admissions patients," "unruly" and "disruptive" patients. Whether adult Munchausen's was a self-standing, diagnosable, and specifically identifiable "disorder" was no longer in question, since so many physicians had seen, had treated, and had been repeatedly deceived and abused by just such patients. Adult Munchausen's could now be understood also as a social relation, as a means of empowerment by which physicians and the medical establishment in general could enforce their authority over those who would callously challenge and impugn it.

It is precisely this means of expressing medical power that engenders and perpetuates MBPS as well. MBPS is constructed as a medical "enigma," one that can be recognized, not to say diagnosed, only by a specially trained physician. Like adult Munchausen's, MBPS is said to consist in a series of very loosely and inconsistently related behavioral patterns, but, in this case, the behavior is said to involve the dynamics of the family, as well as that of the medical environment. Once the set of behavioral patterns became articulated by Meadow (1977), it was designated as a disorder and was inseparably linked to the growing awareness—popular and professional—of increased child abuse, unexplained infant deaths, child molestation, and indeed, a broad variety of difficult to diagnose children's disorders and syndromes. Along with spiraling divorce rates, family dysfunction, single-parent families, substance abuse, economic uncertainty, and evolving parenting roles, MBPS was virtually guaranteed its place as a major and threatening disorder.

RECENT EXTENSIONS

This continuing social threat of MBPS is, in effect, what lends the disorder its central causality as a disorder, thereby empowering the medical profession and related agencies to counter its spread and its "potentially lethal effects." It is precisely the widespread sensibility to these "lethal effects" that has reinvigorated the initial suspicions among the justice and law enforcement communities. The criminal aspect of MBPS has, moreover, been heightened by the dissemination of information and disinformation in the media as well as by a virtual explosion of warnings and alerts on a series of Internet web sites. Not only is this "received knowledge" recycled through usual professional sources, such as journals and books, but Internet users can receive a stream of "updates"— clinical and otherwise—on "medical sleuthing" (*Physician's Weekly*, 1996) to discover new deviations and formulations of MBPS. Feldman (1994; Feldman and Ford, 1994) has his own website to update concerned persons about this dreaded disorder, while also making available a selection of his own related books for sale (Feldman, 1998).

Evidence of the expansion of the MBPS awareness among members of the justice and law enforcement community increased dramatically with the publication and distribution of a number of articles and pamphlets available on the Internet and from the usual published sources. One of the most widely distributed pamphlets, written by Donna Rosenberg (1997) largely recounts her 1987 article. Now, as an official publication of the Justice Department, there is a much stronger emphasis on the investigation, control, and enforcement of MBPS "perpetrators." Effectively, Rosenberg's earlier pronouncements, which were generally directed to physicians, are now pointed to an extremely broad law enforcement community. They thereby attain a degree of legitimacy and authority by just such an extension. Interestingly, it is the Administrator of the Office of Juvenile Justice and Delinquency Prevention, of the Justice Department, Shay Bilchik, who, to bring attention to Rosenberg's account, invokes precisely the "lurid tabloid headlines of child abuse" (Rosenberg, 1997) and neglect. This once again confirms the societial urgency of this ever-growing disorder, one that has extended beyond the confines of professional journals and has now achieved Justice Department standing. Already in multiple government printings, the warning call to individuals and agencies is stated in highly dramatic, and now fully authoritative, terms:

> Munchausen's syndrome by proxy . . . is a form of child abuse in which the caregiver fabricates the child's purported illness. Its victims may be at risk for serious injury and even death. Diagnostic criteria are detailed, and investigative techniques noted. Neglecting children may be criminal. We must not compound that crime with our own neglect of its victims. This guide is a useful tool to ensure that does not occur [Foreword].

In keeping with this sense of official urgency, the FBI has issued a new report on MBPS, which greatly expands—in size and scope—the information about, and the widening danger of, the syndrome (Artingstall, 1995).[1] The text begins with the solid assumption that MBPS is a "criminal act" and that it is widely recognized as such by "the criminal justice community" as well as by the "medical community," which as it "becomes increasingly familiar with MSBP and its warning

---

1. The article can be accessed on the Internet at http://www.fraud-watch.com/leb_msbp.htm. Interestingly, the fraud-watch website alerts insurance companies, hospitals, legal and medical professionals, and other concerned parties as to the possible use and abuse of MBPS diagnoses in medical malpractice suits, personal injury claims, child custody cases, and sexual abuse claims involved in divorce proceedings and other tort litigation.

signs, doctors and medical staffs seem to be more inclined to request the assistance of local law enforcement agencies" (p. 1). In this very confusing study, the author reports that "during the past several years, a number of variations to the normal offender patterns have emerged" and then goes on to cite an article by Alexander, Smith, and Stevenson (1990). Seemingly on the basis of this five-page article, which purported to study the serial nature of MBPS, involving five families with a total of 18 children, new and frightening statistics emerge. The general profile for "maternal perpetrators" of MBPS now appears indeed to be a significant variation of the already questionable "norm":

80 percent possessed backgrounds in health professions
80 percent manifested Munchausen's syndrome (self-inflicted injury) themselves
80 percent received psychiatric treatment prior to diagnosis
60 percent of the mothers attempted suicide. Denial persisted in most cases [Artingstall, 1995, p. 2].

The article goes on to enumerate several procedures intended to help in prosecuting offenders, most of which seem ill conceived. One recommendation is that "law enforcement officers generally should refrain from interviewing the victim" (p. 4). This recommendation is urged for a very significant reason: infants are preverbal and thus cannot respond to questions. Other problems might ensue if the offender were tipped off and flee the area. Thus, "evidence collected should be established prior to informing the subject of the investigation" (p. 4). Recalling that "9 to 31 percent of all MBPS victims die at the hands of their perpetrators" (p. 4), the law officers are warned that courts often fail to "enact protective measures to preclude a suspect from relocating" (p. 4). To avoid the possibility of flight, then, "investigators should ensure that adequate measures to protect the victim are in place via social services or judicial avenues before informing subjects that they are under suspicion" (p. 4). Of course, the logic governing this procedure is painfully simple: "If not arrested, offenders who believe they are under suspicion might become more cautious" (p. 4).

Not only will an offending mother become more cautious and perhaps take her child victims elsewhere, but she might "seek assistance by accessing public shelters provided for victims of domestic violence" (p. 5). Shelters are said to be a favorite kind of hideout for MBPS offenders, since shelter personnel usually will not provide information to outside agencies, resolutely protect their residents, and provide a support system to reinforce the MBPS mother's "fictitious explanation of the child's injuries or illness" (p. 5). Of course, being naturally supportive of each other, shelter residents might confirm the "offender's" non-fictitious explanations as well, which would make apprehension and prosecution even more difficult.

In another variation on the standard profile, the FBI reports that MBPS offenders are often "upper-class, well educated" persons. This assessment might come as a considerable shock to Meadow (1995) who was terribly offended by MBPS perpetrators, who lived in public housing that featured unleashed Alsatians, beer-swilling, *Gun Weekly*-reading, unempathetic macho-man husbands with no communication skills at all. This claim also contradicts the 100% total of "low intellectual functioning" women collected by Schreier and Libow in their psychometical study (p. 173).

In any case, this FBI article seems to confirm Asher's (1951) cry, nearly 50 years earlier, for greater cooperation among judicial and law enforcement agencies. It concludes that these agencies should strive to obtain hard evidence even when the suspect is not informed that she is a suspect, since "most courts are unwilling to remove a child from a parent's custody without concrete evidence to support charges of child abuse" (p. 2).

The greatly increased concern about MBPS by the law enforcement community seems to have affected even the dynamics of the disorder itself. In the early formulation of MBPS, Schreier and Libow (1993a) urged that child protection services, the police, and other agencies, be called in to aid in the management of MBPS and to help secure prosecutions of the perpetrating mothers. More recently, however, Schreier (1996) has argued that law enforcement officials may, in fact, be a component of the etiological dynamics of MBPS. What was formerly held to be the exclusive axis of MBPS, the mother–doctor dyad, now is extended to include law enforcement personnel, particularly when it appears that the mother is attempting to gain custody of the child. On this subject, Schreier states, "we need to change the definition of MBP [formerly, MBPS] by expanding the 'target' audience of the mother to include police investigators, child protection workers, lawyers, and school personnel" (p. 986).

The inclusion of others as dyadic placeholders certainly justifies Schreier's own more generalized conception of Munchausen mothers, which now includes Meadow's (1985) category of "another form of attention seeking behavior" (p. 538). Schreier's theory now appears to have devolved into an attempt to construe MBPS theoretically in two ways: On one hand, he wishes to retain it as a psychiatric disorder—MBPS, properly speaking, as he described it in *Hurting for Love* (Schreier and Libow, 1993a). Indeed, he reiterates this characterization in the 1996 essay by saying that "Munchausen by proxy Syndrome is a particular form of perversion . . . where that term is used in the modern psychoanalytic sense" (p. 989). He then refers this specific usage to Kaplan (1991). But, by the same token, he has dropped the "S"—for syndrome—by calling MBPS simply MBP, thereby bringing it more into accord with Meadows's (1995) usage, which sees it not as a psychiatric syndrome, but as a behavioral disorder. Meadows writes: "I think it is much more to do with the sort of circumstances of the mother at the time. You know, if her life is good, with a good partner, or perhaps with a job, she copes with the child, whereas if things are tough, then this comes out" (p. 99) Thus reconsidered, Munchausen by Proxy Syndrome is at once a form of child abuse and a psychiatric disorder, as well as merely "another form of attention seeking behavior."

Interestingly, this reformulation seems to be a classical case of throwing out the baby with the bath water. All the excruciatingly detailed elements of the earlier proposed etiology (Schreier and Libow, 1993a), which so closely associated the Munchausen mother with the dyadic doctor—the mother's extensive knowledge of medical vocabulary, her interests in hospital procedures, her intimate awareness of the child's every cough, complaint, and sneeze, her profound respect and desire for the pediatrician, obstetrician, or gynecologist, her background of employment in the health-giving professions—all these concerns now seem to be suspended, so as to permit a variety of potential professional placeholders (i.e., other professions in addition to the doctor who might provide the needed attention) within the previously elaborated etiology. This expansion, in turn, would drastically change the specifics of the mother's behavior toward the placeholder. What, for example, if a fetishizing, manipulative mother desired to impress a school supervisor? Would she report the child as being truant or as having a learning disability? If the mother wished to impress a law enforcement official, would she try to get arrested herself, or report the child missing, or report the child's bad habits, or report that the child demonstrated criminal tendencies?

Having extended the "target audience of the mother" from the doctor to virtually any transferential figure who might "occupy positions of power in society" (Schreier, 1996, p. 986), the distinctive Munchausen formation becomes effectively eviscerated of all specific content at the very moment it is so broadly extended. What remains is a manipulative person who seeks attention from somebody who can be construed to hold power of some kind: that is, probably anybody. The spread of such a "target audience" might now include—as Kaplan (1991) suggested—toreadors, hair dressers, actors, female lovers, not to mention postmen, landlords, real estate agents, and astronauts. And one shudders to think of the various manipulations, mutilations, machinations, and kiddie fashion shows, that might be staged in order to garner the attention of this virtually infinite, new target audience.[2]

Not only are MBPS sufferers now allowed to choose different power sources, but the disorder itself is claimed to have emerged much earlier than previously thought. Libow (1995) states that a group of adults ranging in age from 33 to 71 have provided a "first look" at childhood victims of MBPS—that is, themselves—dating back, in some cases, over 60 years. Libow asserts that this "first look" will help to establish that MBPS abuse has a much longer history than previously thought. The study's methodology, however, is so poorly conceived that such a claim seems entirely baseless, if not pointless.

To begin with, the primary method consisted of reviewing self-report data. To what extent self-report data are reliable in general is highly questionable, but the way it is structured here and the ambivalently constructed nature of the disorder itself renders this particular survey largely suspect. The subjects of the survey were a group of 12 adults who initiated contact with Libow "after learning of the author's work in this area through television or newspaper coverage" (p. 1132). She mentions in the very first line of the "Methods" section of her paper that these adults "identified themselves as victims of childhood Munchausen by Proxy syndrome." Her methodological suspicion extends to the "difficulty of verifying their abuse histories"—but, given this difficulty,

---

2. This kind of expansion is also resisted by David P. H. Jones (1996). Though still acknowledging MBPS as a valid diagnosis, Jones argues that it can be extended to any form of parental behavior that involves the use or abuse of a child, in virtually any relationship of power. But, with this extension, Jones prefers to consider the particular forms of abuse involved in the "use" of a child, rather than in terms of a "fabricated presentation," as a "medical label" involving the child.

"their experiences were accepted at face value, as self-report data." Even though Libow dismisses the possibility of "recovered, fragmented or dissociated memories" (p. 1135) playing a role in this survey, that these memories were not of this nature is never fully established. After all, the determination of the type of memories these were was made on the basis of self-report and the questionnaire. Given the enormous complexity (and controversy) surrounding the issue of recovered memory, ruling out recovered memory as a factor seems at the very least, groundless. If, in fact, these were dissociated, fragmented, or revovered memories, the nature of the reports and "events" themselves would appear in a very different light.

The methodological questions surrounding the reliability of self-report data are less than remarkable, because these data were ventured as the only material available. What is remarkable, however, is that the diagnosis of MBPS was delivered by this disparate group of aging "sufferers" consequent to their watching a television show or reading a newspaper. After the endlessly repeated claims that even child psychologists, pediatricians, psychiatrists, general practitioners, social workers, health care professionals, judges, and lawyers were completely incapable of diagnosing this disorder—that it was exponentially more difficult to diagnose than other forms of child abuse—12 self-selected sufferers were fully capable of diagnosing this complex disorder themselves. Yet, in seeming qualification of this remarkable exercise in self-diagnosis, two of the potential subjects of the survey were excluded from the data collection at the very start "because their obvious thought disorder made it impossible to collect meaningful and coherent information" (p. 1132). It is unclear, however, how these "obvious" thought disorders were diagnosed or determined, since no further information is offered; it is suggested in the article that these determinations were made in the course of telephone conversations.

With an already convinced group of Munchausen sufferers who had contacted her, Libow proceeds to mail out a questionnaire that confirms their own self-diagnoses by specifying the very symptoms of the disorder, and to a great extent, what she had a priori hoped to receive—evidence of earlier abuse conforming to the etiology and dynamics of MBPS. Thus, she induces the panel of 10 to respond entirely within and according to the very diagnostic terms she might have hoped to establish: patients were asked pointed questions about their childhood awareness of "abuse," efforts to "seek help," "perceived motivations of the abuser," the role of the "other parent," and "the abuser's later functioning." Armed with this set of concepts and terminology, and absent medical records, how could the respondents not respond to what Libow suggested? The results were guaranteed before the fact.

Even with this front-loaded approach directed to self-diagnosed MBPS sufferers, very few of these cases seem to conform to the conventional MBPS diagnostics—unless, that is, the diagnostic indicators and symptoms are extremely and selectively edited. For example, "Subject B" had been subjected to injuries inflicted on her by her mother; she was bashed with a hammer and suffered bone fractures and osteomylitis. The mother also rubbed coffee grounds into the child's open wounds. If the mother were, in fact, a father, and a truck driver, rather than a nurse, would this make any difference at all in diagnosing the case as physical child abuse, rather than MBPS? That the mother rushed the child to a hospital after these injuries were inflicted really does not prove conclusively that she was suffering from MBPS. All that it proves is that the staff of the hospitals to which she was rushed, "about 23 times," were incapable of spotting a case of severe child abuse.

The uncertainty of a MBPS diagnosis is further exacerbated by the fact that four of the self-diagnosed MBPS sufferers offered their own diagnoses about their mothers. They suggested that their mothers suffered from "manic-depressive illness, major depression or schizophrenia" (Libow, 1995, p. 1139). At the very least, these suggestions would tend to complicate the principal diagnosis of MBPS. Remarkably, Libow goes on to say that "even interviews with other family members will not necessarily confirm or disprove any particular report" (p. 1139), a striking admission, since no interviews were even attempted with other family members. The whole basis for the validity of the argument is summed up several lines further: "The validity of these subjects' self-reports was supported by the personal distress many reported in focusing on their past experiences" (p. 1139).

Self-selected "Subject G," a 71-year-old woman, recalled her abuse (some 60 years earlier). She had been brought up believing that she had tuberculosis and claimed that her mother tried to convince doctors to put her into a sanitarium. Her self-report claimed she had a large abdominal scar, but no explanation. One might be somewhat suspicious of presenting this as a case of MBPS abuse. The subject is remembering events that occurred approximately 60 years earlier. Given the complexity and unreliability of long-term memory, the prevalence and mortal fear of tuberculosis at the time, and the fact that she may have had her appendix removed when she was a young child, all these "data" are virtually useless. Even given the paucity of information presented in this particular account, Libow is inspired to add that "a courageous doctor stood up to her mother and refused to admit her to a TB sanitarium" (p. 1136). It would hardly take much courage for a doctor not to allow someone who does not have tuberculosis into a TB sanitarium.

Two additional cases deserve brief mention. One, a 65-year-old woman, believed (there is no documentation) that she had been poisoned with arsenic by her mother, when she was a child and at intervals thereafter. Milk occasionally had seemed to taste sour, so she put salt in it. Whether the family home had insufficient refrigeration and the milk spoiled was not determined. Likewise, whether her father or brother, rather than her mother, might have slipped rat poison or medicinal arsenic in her milk was not explored. What should be noted here is that, for all the respondents, it was the mother who would have been indicated as the likely abuser—in the TV programs they saw or in the articles they read in the newspapers, if not in the questionnaire forms themselves (which are not specified in detail, other than including several MBPS-related questions, as well as "a checklist of 27 symptoms of Posttraumatic Stress Disorder"). In this particular case, the only "clue" to the mother's being the perpetrator is that she gave the daughter (at what age?) a book (which book?) that contained an account of a mother killing her children with arsenic (Sherlock Holmes? The Wicked Witch? Agatha Christie? *Arsenic and Old Lace*?). This case is listed in "Table 1: Description of Subjects," under "Mode of Abuse": "Chronic arsenic poisoning" (p. 1133).

A final case, presented in a five-sentence summary:

> Subject D: A 33-year-old woman whose mother was preoccupied with bowel and digestive problems. She had three operations by age 6, dozens of physicians, and repeated medical examinations. Her mother overtreated these "medical problems" invasively and excessively with enemas, laxatives, diapers, mineral oil, and so forth. This continued throughout childhood until she ran way from home at age 17 because her mother was urging a colostomy. Her younger half-brother was also the victim of abuse [p. 1134].

Absent documentation of why surgeons would operate three times on a young child and absent documentation from "dozens of physicians" who must, after all, have treated the child, it is extremely difficult to say anything of substance about the case. It might have been a case of parental obsessiveness; it could have been an instance of an extremely difficult to diagnose medical illness in the child; or it may have been that the parent simply had a normal interest the child's health and digestion. Parents often do examine their children's stool, they may give enemas and laxatives, and they not infrequently use diapers and mineral oil. Absent any further documentation or detail, one just does not have a very clear sense of what the relevance of MBPS is here, or, for that matter, child abuse.

A review of the recent material in the field indicates that MBPS has undergone a period of rapid and dramatic inflation, spurred on by the conflation of medical, juridical, and law enforcement interests. Information about MBPS has been widely disseminated through the popular literature and through Internet access. Not only are more people learning about MBPS, but this newly acquired knowledge is generally articulated through a variety of new and, in many cases, unsubstantiated claims. The latest FBI bulletin, for example, states that there has been a near exponential increase in mortality rates, in the presence of Adult Munchausen's in MBPS perpetrators, and in the rate of their suicide attempts. Inspired by the inflation of the disorder, its professional authorities and advocates have likewise expanded its etiology, dynamics, and symptoms. Schreier (1996) sees the formerly limited affective transference to the care-giving doctor now extended to virtually any figure of "power." Libow (1995), following suit, views the disorder as having a much greater historical span than was previously thought, and she also appears to find the range of symptoms virtually coextensive with those belonging to acts of conventional physical child abuse. Most notably, this fully constructed disorder has insinuated itself so thoroughly, so effectively, into the social fabric that it has become a relatively common pretext for criminal prosecution. MBPS has become an "indicator" of psychiatric illness, child abuse, familial dysfunction, failure to thrive, unexplained infant mortality, all of which provoke our deepest, atavistic social fears.

IN LITIGATION: THE YVONNE ELDRIDGE CASE

Even though no definitive statistics are kept on specifically MBPS-related abuse in either civil or criminal law proceedings, there are indications that the number of court cases involving MBPS has significantly increased in the last several years—owing perhaps in part, to more coverage in the media, as well as to its association with divorce cases, child custody cases, and insurance litigation. Mothers are being accused —and, in many cases, tried—in virtually every state in the United States, as well as in Britain, Australia, New Zealand, and on the continent. A number of high profile cases have been reported in detail, particularly the Ellen Storck case in Suffolk County, New York, the Yvonne Eldridge case in Contra Costa County, California, and the forthcoming Kathy Bush trial in Broward County, Florida.

A review of MBPS court cases, particularly the aforementioned Storck, Eldridge, and Bush proceedings, reveals several common characteristics. A large percentage of mothers come from modest or low-income backgrounds, and in many cases they are single parents (it should be noted, however, of the three mothers just mentioned, Storck alone was a single mother). In almost all cases, the defendants are inadequately represented and often face a well-financed prosecution, able to draw on numerable "expert" witnesses, who are oftentimes nationally known figures in their areas of medical specialization. Being of modest means, and usually defended by a single, court-appointed legal defense counsel, the defendants seldom have the financial means to counter such expert testimony. Their defense counsels are usually juvenile or family court lawyers relatively unfamiliar with the complex medical procecdures and terminology typically involved in Munchausen cases. Professional testimony in the prosecution of many such cases is pointedly intended to assure the accuracy of the standard MBPS diagnosis and to emphasize dramatically the seriousness of this as a novel and dangerous form of child abuse. It is characterized by a unique set of psychiatric and behavioral markers and is routinely portrayed as a form of abuse with a particularly high morbidity and mortality rate. Oftentimes, there is a personal conflict with a physician who, in turn, makes the initial accusation of MBPS.

Although these common factors appear in a number of cases, particularly, in the Ellen Storck case, the Yvonne Eldridge case is perhaps most typical in the way in which it was first reported, then unfolded, and subsequently prosecuted. In early 1986, Yvonne Eldridge was granted a California state license to be a foster mother. In 1988, Yvonne and her husband, Dennis, were honored by Nancy Reagan at the White House as one of six "great American families," for their work with severely fragile foster children, many of whom were diagnosed as being addicted to crack-cocaine or methamphetamine drugs, or as being HIV/AIDS infected. Mrs. Eldridge was a participant in the San Francisco Department of Child Services "Baby Moms" Program, which was then being developed as a means of providing at home care for high-risk babies, many of whom were described by another "Baby Moms" foster parent as "often just one step away from the hospital" (Serr et al., 1997).[3] In the course of Mrs. Eldridge's almost 10-year-long participation in the program, she cared for approximately 40 children, of whom about 10 were at the very start characterized as suffering from life-threatening conditions.

Late in 1991, formal accusations were made against Mrs. Eldridge for abusing one of the children in her care, "Foster Child 1." The charges were brought by Dr. Mark Usatin to the Kaiser Walnut Creek Hospital's child abuse and neglect team, and the county child protection services were notified on October 15, 1991. As is typical in many of these alleged Munchausen cases, there were initial claims of misconduct directed against the physician. From sworn declarations filed with the motion for retrial, Mrs Eldridge alleged that Dr. Usatin had made several flirtatious advances toward her that culminated in a sexual advance and a proposition. The advance was stated to have been witnessed by Mrs. Eldridge's daughter, who had herself claimed that Dr. Usatin had placed his hand on her bare thigh a year earlier. These allegations were made in the sworn declarations of Tamara Eldridge O'Connor and Lucille Chapman (Serra et al., 1997) and reported in the sworn statement of Betty Autange, as well as in Dennis Eldridge's letter, filed as an exhibit for the motion. Mr. Eldridge's letter directly connects the rejected advances with "Foster Child 1's" removal from Mrs. Eldridge's care and the accusation of child abuse. As Mr. Eldridge stated:

> In the summer of 1991 Dr. Usatin made two unwanted sexual advances toward my wife. The first encounter was witnessed by Yvonne's mother, Lucille Chapman. The second encounter occurred in October of 1991. Dr. Usatin told my wife, 'Yvonne you are a beautiful woman and you need to have more sex.' My wife pulled away from Dr. Usatin and informed him that she was happily married and as far as she was concerned he could get lost.

---

3. In opposition to the motion for a new trial, the prosecution prepared a document attempting a point-by-point rebuttal of the motion (Lungren et al., 1998). Material relevant to the testimony of Drs. Albin and Usatin appears on pp. 10–64.

Within a matter of days, Dr. Usatin turned my wife in with the allegation that she broke "Foster Child 1's" hip. We later learned that it was a misdiagnosis and "Foster Child 1's" hip was never broken. "Foster Child 1" was kept in traction for one month before Kaiser realized their mistake. At this point Yvonne and I thought the matter would be dropped and we would be allowed to take "Foster Child 1" home. Little did we know that this was the beginning of a four and one half year nightmare that would end with my wife being falsely convicted of child abuse.

In September1992, the Walnut Creek Police Department accused Mrs. Eldridge of child abuse, in what the local news media referred to as a seemingly "twisted attempt to gain attention from the medical community" (Burnson, 1998). By November of 1992 the Contra Costa County District Attorney's Office had investigated the case but declined to charge her with the abuse and the deaths of three medically fragile foster AIDS children in her care (these children were so ill that even professional nurses involved in the Baby Moms program refused to accept them as foster children). Faced with a wrongful death suit, the state of California compensated the natural parents of the children to the sum total of $100,000. Without any admission of guilt, Mrs. Eldridge voluntarily surrendered her foster care license. In November of 1994 the State Attorney General's Office intervened and brought about a grand jury indictment of Mrs. Eldridge on two counts of felonious child abuse. In June of 1996 a Contra Costa County jury deliberated for five hours before convicting her of willful cruelty to two of her foster children, "Foster Child 1" and "Foster Child 2."[4] A month later, in July of 1996, Judge Peter Spinetta sentenced Mrs. Eldridge to three years and four months in prison, but pending her motion for a new trial, she was released on a property bond, posted by her parents. In January of 1998,

---

4. Although our account of the Eldridge trial has been limited to testimony concerning "Foster Child 1," "Foster Child 2" also figured importantly in the trial and subsequent conviction. Highlighting the fragile health of "Foster Child 2," who was also a crack-cocaine baby, medical records indicate that the child was born prematurely in a toilet with a birth weight of one pound five ounces; she showed signs of mental retardation and suffered from repeated bouts of pneumonia, chronic lung disease (bronchopulmonary displasia), apnea, chronic reflux, malnutrition, inability to feed orally, and a variety of other disorders related to in utero insult. "Foster Child 2's" primary physician, Dr. Bruce Nickerson, a pediatric pulmonologist, then at CHO—prior to her having been placed with Mrs. Eldridge—fully exculpated Mrs. Eldridge from any MBPS-related child abuse in his grand jury testimony. It is not clear why, at the trial, defense counsel failed to call him as a witness.

the same judge reviewed the motion for a retrial, now prepared by a new defense team. On review, he threw out the previous conviction and granted Mrs. Eldridge a new trial, tentatively scheduled for January, 1999.

Although the preceding summary seems to indicate a conventional child abuse proceeding, the Eldridge case is distinctive in that, from its very inception, it was brought forth as a clear-cut case of Munchausen by Proxy Syndrome. As early as 1989 Dr. Usatin had claimed that there was no doubt in his mind that Mrs. Eldridge was suffering from MBPS (Serra et al., 1997, p. 223).[5] These accusations became concrete and were advanced by Dr. Usatin in October of 1991. He accused Mrs. Eldridge of breaking "Foster Child 1's" hip and failure to feed "Foster Child 2" sufficiently. Following the removal of "Foster Child 1" from the Eldridge's care, Mrs. Eldridge tried to regain custody of "Foster Child 1" in juvenile court. As Mrs. Eldridge's husband wrote, however, in a letter entered as a defense motion exhibit—treated under California law as the equivalent of sworn testimony, that is, subject to the rules of perjury—"Dr. Usatin and Dr. Schreier went to juvenile court and coinvinced the judge that we should never be allowed to have custody of 'Foster Child 1' again." Mrs. Eldridge was further implicated in MBPS behavior by virtue of a brief police station discussion with Dr. Schreier, at the instigation of one of the investigating detectives, Mike Gorman. According to the same letter, "Dr. Schreier made the outrageous statement that my wife had Munchausen's syndrome by Proxy solely on the word of Detective Gorman and Dr. Usatin" (Serra et al., 1997).

These accusations of Munchausen permeated much of the grand jury testimony and, according to the reasons advanced in the Motion for Retrial, were the primary cause for Mrs. Eldridge's subsequent indictment and conviction of child abuse:

> MSBP was a pervasive theme throughout the course of the grand jury proceedings. The seed that Mrs. Eldridge had MSBP and that caused her to fabricate, exaggerate and cause symptoms in "Foster Child 1" and "Foster Child 2" was improperly planted in the minds of the grand jurors. . . . MSBP evidence is the type of evidence that is inherently misleading to a lay person and the misleading nature of this evidence likely contributed to the grand

---

5. The same source states that "Dr. Keller made reference to a discussion he had had with Dr. Usatin in 1989 with respect to Dr. Usatin's suspicion that Mrs. Eldridge might have MSbP" (p. 233).

jury's decision to return an indictment against Mrs. Eldridge. As such, Mrs. Eldridge was denied her right to due process and the indictment should be dismissed [Serra et al., pp. 233–234].

The grand jury was informed at length about MBPS by Dr. Schreier. Indeed, his expert testimony amounted to some 76 pages of the grand jury transcript. He discussed a broad range of MBPS subjects: its definition, the role of the child in the dynamic, how mothers with MBPS present themselves both to the community and to the doctors. He was particularly careful to point out "the guidelines that are found in almost every case which may provide the clue" (p. 233). Further MBPS-related testimony was given by other key medical figures in the case against Mrs. Eldridge, including the two most condemning witnesses, Dr. Usatin and Dr. Albin; and references to MBPS were also made by Drs. Keller, Petru, Lewis, and Nickerson. It should be stressed that there was not a single eyewitness account of Mrs. Eldridge's alleged acts of abuse by these witnesses or, for that matter, by any other witnesses. One could say that the MBPS perpetrator's diagnosis was itself delivered by proxy, as is so often the case.

Even though no direct MBPS testimony was admitted into the subsequent trial evidence,[6] and in his grand jury testimony Dr. Schreier had made no comments as to whether Mrs. Eldridge did or did not have MBPS, the trial itself resonnated with the classic Munchausen orchestration. Accusatory testimony was largely directed to the particular signs and symptoms of Munchausen, that is, to what "provides the clue": the (foster) mother was accused of excessive concern about the children, influencing doctors to perform unnecessary surgery and other unnecessary invasive procedures, demanding medication, expressing irritation with the medical staff, inducing infections, tampering with medical catheters and feeding tubes, inducing weight loss, and so on. As in the witch trials and hysteria examinations, Mrs. Eldridge was, moreover, confronted by a formidable battery of medical authorities, many of whom had testified about MBPS in the earlier grand jury hearing. They comprised a substantial legal staff provided by the State Attorney

---

6. It was a defense tactic in the regular trial that MBPS was a "character" issue and thus that MBPS testimony should be explicitly excluded, since the major portion of the proceeding would thereby devolve into an attempt to impugn—and to defend—Mrs. Eldridge's character. This tactic may well have been prompted by the negative effects that the MBPS testimony had on the grand jury hearing.

General's office and by Children's Protective Service officials. Mrs. Eldridge, now indigent, was represented by a public defender who, possibly overwhelmed by the sheer bulk of medical records, expert testimony and by lack of resources, presented only one defense witness on her behalf: Mrs. Eldridge herself. She unfortunately, was unable to testify to her own best defense, her good character.

According to the motion presented for a new trial, the witnesses who seemed to be most suspect in their testimony were those who were most adamant about the MBPS diagnosis in their grand jury testimony and in other dealings with Mrs. Eldridge: Dr. Usatin and Dr. Albin. Dr. Usatin had professional medical dealings with "Foster Child 1" as early as 1987, when he had accused Mrs. Eldridge of taking an excessive interest in the care of the child. He noted that Mrs. Eldridge had had a series of tests performed on the child that were, in his words, "negative," therefore implying that Mrs. Eldridge was subjecting the child to unnecessary testing—a significant "clue" to the presence of MBPS. On further examination, however, a discharge summary by Dr. Herbert, at Children's Hospital Oakland, indicated the child tested positive for "minor reflux," which would substantiate Mrs. Eldridge's concerns about the child's vomiting.

These accusations of unduly influencing other physicians continued in a number of incidents involving "Foster Child 1." An important example is Dr. Usatin's claim that Mrs. Eldridge led Dr. Tarnoff (a pediatric heart specialist) to believe that the child was too sick, owing to her pulmonary condition, to risk surgery to close the hole in her heart (a congenital defect). Further observation of Tarnoff's report on the patient's progress indicates that it was Tarnoff himself who stated that heart surgery was necessary and would be helpful for her pulmonary problems, "but will have to be done at some significant risk" (Serra et al., 1997, p. 85).[7]

Several other disorders were reported in Usatin's testimony as having been fabricated by Mrs. Eldridge, especially an immunodeficiency disorder and apnea. Regarding the former, Usatin flatly denied that "Foster

---

7. Other misreadings involve a phone message from Childrens Hospital, San Francisco, where Dr. Usatin claimed in court testimony that "Foster Child 1" was bleeding; in fact the report stated that the child was eating and had no bleeding. He went on to state that Mrs. Eldridge apparently did not want to wait to see the hospitalized sick child, yet review of the message shows that she did not want to awaken her.

Child 1" had any immunodeficiency disorder, and went on to describe a healthy, happy newborn, ending his generally benign assessment with the somewhat condemning statement that the difficulty "came on later, when she was rehospitalized" (p. 88). In actuality, however, it turned out that the Kaiser Walnut Creek Hospital medical staff itself showed concerns that the child might have an immunodeficiency disorder. In the case of "Foster Child 1's" apnea, Usatin once again accused Mrs. Eldridge of totally fabricating the disorder in the child. This claim was confirmed by Usatin's actions at the time, for he further testified that he had discontinued apnea monitoring on June 9, 1988 because no apnea episodes were reported to him. Contrary to this claim, however, there were at least four reports of apnea episodes predating the discontinuance of the apnea monitor: one, reported by another physician, Dr. Molloy, of the Contra Costa County Health Services Evaluation, as well as a phone message from Mrs. Eldridge to Dr. Usatin reporting three additional instances.

Another point of Usatin's testimony was that Mrs. Eldridge had created the illusion that "Foster Child 1" had more medical problems than would be expected for a child who was in reasonably good condition. As far as Dr. Usatin was concerned, the only problem was that the child was not growing or thriving. This, once again, was clearly contrary to the facts. On further examination by Dr. de Lorimer, it was observed that she had edema (a physically observable swelling, which Mrs. Eldridge could not have invented), hypochloremic alkalosis (which results from vomiting), and the suspicion of enteral dysmotility (which causes undigested material to remain in the stomach). On the basis of this evidence, it seems clear that Mrs. Eldridge was hardly creating an illusion of poor health but simply was responding to symptoms that were later verified by medical tests.

Continuing lower GI problems for "Foster Child 1" were diagnosed by Dr. Usatin's colleague, Dr. Dixon, who remarked, early on in 1989, that "etiologies for her retching and vomiting are numerous. Children with chronic neurologic problems often have altered gastrointestinal motility... [even] in children with normal pressure hydrocephalus..." (p. 94). Not only did "Foster Child 1" have hydrocephalus, but Dixon's diagnosis confirmed the earlier diagnosis of Dr. de Lorimer. Dr. Usatin, however, testified at the trial that he thought that Dr. Dixon was "confused" and that he was "trying to go through the laundry list" of etiological indicators. This tendency to dismiss reasoned medical diagnosis and decisions ultimately resulted in Usatin's claim that, by December of 1989, Mrs. Eldridge had convinced Dr. de Lorimer to perform a 90% colectomy on "Foster Child 1." De Lorimer's strong response to this assertion was that he would never perform surgery just upon a mother's request, and indeed, even if a gastroenterologist had suggested it, he would ask, "Well, why? What—what do you accomplish with that?" (p. 99).

Following a number of other questionable accusations by Dr. Usatin—one concerning Mrs. Eldridge's "invented" reports of seizures, which could have well been side effects of the medication "Foster Child 1" was receiving (pp. 105–107)[8]—two events in particular led to her finally being accused of child abuse and ultimately to her trial and conviction. The first of these was the report on September 27, 1991, that "Foster Child 1" had a broken hip. This report was read into the trial record by Dr. Usatin. The conclusion of the attending physicians was that "Foster Child 1" should be admitted and placed in traction. Only problem was that "Foster Child 1" did not have a broken hip. The misdiagnosis—later acknowledged by Dr. Usatin (p. 111)—was made by the emergency room team of physicians. Regardless, this event brought into focus all Usatin's concerns, particularly those related to an ongoing pattern of suspected MBPS abuse.

The second event, shortly following the "broken hip," was the accusation implied by Dr. Usatin's testimony that Mrs. Eldridge was responsible for a pinhole discovered in "Foster Child 1's" subcutaneous venous catheter. Testimony by a Kaiser nurse made it clear, however, that Mrs. Eldridge had not been at the hospital until after the leak was detected. Dr. Usatin's original testimony was never challenged by the defense counsel, and the jury was left with the impression that she was, in fact, responsible for the suspected tampering.

Clearly, Dr. Usatin's testimony—here only briefly summarized—was forgetful, convoluted, and inaccurate. It was, however, marked by a significant MBPS "clue": the case was so complicated that he and other physicians seemed unable to keep up with the details, diagnoses, and

---

8. Among the many medications being prescribed for "Foster Child 1" at the time, those which have "tremors and twitching" as distinct side effects include Atarax, Dilantin, and Tegritol. Other drugs prescribed for "Foster Child 1" during this period included Cimetidine, Tagamet, Lasix, Aldactone, Inderal, Somophyline, and Gantrisin (the latter two being known to cause convulsions).

treatments; and much of this confusion was the result of the mother's dissembling behavior. She led him and others down the wrong road, she made decisions about the child's treatment and progress; she reported symptoms that didn't make sense and even ordered unnecessary surgery. This utter confusion was seemingly attested to by Usatin himself:

> I had been concerned for two years over the inability to explain what was going on with "Foster Child 1" and why she was having so many complications and problems that we are unable to explain. I had shared this concern with our child abuse and neglect team at that time. . . . I had concerns that things just didn't add up. But each time there would be some little thought that would make me think there is something to this. Maybe there is something to this child. Maybe we're not smart enough. Maybe there is something that all these people at UCSF how many the UCSF [sic]. Believing there is something missing. We tend to believe parents. We believe what they tell us. We believe that Mrs. Eldridge . . . [p. 111].[9]

In the absence of any concrete evidence concerning possible physical child abuse—other than "Foster Child 1's" being misdiagnosed as having a broken hip by her physicians and consequently being placed in traction for a month—the only "preponderance of evidence" is Mrs. Eldridge's MBPS "profile." This profile is meticulously elaborated through a set of judgments and exclusions that can only lead to Mrs. Eldridge's being transformed into a MBPS "perpetrator." In fact, the profile is given even more concrete meaning by the failure to discover specifically "real" instances of child abuse, thereby resulting in Mrs. Eldridge's being so clever and manipulative that even the doctors were outwitted and perplexed in their analyses. The very vagueness of the case in general—its twists and turns, its unexplainable problems—is precisely what leads inevitably to the conclusion of some deception, some tampering, that could not have possibly been forseen or discovered by doctors, who, after all, "tend to believe parents."

If the case against Mrs. Eldridge was largely borne by Dr. Usatin's testimony (as improbable as that may seem), his testimony was amplified by Dr. Catherine Albin, a pediatrician at the Stanford University Hospital who belonged to their child abuse prevention center. Never having personally examined "Foster Child 1," she was nevertheless cho-

---

9. The Motion for Retrial goes on to say that "a defense objection was sustained as the court noted that the witness was descending into a narrative" (p. 112).

sen by the prosecution to review and analyze the relevant medical records, procedures, and testimony concerning the case. Albin began her review of the records with "Foster Child 1's" birth in March of 1987. Unlike Usatin, Albin took the general position that "Foster Child 1" was much healthier than the mother's and attending physicians' reports would indicate. Her testimony later served to minimize subsequent concerns, worries, and negative evaluations by Mrs. Eldridge. Of the concatenation of early reports commented on by Dr. Albin concerning the general condition of "Foster Child 1," several deserve mention.

The first of Albin's remarks denied the child's very fragile medical condition at birth. This rather optimistic assessment testified to the "fact" that the child had never been on a ventilator, had never required mechanical ventilation, and had not been really at risk by being placed with her biological parents. The medical records indicate something entirely different: during the first hour of her life, "Foster Child 1" experienced a period of "grunting, flaring, retraction and tachypnea (an abnormal frequency of respiration)." And, although she did not require "mechanical ventilation," the child was kept in ICU for nearly a month. All the symptoms were the result of what was later diagnosed as a lung disease. Beyond these serious symptoms, it was also discovered that "Foster Child 1" had feeding problems and a severe GI disorder, which was later diagnosed as an "absorption problem" related to a severe neurological disorder.

> Simply put, "Foster Child 1's" constipation, absorption, and feeding problems began at birth, the probable result of one of the many in utero insults she experienced such as her birth mother's smoking, drinking, or using drugs during pregnancy. This all occurred long before "Foster Child 1" came to live with the Eldridges [Serra et al., 1997, pp. 10–11].

Add to these conditions an immunodeficiency disorder, a minor cleft in her palate, and a sacral dimple (an indication of neonatal insult, suggesting a neurological disorder), and one might well question Albin's report of a child who appeared to be relatively normal and healthy.

Another instance of Dr. Albin's attempts to minimize these indications was her denial that the "Foster Child 1" had hydrocephalus. Hydrocephalus was, in fact, indicated by a number of specialists in the field who had performed extensive tests on the child, including multiple cranial ultrasound examinations. After spending the month of September 1987 in the Childrens Hospital of San Francisco, she was assesed with failure to thrive and probably hydrocephalus. With these findings in hand, Dr. Albin simply dismissed them and concluded that "Foster Child 1" never had hydrocephalus. She even went so far as to state that another pediatrician's assessment of the child's having a history of hydrocephalus was incorrect. This claim was especially effective in the events leading to Mrs. Eldridge's conviction, since the defense counsel never provided expert testimony from qualified specialists in the field to counter Dr. Albin's testimony—who was, after all, a pediatrician—not even from those specialists who had treated "Foster Child 1" in the first place.

Early in the life of "Foster Child 1," there were also complications with her ability to feed as well as instances of reflux, vomiting. The actual physical causes for the vomiting were testified to by a number of examining doctors who had based their assessments on a variety of tests. Even presented with this medical evidence, Dr. Albin gave the distinct impression that the vomiting and the range of medical procedures meant to address it were initiated solely by Mrs. Eldridge herself. From further review of the records, it is clear that Mrs. Eldridge did report one episode of emesis, precisely that report which effectively alerted her physician at Childrens Hospital Oakland, Dr. Nancy Lewis, to admit "Foster Child 1" and, after subsequent testing, to recommend surgical intervention to prevent further reflux. This condition further alerted doctors at CHO to the seriousness of the child's health. Eventually, Dr. de Lorimer, a pediatric surgeon, performed a Nissen fundoplication (a procedure that binds the upper part of the stomach to physically prevent vomiting). These physician-initiated procedures did not in any way discourage Dr. Albin from continuing to claim that the procedures and the initial diagnosis were whole-cloth creations orchestrated by Mrs. Eldridge. After lengthy conversations with the court, concerning how she was able to surmise that the reports of vomiting were coming exclusively from Mrs. Eldridge, Dr. Albin said, "Well, you can either assume that Mrs. Eldridge said them, or that Dr. Usatin made them up. You got two choices" (p. 44).

With Dr. Albin's brief summation of the situation, the traditional "dyad" is forcefully reasserted: the mother is deceitful and the physician is truthful. Let the facts speak for themselves: *res ipsa loquitur.*[10] Indeed,

---

10. For an excellent discussion of the weakness of such a defense in tort cases—much less in child abuse cases—see Bergeron (1996). Bergeron presents a detailed and critical account of the Ellen Storck case.

the entire case is built on the effort to articulate the dynamics of the typical MBPS mother—in the absense of any direct observation to the contrary and contrary to the medical documentation—in the person of Mrs. Eldridge. If Mrs. Eldridge was guilty of anything, it was of being susceptible to the abstract and fabricated MBPS template imposed on her by her accusers. She was seen as medically sophisticated and resistant to hospital personnel, yet she was also cooperative and helpful with them; she had her own ideas about treatment; she challenged doctors; she spent "excessive" time in hospital settings; there was a high rate of morbidity and mortality among her foster siblings; she influenced physicians to intervene with medical and surgical procedures; she had a disabled husband; she desired a powerful and caring physician (at least apparently in Dr. Usatin's mind); she enjoyed the national recognition she received for being such a careful, loving foster mom; and, most damningly perhaps, she resolutely denied the MBPS charge itself.

Of course, if one removes the affabulated MBPS template from the person of Mrs. Eldridge, none of the foregoing suggests that she would abuse or neglect a child. In reality, there are numerous and perfectly intelligible reasons for these MBPS profile designations, these MBPS "signs" or "symptoms." Mrs. Eldridge was familiar with medical terminology because she had been extensively trained in medical and emergency procedures by the San Francisco "Baby Moms" program. Also, she had fostered approximately 40 medically compromised children, at least 10 of whom were designated as severely ill, life-threatened cases. It would be difficult *not* to become familiar with medical terminology and procedures in the course of such a program of care. Nor, given these circumstances, would it be difficult not to spend a great deal of time in physicians' offices or in hospital settings, even to suggest courses of possible treatment. Her desire for recognition, if in fact this were the case at

---

Other works challenging the MBPS diagnosis and etiology have recently appeared, for example, in England, in an article by Clive Baldwin (1996). Basing his work partially on Ivan Illich's sociological writings dealing with the progressive medicalization of society, Baldwin is currently conducting research questioning the legitimacy of the MBPS diagnosis. Morley (1995) and Fisher and Mitchell (1995) also question the legitimacy of the MBPS diagnosis. In the United States, Thomas M. Ryan (1997) like Bergeron, has strongly criticized both the *res ipsa loquitur* doctrine and the very plausibility of the MBPS diagnosis itself. An association formed to counter the widespread abuse of MBPS allegations—Mothers Against Munchausen Syndrome by Proxy Allegations—maintains an informative and regularly updated website on the internet: http://www.msbp.com.

all, would be entirely justified. Who would not desire some recognition for spending countless days and nights looking after desperately sick foster children? Who would not become irritated with nurses and physicians who accused her of creating line infections and puncturing a feeding tube, when there was perfectly good evidence she had not done so, including the fact that she was not present in the hospital when the tube was punctured? And, as for the line infections, later evidence revealed that the child frequently suffered from diarrhea and that it was the hospital staff who had, allegedly, permitted fecal matter to infect the child. Finally, with the preponderance of evidence against her having abused two foster children, why should her denial of abuse be in any way condemning?

The same MBPS template was affixed to the persons of Ellen Storck and Kathy Bush. In Ellen Storck's case, there was not a single eyewitness to her alleged child abuse, and her son Aaron has always and continues to insist on his mother's innocence, as do her three other children, Joshua, Courtney, and Dana Drew. Indeed, it was precisely this lack of any direct evidence that moved Judge Freundlich to invoke the *res ipsa loquitur* argument, a position usually reserved for tort decisions. Like Yvonne Eldridge, Ellen Storck was found guilty of being susceptible to classification under the taximonic framework of MBPS. Whether she had, in fact, in any way abused her child was simply never established. The evidence seems to the contrary since Aaron was hospitalized on several occasions for apnea, fast heart beat, central nervous system dysfunctions, appendicitis and osteomyelitis, all of which supported the testimony of her long-time pediatrician, Dr. Vincent J. Paluci. The welter of theories, unfounded medical assumptions, speculative etiologies, and suspected behavioral patterns offered during the trial simply pointed directly to her as an abuser, as an MBPS sufferer.

Perhaps the same fate awaits Kathy Bush. While Ellen Storck sought to avoid radical surgical procedures on her child, Kathy Bush is alleged to have induced physicians to perform more than 40 surgical operations on her child, including removal of the child's gall bladder, appendix, and part of her intestines. Although the child had been outplaced by the Florida State Department of Health and Rehabilitative Services, her health had significantly improved for the period of eighteen months prior to outplacement. Nonetheless, the Broward County Assistant State Attorney, seemingly confirming the prosecutor's charge that the "doctors took her mother's diagnoses at face value," claimed that this was clearly a case of MBPS. Outside of the standard MBPS accusations, little specific detail about the case is available, largely because it has not yet come to trial. But the standard die has been cast. In the words of an expert prosecution witness, Dr. Herbert A. Schreier, "This woman fooled the media, she fooled the President's wife, she fooled the Congress, and . . . many, many doctors" (Sharp, 1997, p. 1).

CONCLUDING NOTE

In the final analysis, it is hardly our intention to deny that children are abused and that mothers abuse their children—perhaps more frequently than even Schreier and Libow believe.[11] Rather, what we have tried to argue against is the institutionalization—indeed, the criminalization—of the disorder by force of taxonomic classification. The alleged MBPS "abuser/mother" is assigned a set of characteristics, a largely affabulated etiology, and an inadequately conceived psychological profile and is consequently identified, treated, and punished as a particularly egregious child abuser. But all these classifications have weight only within a very narrow medical-psychiatric discourse, within the closed confines of medical institutions, which in the end serve as the only means of validating these taxonomic designations.

But child abuse entails a far more complicated and dynamic set of behaviors and activities than can ever be expressed, much less understood, in the abbreviated and reductionistic terms of such categorial formulations of MBPS. It would be patently absurd to believe that any mother living in the real world could possibly have demonstrated precisely the behavior that conforms to the etiological construct and to the theoretical models elaborated by Schreier and Libow and the tradition they draw upon. Real-world mothers are at the very least too preoccupied to act out such a scenario. Given that the majority of the "MBPS mothers" discussed in the literature happen to live in what appears to be borderline poverty, often without financial or emotional support from

---

11. Indeed, a recent study published by the U.S. Advisory Board on Child Abuse and Neglect indicates that more young children die at the hands of their parents than in car accidents, house fires, falls, or drowning. The study concluded that at least 2,000 children die of abuse in the U.S. every year, and that at least 18,000 are permanently disabled and 142,000 are seriously injured (*Newsday*, Thursday, April 27, 1995, p. A17).

a spouse; that they live with diminished family ties and may themselves come from dysfunctional families; that they suffer an inordinate amount of stress in the simple day-to-day management of their lives and homes; that many of these women are themselves ill or have been substance abusers—it is not surprising that many fail in their responsibilities toward their children and out of frustration bring harm upon them. It is just as likely that these same women, so sorely disadvantaged, would express their own affection for their children by seeking health care when needed. Perhaps feeling disproportionately, but understandably, responsible for the care of their children, they would seek help for relatively minor concerns, "transient" illnesses or disorders, which may very well lessen in severity during the course of an evening or the wait for admission. By the same token, their children may present few symptoms at the time of diagnosis, something doubtless frustrating to physicians. It would take but a few visits of this nature to generate suspicions about the mother, and such suspicions are routinely reported to social service agencies as possible indicators of MBPS behavior. Should a mother deny such behavior, her very denial could be construed to corroborate her illness and dereliction.

On the other hand, some mothers—and fathers—may use medical instruments or various medications to abuse their children, as is the argument expressed in virtually all the professional literature. Many people may have even seen frightening scenes of mothers on TV being videotaped while trying to smother their own children. But this behavior does not constitute a specified illness; it suggests only that certain people use a specific means or instrumentality to abuse their children. The legitimate category for all these acts is child abuse. To limit unduly the complexity, the motives, the social and economic considerations, the possible relevance of diverse psychopathologies, the broad range of physical disorders, to a single profile—MBPS—severely restricts the understanding and eventual treatment of this sort of child abuse.

> The name of this syndrome evokes a hysteria and it is the responsibility of the public and those that represent the public to question the motives of the accusing hospital and physician. If it is in fact abuse, call it by its real name ... suffocation, poisoning, tampering with urine sample, etc. ... offer substantial proof! [M.A.M.A. 1998, p. 3].

By the same token, the "disordered mother," so factitiously diagnosed, remains an object to be manipulated and dispensed with, if not incarcerated. She is treated according to the priorities of medical and institutional power, rather than according to her actual needs, needs that, as we have stressed at length, still remain painfully obvious even to the most inexpert observer.

What we find troubling about much of the MBPS literature, and about the work of Schreier and Libow in particular, is that such a concern to impress what is merely a taxonomic designation on a group of women—who may or may not have abused their children—effectively forecloses the realistic assessment and treatment of the individual case at hand. What is basically only a nominal entity—the MBPS disorder"—is alleged to have a specific etiology, symptomatology, and diagnosis. When examined closely, however, none of these determinations present themselves or in any way describe a unique disorder. These determinations are but a compilation of a variety of indications, taken from a variety of individuals, issuing from a variety of personal and familial situations, all recycled through the expected configuration assigned them by the literature that extends from the early to the by-proxy form of Munchausen. That "denial" of "typical" behavior should be so prevalent in adult Munchausen or in MBPS can hardly be a mystery to anyone. Why a mother should fetishize a child for the delectation of a sensitive and intelligent, care-giving obstetrician or pediatrician, or any other figure of professional power, so as to receive his affection and respect, however, shall forever remain a mystery. The study of child abuse—and the study of closely associated psychiatric and somatic disorders—deserves a far more extensive and realistic analysis than that conducted under the name of the Baron von Munchausen.

REFERENCES

Alexander, F. G. & Selesnick, S. T. (1966). *The History of Psychiatry: An Evaluation of Psychiatric Thought and Practice from Prehistoric Times to the Present.* New York: Harper & Row.

Alexander, R., Smith, W. & Stevenson, R. (1990). Serial Munchausen's syndrome by proxy. *Pediat.*, 86:581–585.

American Psychiatric Association (1952). *Diagnostic and Statistical Manual of Mental Disorders*, 1st ed. Washington, DC: American Psychiatric Association.

American Psychiatric Association (1968). *Diagnostic and Statistical Manual of Mental Disorders*, 2nd ed. (DSM-II). Washington, DC: American Psychiatric Association.

American Psychiatric Association (1978). *Diagnostic and Statistical Manual of Mental Disorders*, 3rd ed. (DSM-III). Washington, DC: American Psychiatric Association.

American Psychiatric Association (1985). *Diagnostic and Statistical Manual of Mental Disorders*, 3rd ed. rev. (DSM-III-R). Washington, DC: American Psychiatric Association.

American Psychiatric Association. (1994). *Diagnostic and Statistical Manual of Mental Disorders*, 4th ed. (DSM-IV). Washington, DC: American Psychiatric Association.

Arms, S. (1975). *Immaculate Deception: A New Look at Childbirth in America.* Boston: Houghton Mifflin.

Armstrong, L. (1993). *And They Call It Help: The Psychiatric Policing of America's Children.* Reading, MA: Addison-Wesley.

Armstrong, L. (1994). *Rocking the Craddle of Sexual Politics: What Happened When Women Said Incest.* Reading, MA: Addison-Wesley.

Artingstall, K. A. (1995). Munschausen syndrome by proxy. *FBI Law Enforce.Bull.,* August.

Asher, R. (1951). Munchausen's syndrome. *Lancet,* 1:339–341.

Baldwin, C. (1996). Munchausen syndrome by proxy: Problems of definition diagnosis and treatment. *Health and Social Care in the Community,* 4:159–65.

Barker–Benfield, G. J. (1978). Sexual surgery in late nineteenth-century America. In C. Dreifus (ed.), *Seizing Our Bodies: The Politics of Women's Health.* New York: Vintage Books.

Barrow, J. D. (1991). *Theories of Everything: The Quest for Ultimate Explanation.* Oxford, UK: Oxford University Press.

Barstow, A. L. (1994). *Witchcraze: A New History of the European Witch Hunts.* San Francisco: Pandora/Harper.

Baudrillard, J. (1983). *Simulations,* trans. P. Foss, P. Patton & P. Beitchman. New York: Semiotext.

Baur, S. (1988). *Hypochondria: Woeful Imaginations.* Berkeley: University of Califiornia Press.

Bentham, J. (1969). Panopticon papers. In: M. P. Mack (ed.), *A Bentham Reader.* New York: Pegasus, pp. 189–208.

Bergeron, M. L. (1996). Hegemony, law and psychiatry: A perspective on the systematic oppression of "rogue mothers." *Feminist Legal Studies,* 4:49–72.

Booth, S. S. (1975). *The Witches of Early America.* New York: Hastings House.

Boros, S. J. & Brubaker, L. C. (1992). Munchausen syndrome by proxy: Case accounts. *FBI Law Enforce. Bull.,* 61:16–20.

Brenner, C. (1957). *An Elementary Textbook of Psychoanalysis.* Garden City, NY: Doubleday.

Breuer, J. & Freud, S. (1893). On the psychical mechanisms of hysterical phenomena: Preliminary communication. *Standard Edition,* 2:3–17. London: Hogarth Press, 1955.

Breuer, J. & Freud, S. (1893–95). *Studies on Hysteria, Standard Edition,* 2. London: Hogarth Press, 1955.

Brodie, B. C. (1837). *Lectures Illustrative of Certain Local Nervous Affections.* London: Longman.

Brown, P. (1990). The name game: Toward a sociology of diagnosis. *J. Mind Behav.,* 11:385–406

Burdeau vs. McDowell (1921). 246 U.S. 646.

Burgess, R. L. & Draper, P. (1989). The explanation of family violence: The role of biological, behavioral, and cultural selection. In L. Oblin & M. Tonry, (ed.), *Family Violence, Vol. 11.* Chicago: University of Chicago Press, pp. 59–116.

Burnson, R. (1998). Foster mom convicted of abuse wins reversal. *Times Martinez Bureau,* Jan. 17, pp. 1–4.

Butcher, J. N. (1990). *MMPI-2 in Psychological Treatment*. New York: Oxford University Press.

Caplan, P. J. (1989). *Don't Blame Mother: Mending the Mother–Daughter Relationship*. New York: Harper & Row.

Caplan, P. J. (1991). How *do* they decide who is normal? The bizarre, but true, tale of the DSM process. *Canadian Psychol. [Psychologie Canadienne.]* 32:162–170.

Caplan, P. J. (1994). *The Myth of Women's Masochism*. Toronto: University of Toronto Press.

Caplan, P. J. (1995). *They Say You're Crazy: How the World's Most Powerful Psychiatrists Decide Who's Normal*. Reading, MA: Addison-Wesley.

Chapman, J. S. (1955a). Missing hospital patient. *J. Amer. Med. Assn.*, 157:182.

Chapman, J. S. (1955b). Hospital patient. *J. Amer. Med. Assn.*, 159:213–214.

Chapman, J. S. (1957). Peregrinating problem patients: Münchausen's syndrome. *J. Amer. Med. Assn.*, 165:927–933.

Charcot, J.-M. (1890). *Oeuvres complètes de J.-M. Charcot: Leçons sur les maladies du system nerveux, recueillies et publiées par MM. Babinski, Bernard, Féré, Golnon, Marie & Gilles de la Tourette*. Paris: Lecrosnier.

Chesler, P. (1972). *Women and Madness*. Garden City, NY: Doubleday.

Cheyne, G. (1733). *The English Malady*. London: Tavistock, 1991.

Chodorow, N. (1989). *Feminism and Psychoanalytic Theory*. Cambridge: Polity.

Chorover, S. L. (1974). *From Genesis to Genocide*. Cambridge, MA: MIT Press.

Clark, M. J. (1981). The rejection of psychological approaches to mental disorder in late nineteenth-century British psychiatry. In A. Scull (ed.), *Madhouses, Mad-Doctors, and Madmen: The Social History of Psychiatry in the Victorian Era*. Philadelphia: University of Pennsylvania Press, pp. 271–312.

Clarke, E. & Melnick, S. C. (1958). The Munchausen syndrome or the problem of hospital hoboes. *Amer. J. Med.*, 25:6–12.

Clyne, M. B. (1955). Munchausen syndrome. *Brit. Med. J.*, Nov. 12:1207.

Cramer, B., Gershberg M. R. & Stern, M. (1971). Munchausen syndrome: Its relationship to malingering, hysteria, and the physician–patient relationship. *Arch. Gen. Psychiat.*, 24:573–578.

Curran, J. P. (1973). Hysterical dermatitis factitia. *Amer. J. Dis. Children*, 125:564–567.

Dain, N. (1994). Psychiatry and anti-psychiatry in the United States. In M. Micale & R. Porter (ed.), *Discovering the History of Psychiatry*. New York: Oxford University Press, pp. 415–444.

Decker, H. S. (1991). *Freud, Dora, and Vienna 1900*. New York: Free Press.

Didi-Huberman, G. (1982). *Invention de l'hystérie: Charcot et l'iconographie photographique de la Salpêtrière*. Paris: Éditions Macula.

DiVasto, P. & Saxon, G. (1992). Munchausen's syndrome in law enforcement. *FBI Law Enforce. Bull.*, April:11–14.

Doty, L. (1997), Help for health decision challenges. *J. Florida Med. Assn.*, 84: 391–396.

Dreifus, C. (1978). Sterilizing the poor. In C. Dreifus (ed.), *Seizing Our Bodies: The Politics of Women's Health*. New York: Vintage Books, pp. 105–109.

Drinka, G. F. (1984). *The Birth of Neurosis: Myth, Malady, and the Victorians.* New York: Simon & Schuster.

Ehrenreich, B. & English, D. (1973). *Witches, Midwives, and Nurses: A History of Women Healers.* Old Westbury, NY: Feminist Press.

Eisendrath, S. J. (1989). Factitious disorder with physical symptoms. In *Treatments of Psychiatric Disorders.* Washington, DC: American Psychiatric Association, pp. 2159–2164.

Emery, J. L. (1993). Child abuse, sudden infant death syndrome, and unexpected infant death. *Amer. J. Dis.Children,* 147:1097–1100.

Eyer, D. E. (1992). *Mother–Infant Bonding: A Scientific Fiction.* New Haven, CT: Yale University Press.

Faludi, S. (1992). *Backlash: The Undeclared War Against American Women.* New York: Doubleday.

Feldman, M. D. (1994). Denial in Munchausen by proxy syndrome: The consulting psychiatrist's dilemma." *Internat. J. Psychiat. in Med.,* 24:121–128.

Feldman, M. D. (1998). Dr. Marc Feldman's Munchausen syndrome and factitious disorders page. http://ourworld.compuserve.com/home-pages-marc feldman2/

Feldman, M. D. & Ford, C. V. with Reinhold, T. (1994). *Patient or Pretender: Inside the Strange World of Factitious Disorders.* New York: Wiley.

Fisher, G. C. & Mitchell, I. (1995). Is Munchausen syndrome by proxy really a syndrome? *Arch. Dis. Childhood,* 72:530–534.

Fiske, J. (1987). *Television Culture.* London: Methuen.

Foreman, D. M., & Farsides, C. (1993). Ethical use of covert videoing techniques in detecting Munchausen syndrome by proxy. *Brit. Med. J.,* 307:611–612.

Foucault, M. (1965). *Madness and Civilization: A History of Insanity in the Age of Reason.* New York: Random House.

Foucault, M. (1979). *Discipline and Punish: The Birth of the Prison.* New York: Random House.

Foucault, M. (1988). *The Care of the Self: The History of Sexuality, Vol. 3.* New York: Random House.

Freud, S. (1894). The neuro-psychoses of defense. *Standard Edition,* 3:45–68. London: Hogarth Press, 1962.

Freud, S. (1905). Fragment of an analysis of a case of hysteria ('Dora'). *Standard Edition,* 7:7–122. London: Hogarth Press, 1953.

Freud, S. (1912), The dynamics of transference. *Standard Edition,* 12:99–109. London: Hogarth Press, 1958.

Freud, S. (1913). Totem and taboo. *Standard Edition,* 13:1–16. London: Hogarth Press, 1955.

Freud, S. (1915). Observations on transference-love. *Standard Edition.* 12:157–171. London: Hogarth Press, 1958.

Freud, S. (1916–1917). *Introductory Lectures on Psychoanalysis. Standard Edition* London: Hogarth Press, 1963.

Freud, S. (1923). The ego and the id. *Standard Edition,* 19:12–66. London: Hogarth Press, 1961

Freud, S. (1925). Some psychical consequences of the anatomical distinction between the sexes. *Standard Edition,* 19:248–258. London: Hogarth Press, 1961.

Freud, S. (1926a). Inhibitions, symptoms and anxiety. *Standard Edition,* 20:87–174. London: Hogarth Press, 1959.

Freud, S. (1926b). The question of lay analysis. *Standard Edition,* 20:183–258. London: Hogarth Press, 1959.

Freud, S. (1927). Fetishism. *Standard Edition,* 21:152–157. London: Hogarth Press, 1959.

Freud, S. (1931). Female sexuality. *Standard Edition,* 21:225–243. London: Hogarth Press, 1961.

Freundlich, D. (Hon.) (1993). Memorandum decision fact finding. *Family Court of the State of New York,* Suffolk County (Feb. 22).

Gavin, H. (1838). *On the Feigned and Factitious Diseases of Soldiers and Seamen, on the Means Used to Simulate or Produce Them, and on the Best Modes of Discovering Impostors.* Edinburgh: University of Edinburgh Press.

Gawn, R. A. & Kauffmann, E. A. (1955). Munchausen syndrome. *Brit. Med. J.,* Oct. 29:1068.

Goffman, E. (1961). *Asylums: Essays on the Social Situation of Mental Patients and Other Inmates.* Garden City, NY: Anchor Books.

Gosselin, C. & Wilson, G. (1980). *Sexual Variations: Fetishism, Sadomasochism, and Transvestism.* New York: Simon & Schuster.

Gould, S. J. (1981). *The Mismeasure of Man.* New York: Norton.

Groves, J. E. (1978). Taking care of hateful patients. *New Eng. J. Med.,* 298:883–887.

Grünbaum, A. (1984). *The Foundation of Psychoanalysis: A Philosophical Critique.* Berkeley: University of California Press.

Guillain, G. (1959). *J.-M. Charcot, 1825–1893: His Life-His Work,* ed. & trans., P. Bailey. New York: Hoeber.

Hanson, F. A. (1993). *Testing Testing: Social Consequences of the Examined Life.* Berkeley: University of California Press.

Hartmann, B. (1987). *Reproductive Rights and Wrongs: The Global Politics of Population Control and Contraceptive Choice.* New York: Harper & Row.

Hilts, P. J. (1994a). Hospital is accused of illegal experiments. *New York Times,* Jan. 21, p. A12.

Hilts, P. J. (1994b). Hospital put on probation over tests on poor women. *New York Times,* October 5, p. B9.

Hinsie, L. E. & Cambell, R. J. (1996). *Psychiatric Dictionary*. New York: Oxford University Press.

Holmes, S. W. (1951). Munchausen's syndrome. *Lancet*, Jan.–June:638.

Hopkins, M. (1647). The discovery of witches . In A. E. Green (ed.), *Witches and Witch-hunters*. Yorkshire: S. R. Publishers, 1971.

Hughes, M. C. (1984). Recurrent abdominal pain and childhood depression. *Amer. J. Orthopsychiat.*, 54:146–155.

Irigaray, L. (1985). *The Sex Which Is Not One*. Ithaca, NY: Cornell University Press.

Janssen-Jurreit, M. (1982). *Sexism: The Male Monopoly on History and Thought*, trans. V. Moberg. New York: Farrar, Straus & Giroux.

Jones, D. P. H. (1996). Munchausen syndrome by proxy: Is expansion justified? *Child Abuse & Neglect*, 20:983–984.

Kaplan, L. J. (1991). *Female Perversions: The Temptations of Emma Bovary*. New York: Doubleday.

Kaufman, K. L., Coury, D., Pickrel, E. & McCleery, J. (1989). Munchausen syndrome by proxy: A survey of professionals' knowledge. *Child Abuse & Neglect*, 13:141–147.

Kawamoto, L.(Hon.) (1996). Order. *In the interest of J. N., a minor (People of the State of Illinois), No. 1-95-1958, consolidated with 1-95-2049 and 1-95-2357, Court of Appeals, Cook County, 92 J 7049.*

Kerr, J. (1993). *A Most Dangerous Method: The Story of Jung, Freud, and Sabina Spielrein*. New York: Knopf.

King, H. (1993). Once upon a text: Hysteria from Hippocrates. In S. L. Gilman, H. King, R. Porter, G. S. Rousseau & E. Showalter (ed.), *Hysteria Beyond Freud*. Berkeley: University of California Press, pp. 3–90.

Kirk, S. A. & Kutchins, H. (1992). *The Selling of DSM: The Rhetoric of Science in Psychiatry*. New York: Aldine de Gruyter.

Klaits, J. (1985). *Servants of Satan: The Age of Witch Hunts*. Bloomington: Indiana University Press.

Kors, A. C. & Peters, E. (ed.) (1971). *Witchcraft in Europe 1100–1700: A Documentary History*. Philadelphia: University of Pennsylvania Press.

Kraepelin, E. (1907). *Clinical Psychiatry*, ed. & trans. A. R. Diefendorf. Delmar, NY: Scholars' Facsimilies & Reprints, 1981.

Laing, R. D. (1962). *Self and Others*. London: Penguin, 1990.

Lawrence, L. & Weinhouse, B. (1994). *Outrageous Practices: The Alarming Truth about How Medicine Mistreats Women*. New York: Fawcett Columbine.

Leehan, J. & Wilson, L. P. (1985). *Grown-up Abused Children*. Springfield, IL: Charles C. Thomas.

Levin, A. V. & Sheridan, M. S. (eds) (1995). *Munchausen Syndrome by Proxy: Issues in Diagnosis and Treatment*. New York: Lexington Books.

Libow, J. A. (1995). Munchausen by proxy victims in adulthood: A first look. *Child Abuse & Neglect*, 19:1131–1142.

Lidz, T., Miller, J., Padget, P. & Stedem, A.F. A. (1949). Muscular atrophy and pseudologica fantastica associated with islet cell adenoma of the pancreas. *Arch. Neurol. & Psychiat.*, 62:304–313.

Light, M. J. & Sheridan, M. S. (1990). Munchausen syndrome by proxy and apnea—A survey of apnea programs. *Clin. Pediat.*, 29:162–168.

Lipsitt, D. R. (1970). Medical and psychological characteristics of "crocks." *Internat. J. Psychiat. Med.*, 1:15–25.

Lloyd, T. O. (1970). *Empire to Welfare State: English History 1906–1967.* London: Oxford University Press.

Lothane, Z. (1992). *In Defense of Schreber: Soul Murder and Psychiatry.* Hillsdale, NJ: The Analytic Press.

Lungren, D. E. et al. (1998). *The People of the State of California vs. Yvonne Eldridge, In the Superior Court of the State of California for the County of Contra Costa, No.942154–6. Opposition to motion for new trial* (1/16/98).

M.A.M.A. (1998). Mothers against Munchausen syndrome by proxy allegations, Jan. 20, http://www.msbp.com/

Macaulay, T. B. (1906). *The History of England: From the Accession of James II,* 4 vols. New York: Dutton.

Mackay, C. (1841). *Extraordinary Popular Delusions and the Madness of Crowds.* New York: Farrar, Straus & Giroux., 1932.

Markantonakis, A. (1989). Munchausen syndrome by proxy. *Brit. J. Psychiat.*, 155:130–131.

Martin, P. A. (1975). The obnoxious patient: Tactics and techniques in psychoanalytic therapy. In P. L. Giovacchini (ed.), *Countertransference,* Vol. 2. New York: Aronson.

Masson, J. M. (1984). *The Assault on Truth: Freud's Suppression of the Seduction Theory.* New York: Farrar, Straus & Giroux.

McClure, R. J., Davis, P. M., Meadow, R. & Sibert, J. R. (1996). Epidemiology of Munchausen syndrome by proxy, non-accidental poisoning, and non-accidental suffocation. *Arch. Dis. Childhood,* 75:57–61.

McCullough, V. B. (1992). *Testing and Your Child.* New York: Penguin Books.

Meadow, R. (1977). Munchausen syndrome by proxy: The hinterland of child abuse. *Lancet,* Aug. 13:343–345.

Meadow, R. (1985). Management of Munchausen syndrome by proxy. *Arch. Dis. Childhood,* 60:385–393.

Meadow, R. (1995). Munchausen syndrome by proxy. *Medico-Legal J.,* 63(3):89–105.

Menninger, K. A. (1934). Polysurgery and polysurgical addiction. *Psychoanal. Quart.,* 3:173–199.

Miller, (Judge). (1987). Family Court. *New York Law J.,* March 3, p. 13.

Millet, K. (1991). *The Loony-Bin Trip.* New York: Touchstone.

Mohr, J. C. (1978). *Abortion in America: The Origins and Evolution of National Policy.* New York: Oxford University Press.

Morley, C.J. (1995). Practical concerns about the diagnosis of Munchausen syndrome by proxy. *Arch. Dis. Childhood*, 72:528–530.

Newsday (1995). April 17, p. A17.

Nietzsche, F. (1974). *The Gay Science*, ed. & trans. W. Kaufmann. New York: Random House.

Notestein, W. (1911). *A History of Witchcraft in England, From 1588 to 1718*. New York: Apollo Editions, 1968.

Oakley, A. (1976). *Woman's Work: The Housewife, Past and Present*. New York: Vintage.

O'Shea, B. M., Lowe, N. F., McGennis, A. J. & O'Rourke, M. H. (1982). Psychiatric evaluation of a Munschausen's syndrome. *Irish Med. J.*, 75(6):200–202.

Parnell, T. F. & Day, D. O., (eds.) (1998). *Munchausen by Proxy Syndrome: Misunderstood Child Abuse*. Thousand Oaks, CA: Sage.

Penfold, S. P. & Walker, G. A. (1983). *Women and the Psychiatric Paradox*. Montreal : Eden Press.

Physicians Weekly (1996). 13(27):1.

Porter, R. (1991). Introduction. In G. Cheyne, *The English Malady*. London: Tavistock/Routledge.

Priest, W. M. (1951). Munschausen's syndrome. *Lancet*, Feb. 24:474.

Renik, O. (1992). Use of the analyst as a fetish. *Psychoanal. Quart.*, 61:542–563.

Rich, A. (1976). *Of Woman Born*. New York: Norton.

Rogers, D., Tripp, J., Bentovim, A., Robinson, A., Berry, D. & Goulding, R. (1976). Non-accidental poisoning: An extended syndrome of child abuse. *Brit. Med. J.*, 1:793–796.

Rosenberg, D. A. (1987). Web of deceit: A literature review of Munchausen syndrome by proxy. *Child Abuse & Neglect*, 11:547–563.

Rosenberg, D. A. (1994). Review of *Hurting for Love: Munchausen by Proxy Syndrome*. *Child Abuse and Neglect*, 18:1085–1086.

Rosenberg, D. A. (1997). *Child Neglect and Munchausen Syndrome by Proxy: Portable Guide to Investigating Child Abuse*. Washington, DC: US Department of Justice.

Rothman, B. K. (1982). *In Labor: Women and Power in the Birthplace*. New York: Norton.

Ryan, T. M. (1997). Munchausen syndrome by proxy: Misogny or modern medicine? Association of Trial Lawyers of America's Women Trial Lawyers Caucus *Newsletter*, fall:3–4.

Scheff, T. J. (1966). *Being Mentally Ill: A Sociological Theory*. Chicago: Aldine.

Schreier, H. A. (1992). The perversion of mothering: Munchausen syndrome by proxy. *Bull. Menninger Clin.*, 56:421–437.

Schreier, H. A. (1996). Repeated false allegations of sexual abuse presenting to sheriffs: When is it Munchausen by proxy? *Child Abuse & Neglect*, 20:985–991.

Schreier, H. A. & Libow, J. A. (1993a). *Hurting for Love: Munchausen by Proxy Syndrome.* New York: Guilford Press.

Schreier, H. A. & Libow, J. A. (1993b). Munchausen by proxy syndrome: Diagnosis and prevalence. *Amer. J. Orthopsychiat.,* 63:318–321.

Sedgwick, P. (1982). *Psycho Politics: Laing, Foucault, Goffman, Szasz and the Future of Mass Pychiatry.* New York: Harper & Row.

Serra, J. T., Gilg, Z. K. & Wohadlo, K. P. (1997). *People of the State of California v. Yvonne Lucille Eldridge, No. 05-942154-6, Memorandum of points and authorities in support of defendant's motion for new trial.*

Serra, J. T., Gilg, Z. K. & Wohadlo, K. P. (1998). Declarations in support of reply to people's opposition to defendant's motion for new trial, relating to *People of the State of California v. Yvonne Lucille Eldridge, No. 05-942154-6, Memorandum of points and authorities in support of defendant's motion for new trial.*

Sharp, D. (1997). Mother charged in "Munchausen" case. *USA Today,* Health. Sept. 9, p.1; http://www.usatoday.com/life/health/ family/abuse/lhfae003.htm

Short, I. O. (1955). Munchausen's syndrome. *Brit. Med. J.,* Nov. 12:1207.

Simon, B. (1978). *Mind and Madness in Ancient Greece: The Classical Roots of Modern Psychiatry.* Ithaca, NY: Cornell University Press.

Slater, P. (1968). *The Glory of Hera.* Boston: Beacon Press.

Southall, D. P., Stebbins, V. A., Rees, S.V., Lang, M. H., Warner, J. O. & Shinebourne, E. A. (1987). Apnoic episodes induced by smothering: Two cases identified by covert video surveillance. *Brit. Med. J.,* 294:1637–1641.

Stern, T. A. (1980). Munchausen's syndrome revisited. *Psychosomat.,* 21:329–336.

Stone, M. H. (1977). Factitious illness. *Bull. Menninger Clin.,* 41:239–254.

Stretton, J. E. H. (1951). Munchausen's syndrome. *Lancet,* Feb. 24:474.

Sullivan, R. (1994). 2 Hospitals are accused of segregating by race. *New York Times,* May 20, p. B3.

Sulloway, F. J. (1979). *Freud, Biologist of the Mind.* New York: Basic Books.

Sussman, N. (1989). Factitious disorders. In H. I. Kaplan & B. J. Sadock (ed.), *Comprehensive Textbook of Psychiatry, Vol. 2.* Baltimore, MD: Williams &Wilkins, p. 1136.

Sussman, N., Borod, J. C., Canselmo, J. A. & Braun, D. (1987). Munshcausen syndrome: A reconceptualization of the disorder. *J. Nerv. & Ment. Dis.,* 175:692–695.

Szasz, T. S. (1970). *The Manufacture of Madness: A Comparative Study of the Inquisition and the Mental Health Movement.* New York: Harper & Row.

Szasz, T. S. (1974). *The Myth of Mental Illness.* New York: Harper & Row.

Taueber, C. (ed.). (1991). *Statistical Handbook on Women in America.* Phoenix, AZ: Oryx Press.

Tavris, C. (1992). *The Mismeasure of Woman.* New York: Simon & Schuster.

Tierney, L., McPhee, S. & Papadakis, M. A. (1998). *Current Medical Diagnosis and Treatment,* 37th ed. New York: Appleton & Lange.

Todd, J. (1951). Munchausen's syndrome. *Lancet,* March 3:528.

Trebilcot, J. (ed.) (1984). *Mothering: Essays in Feminist Theory*. Totowa, NJ: Ronman & Allanheld.

Tufte, E. R. (1983). *The Visual Display of Quantitative Information*. Cheshire, CT: Graphics Press.

Turner, S. M., Jacob, R. G. & Morrison, R. (1984). Somatoform and factitious disorders. In H. E. Adams & P. B. Sutker (ed.), *Comprehensive Handbook of Psychopathology*. New York: Plenum, pp. 307–345.

Veith, I. (1965). *Hysteria: The History of a Disease*. Chicago: University of Chicago Press.

Victor, R. G. (1972). Self-induced phlebotomy as a cause of factitious illness. *Amer. J. Psychother.*, 26:425–431.

White, M. (1987). Ideological analysis and television. In R. C. Allen (ed.), *Channels of Discourse: Television and Contemporary Criticism*. Chapel Hill: University of North Carolina Press, pp.134–171.

Williams, B. (1951). Munchausen's syndrome. *Lancet*, March 3:527.

Williams, C. & Bevan, V. T. (1988). The secret observation of children in hospital. *Lancet*, 1:780–781.

Wolman, B. B. (1968). *The Unconscious Mind: The Meaning of Freudian Psychology*. Englewood Cliffs, NJ: Prentice-Hall.

Zilboorg, G. & Henry, G. W. (1941). *A History of Medical Psychology*. New York: Norton.

INDEX